A HISTORY OF

KOREA

William E. Henthorn

A History of Korea

WILLIAM E. HENTHORN

A History of Korea

THE FREE PRESS
A Division of Macmillan Publishing Co., Inc.
New York

Collier Macmillan Publishers
London

THE FREE PRESS
A Division of Macmillan Publishing Co., Inc.
866 Third Avenue, New York, New York 10022

Collier-Macmillan Canada Ltd.

First Free Press Paperback Edition 1974

Library of Congress Catalog Card Number: 75–143511

Printed in the United States of America

hardbound printing number
1   2   3   4   5   6   7   8   9   10

paperback printing number
1   2   3   4   5   6   7   8   9   10

For

OSCAR AND VIOLET WURSTER

Preface

This work was undertaken as an intellectual responsibility in response to what was a felt need for a general introduction to the history and culture of traditional Korea. Here, by traditional Korea is meant Korea prior to the reign of King Kojong (r. 1864–1907), penultimate ruler of the Yi dynasty. Events after the reign of King Kojong belong to another era and are properly the subject of another book.

The structural format, such as the use of topical categories and the inclusion of terms in the original and considerable institutional information, has been dictated largely by considerations of the audience for whom this work is intended, namely, university undergraduates studying the history and culture of east Asia.

The answers which a study of a society and culture provide depend to a large extent upon the questions asked. I have endeavored in the discussion and observations of Korean history in Appendix 3, "Postscript," to make explicit some of the theoretical considerations underlying my interpretations.

This work has benefited from the scholarship of many who have preceded me. Although I have used both primary and secondary source materials, I am heavily indebted to modern Korean, and to a lesser extent Japanese, scholarship. I have attempted to indicate this debt by including a summary bibliography instead of the usual reading list or enumeration of works utilized.

I am especially indebted to Marius B. Jansen of Princeton University, who first encouraged me to undertake this task and was generous enough to read and comment upon an earlier version of the manuscript. I should also like to express my appreciation to several scholars for their comments on portions of this work at various stages of its preparation: Yi Sangeun, Korea University; Yi Kibaek, Sogang University; Yi Kwangnin, Sogang University; Richard Pearsons, University of Hawaii; Hugh W. Kang, University of Hawaii, and Fred Lukoff, University of Washington. I am grateful to the Human Relations Area Files for permission to quote from their translation of C. Dallet's *Histoire de l'église de Corée.*

I should like to indicate my gratitude also to the Ford Foundation, the Rockefeller Foundation, the American Philosophical Society, the East-West Center, and Princeton University for past support for study in the general field of Korean history and culture. This work is, of course, my own responsibility, and the support received from institutions and individuals in no way constitutes an indorsement of it nor of the opinions expressed herein.

The encouragement of my wife, Taesoon Lee Henthorn, during the preparation has been my greatest asset.

W. E. H.
Honolulu
January 1971

Contents

5 *Late Silla* 59

6 *Early Koryŏ* 85

9 *Late Chosŏn* *186*

Appendix 1 *The Korean Language* *227*

Appendix 2 *Foundation Myths* *228*

A History of Korea

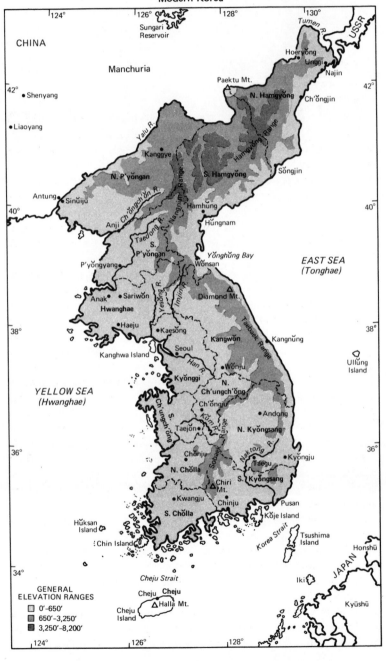

Modern Korea

CHINA

Manchuria

USSR

Tumen R.

Sungari
Reservoir

Shenyang

Liaoyang

Hoeryŏng
Unggi
Najin

Paektu Mt.

42°

N. Hamgyŏng

Ch'ŏngjin

Yalu R.

Kanggye

Hamgyŏng Range

S. Hamgyŏng

Sŏngjin

N. P'yŏngan

Antung
Sinŭiju

Ch'ŏngch'ŏn R.

Nangnim Range

40°

Anji

Hamhŭng

Hŭngnam

Taedong R.

**S.
P'yŏngan**

Yŏnghŭng Bay

*EAST SEA
(Tonghae)*

P'yŏngyang

Wŏnsan

Anak
Sariwŏn

Yesŏng R.

Imjin R.

Diamond Mt.

Hwanghae

Haeju

Kaesŏng

Seoul

Kangwŏn

Kangnŭng

38°

Kanghwa Island

Han R.

Wŏnju

Taebaek Range

Ullŭng
Island

Kyŏnggi

**N.
Ch'ungch'ŏng**

*YELLOW SEA
(Hwanghae)*

Ch'ŏngju

Andong

**S.
Ch'ungch'ŏng**

Kŭm R.

Sobaek Range

N. Kyŏngsang

Taejŏn

Naktong R.

36°

Chŏnju

Kyŏngju

N. Chŏlla

Chiri
Mt.

Taegu

S. Kyŏngsang

Kwangju

Chinju

Pusan

S. Chŏlla

Kŏje Island

Hŭksan
Island

Korea Strait

Tsushima
Island

Honshū

Chin Island

JAPAN

Iki

34°

Cheju Strait

Cheju **Cheju**

Kyūshū

Cheju
Island

Halla Mt.

GENERAL
ELEVATION RANGES

☐ 0'–650'
▨ 650'–3,250'
■ 3,250'–8,200'

124°   126°   128°   130°

1

The Land

The mountainous peninsula of Korea, an extension of the eastern Manchurian high-lands, stretches southeast for some 600 miles through 7 degrees of latitude, with an average width of about 150 miles. To the east, beyond the East Sea (Sea of Japan), the islands of Japan arc out into the Pacific, approaching the peninsula closely in the south. To the west beyond the Yellow Sea stretches the China mainland. The rugged peninsula, its broad northern base anchored in lofty ranges, comprises little more than 85,250 square miles including its offshore islands, an area about three-fifths the size of Japan, two-thirds the size of Italy.

Roughly one-fourth of modern Korea is contained in the great mountainous uplands of northeast continental Korea. Here in the northeast, massive lava floods poured out upon the surface of the earth to form the Kaema Plateau, and it is only in this part of Korea that we find extensive areas which are over 5,000 feet above sea level. Subsequent eruptions on the Kaema Plateau built volcanic cones climaxing in a towering mountain range, crowned by Paektu-san, Korea's highest mountain, which rises over 9,000 feet. This mountain, long sacred to the tribal peoples of northeast Asia and today a symbol of political unity, holds in its caldera a 2-mile-wide crater lake, *Ch'ŏnji* (The Pool of Heaven). On the northern side of the mountain there is a small stream; some way down the slope the stream branches to form the headwaters of two mighty rivers, the Yalu and the Tumen. The Yalu River forms the larger portion of the modern Korea-Manchuria border as it flows southwest to empty into the Gulf of Korea some 490 miles away. On the slopes of Paektu Mountain the broad Tumen River, frozen 5 months of the year, begins its 324-mile arc to the northeast. The lower reaches of the Tumen are full of sand banks which make navigation rather hazardous. Eleven miles before the Tumen empties into the East Sea, the mountainous frontiers of Korea, China, and Russia converge. Here on the eastern flank of the great mountain ranges of the north is the passageway from eastern Manchuria and the Soviet Primore region into the Korean northeast. In the northwest, the broad delta of the Yalu forms Korea's northwest passage, the easiest route of entry into the peninsula from the continent, while the smaller delta of the Tumen in the northeast is practically isolated from the rest of the peninsula by the intervening Hamgyŏng Range on the Kaema Plateau.

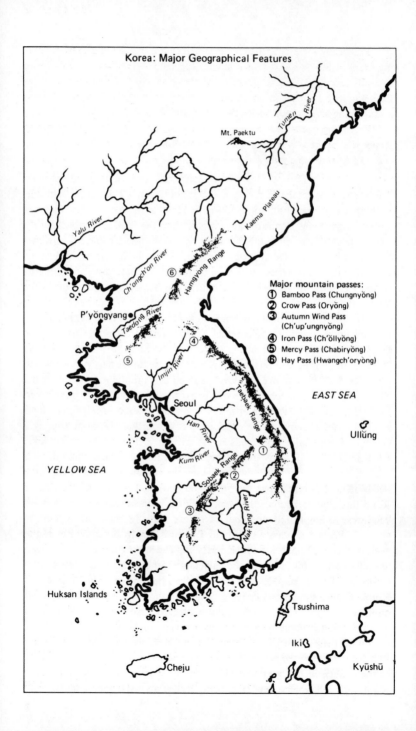

Korea: Major Geographical Features

Mt. Paektu

Tumen River

Yalu River

Kaema Plateau

Ch'ongch'on River

Hamgyong Range

P'yŏngyang

Taedong River

Major mountain passes:
① Bamboo Pass (Chungnyŏng)
② Crow Pass (Oryŏng)
③ Autumn Wind Pass
   (Ch'up'ungnyŏng)
④ Iron Pass (Ch'ŏllyŏng)
⑤ Mercy Pass (Chabiryŏng)
⑥ Hay Pass (Hwangch'oryŏng)

⑥

⑤

Imjin River

④

EAST SEA

Seoul

Han River

Taebaek Range

Ullŭng

Kum River

Sobaek Range

YELLOW SEA

①

②

Naktong River

③

Huksan Islands

Tsushima

Iki

Cheju

Kyūshū

Practically the entire eastern coast of Korea is a mountain barrier fronting the East Sea, a rocky shoreline with rugged, conifer-forested cliffs rising abruptly from the sea. As a result, the rivers which flow eastward into the East Sea drop swiftly and torrentially, carving narrow plains along the coast and forming small coves where they enter the sea.

Extending south from the northeast the high altitudes of the Hamgyŏng Range are broken by a gap. This tectonic line marks the 100-mile Seoul-Wŏnsan corridor, the principal passage from the Korean northeast; a shorter corridor extends north from Wŏnsan to Hamhŭng. Near the 39th parallel of north latitude, just beyond this break in the mountainous eastern coast, begin the Diamond Mountains, 32 miles long and 22 miles wide.

The coastal mountain barrier continues down the eastern coast in the Taebaek Range. The many mountain spurs extending westward like ribs off the Taebaek Range act as natural structural guides for the long rivers which flow into the Yellow Sea. These rivers cut deep channels and defiles in the eastern uplands, and then as they reach the lowlands in the west laden with sands, they wander slowly in great meanders—gradually tearing down the mountains and extending their deltas westward out into the Yellow Sea.

Beginning in the northwest, the most important rivers which empty into the Yellow Sea are the Ch'ŏngch'ŏn River (164 miles), lying about halfway between the Yalu to the north, and the Taedong River (247 miles), flowing past P'yŏngyang to the south; the Imjin (208 miles); the great Han River (292 miles), which flows northward past Seoul in central Korea, and the Kŭm River (250 miles) further south in the modern Chŏlla Provinces, Korea's granary. Excluding the Han, these rivers do not run lengthwise down the country but rather from east to west across the peninsula and have developed as regional rather than national avenues of transportation. There are several large reservoirs which feed rivers in Korea, Pujŏn and Changjin in the northern interior and the Hwachon in central Korea, but only two lakes of any size, Manp'o and Sŏbŏnp'o on the Sosura peninsula, not far from the Korea-Soviet border.

The Taebaek Range branches in the south, extending toward the southwest tip of the peninsula in the Sobaek Range, forming a natural pocket of the southeast portion of the peninsula. Here in this pocket the mighty Naktong River flows southward for some 300 miles, forming a rich and fertile delta area, before it finally empties into the Korea Straits (Tsushima Straits).

The southern coast of the peninsula is a submerged mountain area. As the submergence occurred, thousands of offshore islands formed from the grey granite and basaltic peaks of the submerged mountains, an area which Koreans have appropriately termed "The Sea of Many Islands."

To the southwest, some 50 miles from the mainland, is the volcanic island of Cheju (Quelpart). The island is dominated by lofty Halla Mountain, with its two parasitic volcanoes last recorded active in the early eleventh century. Somewhat to the north, about 80 miles out in the East Sea, is Ullŭng (Dagelet) Island, a dormant volcanic island.

Looking at a map of the Korean peninsula, we find that it widens at the Hwanghae peninsula in the northwest. Here is Korea's closest point with China proper, for the Shantung promontory lies only some 120 miles to the west. The Yellow Sea, bordering the peninsula on the west, is comparatively shallow, with stretching tidal flats and tides which range from 18 to 30 feet. To the east is the much deeper East Sea. Here a narrow continental shelf drops fairly sharply, and the small tidal ranges of 2 or 3 feet present an enormous contrast to the tides of the Yellow Sea. One result of this is that good harbors for deep-draft vessels are developed with difficulty on the western coast, while the eastern coast has excellent natural harbors, the most active of which are Pusan and Pohang in the south; Wŏnsan on Yŏnghŭng (Broughton) Bay and Hŭngnam in the central area; and Sŏngjin, Chŏngjin, and Najin in the north.

In the climatic sphere, we find that although the average monthly temperatures on the peninsula are usually below freezing in the winter, there is a great contrast between the milder season along the southern coast and the more severe winters in the northern interior. During October dry air masses move over Korea from the continent, bringing clear, dry weather, and in March this process begins to reverse itself as warm, wet air masses move in from the Pacific. By July the monsoon season has arrived and the hot, humid summer has begun. The eastern coast is naturally more influenced by maritime factors than is the western portion of the peninsula. The cold Liman current flows southward along the eastern coast of Korea, and in the sea near Pohang it meets a branch of the warm Black current flowing northward. One consequence is the rich fishing grounds off southeastern Korea. The most notable climatic factor is that the rainfall comes almost entirely during the growing season. The ideal conditions for wet-field rice cultivation undoubtedly influenced the transition from a hunting and gathering type of life to a sedentary agricultural life on the peninsula. The southern part of the peninsula is chiefly devoted to wet-field rice, normally followed by a second crop of grain, while in the north a single grain crop, paddy-field rice in the lowlands and barley or millet in the uplands, is the rule. Wet-field rice can be grown throughout Korea. The agricultural potential soon influenced settlement as people concentrated in the river valleys, most of which are in the west, and in the southern part of the peninsula. Fishing has traditionally been the second most important occupation; yet Korea is still predominantly agricultural, with some two-thirds of the population cultivating the arable one-fifth of the peninsula.

Rainfall has been a crucial element in life on the peninsula since the introduction of wet-field rice centuries ago. Not only quantity but timing is of great importance, particularly when the young rice plants are ready for transplanting from the lush seed beds to the main fields in June.

To the modern eye Korea often seems largely a land of denuded hills, particularly in the more densely settled western and southern areas, where the farmers—whose thatched, earthen huts are scattered in hamlets in the narrow mountain valleys—have long since cut the original forests for cooking and for use in the Korean *ondol* system of radiant heating or for making charcoal to sell in the urban areas. Yet the early peoples on the peninsula were acquainted with a different land, a land abundant with a variety of wild life: pheasant, deer, bear, leopard, and the once ubiquitous tiger. Even today, great boar packs still roam the dense forests of the northeast and seals sport among the rocky islands of the southwest, whose shores are sanctuaries for a large variety of waterfowl, including herons, cormorants, ducks, geese, teal, and crane, and in whose offshore waters are found myriads of fish, while schools of whale still range along the coast.

In an overview Korea seems distinctly compartmentalized by the general east-west extension of mountain ranges, which have acted as a regionalizing, isolating factor throughout Korea's history. Entry from one region into another is commonly via high mountain passes, such as Chabi Pass, the passageway between the Korean northwest and the valley of the Han, or Ch'up'ung Pass, a major gateway to the Naktong area.

The present administrative divisions of Korea follow, in general, the natural regional divisions made by the major mountain ranges as does the distribution of principal dialects. The creation of new administrative divisions in north Korea, viz., the division of Hwanghae Province into north and south and the creation of Chagang Province and Yanggang Province from areas of North P'yŏngan and North Hamgyŏng Provinces, is an attempt to focus development in these areas.

The major geographic features of Korea have been important to the history of its peoples in the past as they will surely be in the future. The mountain ranges continue to form an immense natural barrier as they did when the first nomadic hunters and gatherers began to make their way into the peninsula millennia ago.

2
The Archaeological Record

PALEOLITHIC OR PRECERAMIC CULTURE

Korea, we know, has not always been peninsular in character. During the glacial ages of the Pleistocene epoch, when there was a lowering of the level of the seas as a consequence of the vast masses of ice which accumulated on the land, the relatively shallow Yellow Sea became dry, and Korea became a portion of the main continental mass of east Asia. During this period, the island of Cheju also apparently became a part of the continent, as did the islands of Japan, while the East Sea was reduced to a land-locked lake.

While the glacial invasion did not extend into Korea, the lowering of the temperature caused a general receding of the vegetation toward the south. Fossil evidence indicates that Korea's Quaternary flora and fauna were quite similar to the continental flora and fauna of the period. The fossilized bones of a large variety of animals which foraged the land found near P'yŏngyang, and in the northeast at Tonggwanjin and Changdong-ni in North Haymgŏng Province, include the arctic hairy mammoth, the woolly rhinoceros, the bison, the wild cow, several species of deer and swine, and members of the horse, rodent, and goat families.

Increasing evidence of a widespread Paleolithic culture in adjacent areas, in North China, Manchuria, the Soviet maritime provinces, Siberia, and Japan, suggests that further evidence of early man in Korea will be forthcoming in the future. At this date, information is still meager, and rests upon three finds:

1. The Tonggwanjin site, in the Tumen River area, which has been viewed with skepticism since being reported by the Japanese archaeologist Nobuo Naora in 1940.
2. The Kulp'o-ri site, in the same area, discovered in 1962 and reportedly confirmed by geologic stratigraphy.
3. The Sŏkchang-ni site, in South Ch'ungch'ŏng Province, discovered in 1964, which has been radio-carbon dated at 29,000 B.C.

When the last glaciation ended in north Asia, there began a xerothermic period, and the woolly rhinoceros preceded the mammoth to extinction. If

6

the Tonggwanjin site is accepted, then a people using crude tools of bone, deer antlers, and obsidian lived in northeastern Korea when the woolly rhinoceros and the arctic hairy mammoth still foraged the land. The Kulp'o-ri site may well prove to be postglacial and fall in that period when early man in Korea lived under more moderate climatic conditions than the later pottery-making Neolithic peoples, a time when the waters as far north as the Kamchatka peninsula proved favorable for types of marine shellfish now found only in the southern part of the Sea of Japan.

A preceramic phase may be represented by the microlithic industry of the Tumen River area, which apparently entered the Korean northeast as it diffused across north Asia through Manchuria to North America from origins probably in the Gobi region. Although it spread throughout the peninsula in time, the microlithic industry of the Tumen River area was distinctive, for the microliths are well retouched compared with those in other areas of concentration.

NEOLITHIC CULTURES

There is a great plain which stretches across northern Eurasia from the Volga to the Manchurian highlands, a plain which became a natural highway for nomadic peoples and for peoples forced to move by the pressure of other groups coming into the area. It was also a channel for cultural diffusion both eastward and westward. The eastern terminus of this plain is the Manchurian highlands, of which the mountainous peninsula of Korea is but an extension.

The Neolithic period in Korea coincides with that vast and diverse cultural efflorescence which occurred in north Asia in the third and fourth millennia B.C. The diversity was created by many cultural influxes from central Asia, North China, and Manchuria, which were themselves very diverse. Particularly in the adjacent area of Manchuria cultural diffusion from North China, the Gobi region, the Eurasian steppes, and from the forest peoples of the north mingled and mixed with the local culture. The result was a rich blending with considerable regional development.

Current archaeological and linguistic hypotheses indicate the movement of a primitive hunting and fishing people into the peninsula from the northeast around the fourth millennium B.C. These people were gatherers of shellfish and lived in pit dwellings.

Certainly the early population of the peninsula was sparse. The crude and meager cultural levels associated with the early Neolithic sites indicate that the majority of the time was spent in producing food. Earthquakes, frequent as late as the fourteenth century, were a hazard of Neolithic life. The many finds of burnt dwellings suggest the possibility of conquering tribes, and they also raise the powerful and ominous specter of roaming bands of human predators preying on hapless settlements in times of food scarcity. Yet despite all the hazards Neolithic man prevailed, his creativity and inventiveness attested by the pottery, tools, ornaments, and weapons he made.

Recent archaeological work in southeastern Korea reveals that hunting was secondary to fishing and shellfish gathering as a means of producing food until the second millennium B.C., which is about the same time that the development of agriculture is seen in this area. The people in this area had contacts with people in Japan, from whom they obtained decorated pottery, while they produced a grey pottery themselves.

EARLY POTTERY TYPES

We can distinguish three principal modes of life on the peninsula, associated with distinctive pottery types.

Comb Ceramic This type, so-called from the design on its surface, is believed to be Korea's oldest pottery. It is comparatively thin-walled with a smooth surface, and the design from which it derives its name occurs either as a stippled or incised border around the mouth of the vessel or covers the entire surface, as though a comb had been scraped across the surface of the clay in straight or wavy lines before the vessel was fired.

Similar pottery has been found in the coastal district of southern Manchuria, Siberia, northern Russia, Sweden, and the southern Japanese island of Kyūshū. The distribution of the comb ceramic ware in Korea extends around the coast and to the offshore islands as well as along the major rivers. It is believed that it was brought to the peninsula from the northeast and then slowly became distributed throughout the rest of the peninsula, perhaps diffusing westward through the Seoul-Wŏnsan corridor. Comb ceramic ware has often been found with rough-hewn arrowheads, and articles of bone and horn. Its occurrence predominantly along the coast, especially in shellmounds, and the frequent finds of bone fishhooks with it indicate that its makers lived a life dependent mainly upon maritime products supplemented by the yield of the hunt. The later comb ceramic people were not simply fisherfolk, for evidence of agricultural tools in many sites indicates that they raised grain and practiced a primitive agriculture. This was a late development, however, for the majority of the sites lack these agricultural implements.

The comb ceramic ware was contemporary with the late *mumun* ware (described below) for a time; yet the usually marked separation of the sites suggests that they were produced by two different groups of people. The disappearance of the comb ceramic ware from later shellmounds has led to the belief that the comb ceramic "culture" was absorbed by the *mumun* pottery group.

Mumun   The *mumun* or undecorated red or brownish-red pottery, whose name implies that it is entirely without decoration, although this is not always the case, comes in a variety of forms. Both flat-bottomed and round-bottomed types are common, but a distinction of many pieces is the rim, which is rolled outward. A special feature of the flat-bottomed *mumun* pottery is the cow-horn or nipple shaped "handle," which seems symbolic rather than functional. This heavy, thick-walled, coarse pottery has been found in greater quantity and variety than the comb ceramic, and its repeated association with polished stone agricultural implements has led to the belief that the pottery makers followed a primitive agricultural life, augmenting their diet by hunting and fishing. It is believed that the Korean *mumun* ware is related to similar earthenware found in North China, Mongolia, and Manchuria.

Burnished Red   Also known as painted pottery, it is a thin-walled ware made of fine paste and colored or painted red by means of iron—probably obtained from working surface deposits—and is highly polished or burnished. The firing technique used was far more sophisticated than that of the *mumun* or comb ceramic earthenwares. There is little doubt that this decorated ware is related to North China's painted pottery culture and that it was transmitted through Manchuria and into the Korean northeast. It was associated with an advanced agricultural society which knew bronze, as is shown by the finds with this ware of steamers for steaming grain and bronze articles at the Ch'o Island site, near Najin, the most important site containing this ware yet discovered in Korea. This is a much more sophisticated pottery than either mentioned above, and a large variety of forms occurs, including footed basins, jars, bowls, and steamers.

The painted pottery of the Korean northeast has black curvilinear designs on a red background and at the Najin site was associated with a pottery decorated with appliqué bands. Both pottery types are similar to two main groups of Neolithic pottery found at the Sha-kuo-t'un cave near the Bay of Liaotung in southwestern Manchuria, whose painted pottery presumably originates from the Yangshao painted pottery of the Kansu, Honan, and Shensi areas of North China. Similar appliqué-decorated vessels and painted ware have been found in Neolithic sites in southern Manchuria, the Amur River region, and the Soviet maritime provinces. The bronze finds of the Najin site indicate a date for this particular site somewhat later than the Neolithic dating, between the third and mid-second millennium, suggested by Soviet archaeologists for Sha-kuo-t'un and the southern maritime region.

DWELLINGS

For dwellings Korea's Neolithic populace excavated circular or rectangular pits from 10 to 30 feet in diameter and about 3 feet deep. Flat stones or clay firmly tamped down provided a flooring, while clay was also used at times as a caulking or wall material. Posts supported an upright framework, which probably had the shape of a circular or rectangular thatched lodge. Similar semisubterranean dwellings were constructed by Neolithic peoples in the Amur region and the Soviet maritime provinces and in Japan by both the Ainu and the early Japanese peoples.

The majority of early dwelling sites found have been located in relatively low areas. A small Neolithic village, probably occupied around the fifth century B.C., discovered on the bank of the Tongno River just south of the city of Kanggye in North P'yŏngan Province, presents some interesting insights into life at this time. There were six rectangular, semisubterranean dwellings connected to a central groove-lane by individual paths. A small circle of stones near the center of each dwelling provided an open fireplace. Pits and outlines of small structures adjoining the dwellings were probably used for storage. The stone productive implements, working tools, weapons, and ornaments reveal a small, primitive agricultural community which raised grain, made its own cloth, supplemented its larder with the yield of the hunt and fish from the adjacent river, and made a limited variety of small pottery vessels. Stone items, one-half of which were microliths (chiefly drills and points), included arrowheads, axes, crescent-shaped knives, a sickle, plummets for use with fishing nets or lines, mealers for grinding grain, and spindlewhorls for a simple method of spinning. Two of the dwellings had been unoccupied for a brief period, while three others had burned.

The way of life changed slowly, as a small community discovered some 40 miles north of Seoul and radio-carbon dated to the second century attests. This community of pit houses smelted iron ore, knew the potter's wheel, used steamers for their rice, yet still lived in a semisubterranean dwelling; they used more hand-made pottery than wheel-thrown ware and still used a considerable number of stone tools and weapons.

In addition to these apparently permanent dwelling sites, isolated dwellings have been found, chiefly in the mountains. Temporary refuges were also constructed on mountain summits and in similar places of restricted access for refuge in time of crisis. These mountain refuges developed into a characteristic defense for the peoples of the peninsula, and in later historic times these citadels of refuge (*sansŏng*) were located near every major settlement. Two of the more famous are Pukhan *sansŏng* and Namhan *sansŏng*, located north and south of Seoul respectively. The latter was used by the royal court as a refuge from the Manchu invaders in the seventeenth century.

The severity of the Korean winters resulted in a wide variety of heating arrangements in dwellings, which ranged from simple fireplaces or hearths to a method of radiant heating, the *ondol*, or Korean hot floor. Heating methods included heating stones which were put on the floor, fire-chambers adjacent to the main chamber, and central stone or clay fireboxes. The remnants of an *ondol*, the Korean-style hypocaust, whose construction was similar to those currently in use through the peninsula, were found in a Neolithic site at Unggi, North Hamgyŏng Province. In this method of heating, the hot air and smoke from a fire are circulated through chambers beneath a stone floor, heating the entire floor space for some period, as the stone retains the heat. Similar types of radiant heating were known in North China and in the Roman Empire, and the Romans introduced it to England in the first century B.C.

SHELLMOUNDS

A major source of knowledge of Korea's early culture are the shell-mounds. The shellmounds were, of course, refuse heaps. The items discovered in these refuse piles reveal, not primitive groups of nomadic gatherers, but peoples as highly developed as any on the peninsula. The shellmound people were a fisherfolk, who lived near the coastline and major river courses, developing the full equipment necessary to secure an abundance of marine products. From the coastal and river waters they took great harvests of shell-fish. Popular items included varieties of oysters, abalone, clams, sea scallops, and snails, while both coastal and migratory fish, such as cod, flounder, bigmouth, and sea perch, were caught. The shellmound people supplemented their fishing activities by hunting and later by primitive agriculture and domestication of the pig and dog. It is evident from the enormous number of shellmounds that fishing was an important economic activity, which affected the life and culture of the people who developed this specialization. In some areas where the catch was bountiful, small communities settled over long periods of time, as is evidenced by the great size of some of the shellmounds, and developed such specialized equipment as harpoons and nets.

Shellmounds are, of course, rather widespread, occurring in Europe as well as in Asia. In Korea, shellmounds are found along the coastline and in adjacent river deltas around the peninsula, on the numerous offshore islands in the Yellow Sea, and even on distant Ullŭng Island some 80 miles out in the Sea of Japan. The shellmounds began to disappear in Korea around the second century B.C. However, in the south, particularly in the Naktong region, bronze and iron items in the shellmounds indicate they lasted into the first century. Iron implements and coins minted in A.D. 14 during the Wang Mang interregnum (A.D. 9 to 23) have been found in the Kimhae

MATERIAL CHRONOLOGY OF EARLY KOREA

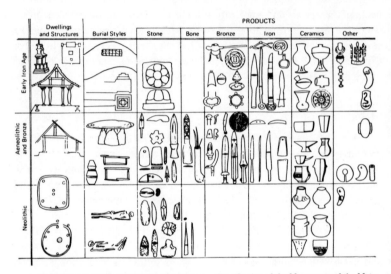

SOURCE: After M. N. Vorob'yev, *Drevnyaya Koreya*, 1961, Table XL, "Chronological Classification of the Monuments of the Material Culture of Korea."

shellmounds in the Naktong River delta. It seems probable that there were two distinct shellmound periods in Korea, an early one coinciding with the early immigrants and a second one beginning perhaps as late as the fifth century B.C.

MANUFACTURED ITEMS

The resourcefulness of Neolithic man in Korea is seen in the wide variety of implements and ornaments he made from bone, horn, wood, shell, stone, and clay, materials he continued to work with even after he became acquainted with metal, partially because of the scarcity of metal.

Bone items include arrowheads, similar to Manchurian types, daggers, axes with two cutting edges, fishhooks, needles of fishbone, and even a fine needle case made from the leg bone of a bird. Animal teeth, particularly the incisor teeth of the wild pig, were used as gaffs, possibly attached to wooden handles. Horn items include a primitive type of pick, probably for digging roots. Scrapers, knives, and ornaments were also made from shells.

Stone items are generally divided into two categories: chipped and polished. Burstone and argillite were popular materials for polished stone implements, while almost any strong stone was used for the chipped implements. Chipped arrowheads, however, fall outside the general category of chipped items and were made primarily from materials whose fracture plane is such that they are best worked by chipping, such as obsidian or flint.

Common ornaments included pierced animal teeth, from which probably derived the comma-shaped ornaments of stone well known from Japanese sites, i.e., the so-called *magatama*, and ornaments made of clay, including a number of small human figurines. With the entrance of a metal culture, we find many of the old forms of ornaments persisting, such as the comma-shaped ornaments and the cylinder beads, but made of semiprecious stone such as jade—not found in a natural state in Korea—and jasper.

Clay was used rather limitedly for plummets, spindle-whorls, and ornaments as well as for pottery, which frugal Neolithic housewives often mended by boring holes in the vessel and tying the pot back together; when beyond repair the fragments were often used as weights for fishing lines.

Tools, of which there are a great variety, show regional characteristics and reflect both the process of diffusion and regional differentiation. The stone semilunar or crescent-shaped woman's knife is also common throughout North China, Mongolia, Manchuria, the Soviet maritime provinces, Japan, and among the Eskimos and Indians of North America.

DOLMEN AND THE ENTRANCE OF A METAL CULTURE

Through the mortuary articles they have yielded, dolmen are a second important source of knowledge of prehistoric Korea. The dolmen are often divided into two categories: *northern* and *southern.*

Northern Dolmen   These extend from Manchuria into the northern portion of the peninsula, where they are concentrated north of the Han River, although many have been found in the south as well, including even on Cheju Island. They are constructed of huge flat stones like a house of cards, i.e., four slabs on the sides and one larger overlapping slab on top. The northern dolmen are of considerable size, one found at Hogadon having upright supporting stones 7 feet high, while the covering slab measured 28½ feet long and 18½ feet wide. The dolmen are quite commonly found in groups of from three to ten. Groups of thirty have been found in South P'yŏngan and Kangwŏn Provinces. A north-south–oriented assemblage of over forty dolmen, arranged in a straight line for over 500 meters with larger stones interspersed at approximately equal intervals between each dolmen, was found in Hwanghae Province. The size and construction of the dolmen are revealing for they imply a high degree of engineering skill and a social organization capable of assembling and directing the considerable manpower necessary to quarry, transport, and erect the huge stone slabs used in their construction.

Southern Dolmen   They are of somewhat different construction from the northern. A small stone chamber is constructed of flat stones, and a boulder is placed on top at ground level, giving the natural appearance of a boulder sitting in the field. The southern dolmen, viewed as a later development of the northern type, are concentrated in the area below the Han River, although they have also been found as far north as the Taedong River. The southern dolmen are linked in both construction and burial items with the cist graves or dolmen of northern Kyūshū. Occasionally the southern dolmen are found in groups, e.g., a group of ten was found on Kŏje Island in South Kyŏngsang Province; yet the majority are scattered individual sites.

It is believed that the dolmen date from about 800 B.C. and continued until about the second century, when they gave way to the various types of urn burials, stone chamber tombs, and tumuli of Korea's Three Kingdoms period.

There were also regional developments in dolmen construction, particularly in the northwest. The size decreased and variant forms appeared. The dolmen have yielded both *mumun* and burnished red earthenware and also chipped stone items, chiefly arrowheads of obsidian or flint, although the majority of the stone items fall into the polished stone category.

The dolmen people knew metal, and as burial items they interred fragile stone ceremonial daggers made of an easily worked stone and patterned after metallic daggers, which were too precious to be buried even by the upper class. As metal became more common, these ceremonial stone substitutes were replaced by bronze and iron items.

Believed to be closely related to the dolmen are the menhir, generally thought to be phallic symbols of fertility, in which case we might associate them with an agricultural society, or symbols of a guardian spirit. In Asia, menhir are widespread and have been found, for example, in Indonesia, Burma, Siberia, Mongolia, and Japan as well as in Korea. It has been suggested that many menhir were subsequently made into stele or monuments, e.g., the famous monument to Koguryŏ's King Kwanggaet'o or, following the introduction of Buddhism in the last quarter of the fourth century, were carved into images of Maitreya, the Buddha of the future. The feeling of later people toward these menhir is suggested by a small 4½-foot-high menhir in North P'yŏngan Province which had eight characters carved on it, which read in part: "an item of antiquity from the time of the creation of heaven and earth. . . ."

METAL CULTURE

The work of Soviet archaeologists in Manchuria and the Soviet maritime region indicates the existence there of a bronze culture dating from the end of the second millennium to the first half of the first millennium B.C. North Korean archaeologists would include the Tumen and Yalu River regions in this culture area. The dating, it should be noted, coincides roughly with the fall of China's Shang-Yin dynasty in 1122 B.C.

Dates given for the entrance of an advanced iron culture into the peninsula are principally based on two types of coins, *ming-tao* (knife money) and *fu-ch'ien* (spade money), minted during the latter half of China's Eastern Chou period, i.e., the Period of Warring States (403–221 B.C.), which have been found in North and South P'yŏngan Province, in the Korean northwest, and in South Chŏlla Province in the southwest. It is clear that an advanced metal culture entered Korea's northwest prior to the fall in 265 B.C. of the Kingdom of Yen, a northern Chinese state where similar coins were minted. A Ch'in dynasty sword with an inscribed date of 222 B.C., unearthed at P'yŏngyang, attests to a continuance of the influx of a metal culture. Associated with this advanced metal culture was a blue-grey, mat-decorated pottery fired at temperatures around 1,000 degrees—a highly fired ware—as well as bronze and iron arrowheads, axes, spearheads, sickles, and crescent-shaped knives of iron. The six sites where the coins were found were located along what is believed to have been an important communications route which came down into the Korean northwest from the middle reaches of the Yalu River.

Another metal culture which entered the peninsula probably around the same time as the knife money is that represented by distinctive bronze articles, generally termed Scytho-Siberian, which have also been found through the peninsula as far south as the Naktong delta region. These articles, which reflect the animal art of the Eurasian steppe, include bronze horse-shaped and tiger-shaped belt clasps and numerous horse trappings; similar belt buckles have also been found in Japan as have been a type of ornamental bell similar to a smaller type of bell found in Korea associated with such articles. The predominant connection with horses reveals a culture related to mobile, nomadic peoples, probably of the great steppes of eastern Asia, such as the Hsiung-nu, and the excellence of the artifacts is noteworthy.

As contacts increased with North China, undoubtedly including through refugees from the wars in China, the peoples on the peninsula began to cast their own versions of Chinese metallic items. This metamorphosed Chinese culture included bronze daggers, spearheads, and mirrors with two knobs on the reverse side—in contradistinction to the Chinese mirror, which has a single knob—and decorated with a zig-zag geometric design resembling a welter of lightning flashes. Some twenty mirrors or their fragments have been found to date: fifteen from Korea, three from Japan, and one each from southern Manchuria and the Vladivostok area. The zig-zag pattern is, it should be noted, a common design found on pottery of the Amur and maritime regions and the Korean northeast, and it has also been found at the lowest level of the Shao-kuo-t'un cave in southwestern Manchuria, near Liaotung Bay.

The movement of people into the peninsula in the fourth to third centuries B.C. coincides with the end of China's Chou dynasty and the rise and fall of the short-lived Ch'in dynasty. This is also the period when the bearers of Japan's Yayoi culture entered northern Kyūshū, where they introduced wet-field rice, wheel-made pottery, and a metal culture. An apparently related people settled in the lower reaches of the Naktong River area, where they later formed the Kaya league. The Kaya people are believed, on rather slender linguistic evidence, to have been a northern people and to have spoken a language similar to that spoken in the Korean-Manchurian state of Koguryŏ and in adjacent areas of Japan yet different from their Chinhan neighbors to the north, who would later form the state of Silla. Third century descriptions indicate that with the exception of the T'amna (Cheju) islanders and the Chinhan people, most of the people on the peninsula spoke related dialects of a common language.

At this point our knowledge of ancient Korea is too meager to generalize on the basis of the few detailed site reports which exist. The evidence to date suggests migration of tribal groups into the peninsula from the maritime provinces and from Manchuria. The painted pottery of the Tumen area suggests migration from North China in a later period. We can also see changes in the mode of life in some areas shifting from fishing to hunting and to agriculture. An early agricultural way of life had apparently begun to develop in the southeast prior to the adoption of wet-field rice agriculture. Unfortunately we have many conjectural opinions and little positive evidence to indicate the origins of wet-field rice agriculture on the peninsula, the relationship between the people of the Korean southeast and the people of Japan during this period, or to answer the many other questions we can ask about early Korea.

Evidence of influences from China at different periods is abundant, particularly on items of metal, although the metallic items believed to be of Scytho-Siberian origin suggest a strong influence of a metal culture from the plains of Manchuria and possible contacts with the Hsiung-nu. There is also some evidence of contacts between the people of the Korean southeast and the Japanese people of southern Honshū and northern Kyūshū during the middle and late Jomon period.

3
The Early Tribal Peoples

The area north of China has been the homeland of many tribal peoples—Mongolian, Turkish, Tungusic, and Manchu. Its history is one of repeated struggles of one tribal group or alliance against the other tribal peoples in the area and, above all, of conflicts between these nomadic and seminomadic people and the sedentary people of the Chinese states, a conflict which has continued into modern times with the entry of a new contender, the Soviet Union. Under the great Chinese empires of Han, T'ang, and Ming, these areas were under varying degrees of Chinese control, while in other periods these areas and the region of North China were under the control of northern peoples, the Ch'itan Liao, the Jürčen Chin, the Mongol Yüan, and the Manchu Ch'ing dynasties. Immediately involved were the peoples of eastern Manchuria and the Korean peninsula, i.e., those tribal peoples who lived in the area bounded by the Liao River to the west and the Sungari and Amur Rivers to the north, the earliest implied boundaries to emerge in the northeast.

This period is, as far as Korea is concerned, chiefly protohistory, a period when we have a few facts and quite a lot of materials which are often of uncertain value. Examples of the latter are the Korean and Japanese works which purport to record the history of this early period but which are more in the way of a foggy sea of legend, myth, and exaggeration with a few firm islands of fact. Our major sources for this period are Chinese records of the first to third centuries, which tell us something of the peoples of Manchuria and Korea.

PUYŎ

Early Chinese descriptions of the northeast indicate that in the second century B.C., the most powerful tribal group in this area was the Puyŏ (c. Fuyü), who lived in the Sungari River area. The Puyŏ tribes were identified by apparently totemistic animals, viz., horse tribe, cow tribe, dog tribe, pig tribe. The chieftains of these tribes, who selected one of their number to be the supreme chieftain, are said to have worn the furs of the fox and the sable

Chronological Overview

The Four Han Commanderies and the Emergence of the Three Korean States

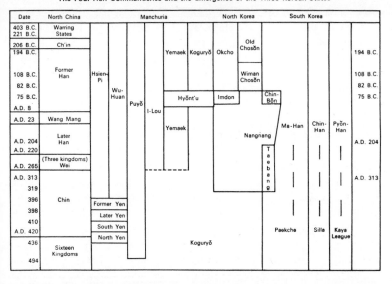

Date	North China	Manchuria	North Korea	South Korea	
403 B.C. / 221 B.C.	Warring States				
206 B.C.	Ch'in		Old Chosŏn		
194 B.C.		Yemaek / Koguryŏ / Okcho			194 B.C.
108 B.C.	Former Han	Hsien-Pi	Wiman Chosŏn		108 B.C.
82 B.C.		Wu-Huan			82 B.C.
75 B.C.		Puyŏ / Hyŏnt'u / Imdon	Chin-Bŏn		75 B.C.
A.D. 8		I-Lou			
A.D. 23	Wang Mang	Yemaek	Nangnang	Ma-Han / Chin-Han / Pyŏn-Han	
A.D. 204	Later Han				A.D. 204
A.D. 220	(Three kingdoms) Wei		Taebang		
A.D. 265					
A.D. 313	Chin				A.D. 313
319					
396		Former Yen			
398		Later Yen			
410		South Yen			
A.D. 420		North Yen	Paekche / Silla / Kaya League		
436	Sixteen Kingdoms	Koguryŏ			
494					

over imported silks, and their hats were ornamented with gold and silver. Under each tribal chieftain were the heads of the tribal villages. Justice was swift and punishment severe. Murderers and adulteresses were killed, and their families were cast into slavery. Thieves were required to recompense their victims twelvefold. It was customary for a younger brother to inherit the wife of his elder brother upon the latter's death, a custom observed by some Mongolian tribes as well. The Puyŏ inhabited a broad plains area and engaged in some agriculture. They also raised fine horses, which, along with red gemstones and furs of the sable, they sent to China, whence they received silks, embroidered cloth, and other products. Sacrifices to heaven were made in the twelfth lunar month, when there were large gatherings and a celebration with feasting, singing, and dancing which lasted for days. Prior to military undertakings a cow would be sacrificed and a prognostication of the outcome made using one of its hooves, presumably by exposing it to fire. Subject to the Puyŏ in varying degrees were the other tribal people of eastern Manchuria and northern Korea, who are briefly described in Chinese sources.

OKCHŎ

The Okchŏ were a small group of tribes who occupied the general area of the modern North Hamgyŏng Province from the Tumen River valley into the Kaema Plateau region, a long narrow and fertile area with mountains to its back and the sea before it. Three groups were recognized: the Eastern, Northern, and Southern Okchŏ, whose speech, dwellings, food, and clothing resembled those of the Koguryŏ peoples. A minor tribal group who never seemed to have entered the stage of a tribal alliance, the Okchŏ lived in scattered villages, each with its own headman, and were subordinate and tributary to the stronger groups of people neighboring them, first to Chosŏn and then in turn to Puyŏ, to Han China, and later to Koguryŏ. The Okchŏ lived in terror of the northern I-lou, who used to raid south by boat during the short summers when the rivers were free of ice. They had an interesting burial custom in which there was temporary burial; later the bones would be disinterred and placed in a family or clan ossiary.

YEMAEK

The Yemaek lived along the upper reaches of the Yalu River. It is recorded that their language and customs were generally the same as those of Koguryŏ, although their clothing was different. They considered themselves to be a branch of the Koguryŏ peoples. Their land was known for the small Korean horse, the leopard, and the tiger, the last being worshipped. Within their area they recognized what were apparently clan boundaries, and they held a harvest celebration in the tenth lunar month, with sacrifices to heaven, drinking, singing, and dancing. The view has been advanced that the Maek or Yemaek people were the founders of the ancient state of Chosŏn and that they originally lived in the lower Liao River area and later moved eastward into Korea about the third century B.C.

I-LOU

The I-lou lived in the forested mountains of the far northeast, and even the Chinese were uncertain of the northern borders of their lands. Like the Okchŏ, they had no supreme ruler, but each village had its own headman. Subordinate to the Puyŏ from Han times to the third century, they practiced some agriculture and produced a coarse cloth but were better known as swine herders. The hides of the pig were used for clothing, while in winter they smeared their bodies with pork grease as protection against chapping by the fierce and icy northern winds. Their dwellings were at least partially subterranean and were entered through a door in the roof. Famed archers, the I-lou used stone arrowheads treated with a deadly poison and were known for their summer raiding activities.

THE NORTHERN TRIBAL PEOPLES AND CHINA

Bordering the Puyŏ to the west were the Hsien-pi, to the southwest the Wu-huan, and further west the nomadic Hsiung-nu, whose chieftains, the

Shan-yü, had gained both the respect and fear of the Chinese. The sweeping, plundering incursions of the Hsiung-nu through China had continued periodically for centuries. A legacy of the period is the long wall of China erected primarily against the Hsiung-nu. The eastward movement of these peoples from the Mongolian plateau area into Manchuria undoubtedly contributed to the rise of the Puyŏ peoples even as their metal culture diffused into eastern Manchuria and the Korean peninsula.

During China's "Spring and Autumn" period (ca. 770–430 B.C.), there had developed in northeastern China on the Gulf of P'ohai the state of Yen. In the ensuing Warring States period (430–211 B.C.), Yen had, through a series of military campaigns in 311–297 B.C., expanded to incorporate the Liaotung Peninsula and southeastern Manchuria. The knife-money and spade-money coins found in northwestern Korea as far south as the Taedong River were probably minted in the state of Yen. At present the general view is that they indicate an ancient trade route in this area. The short-lived Ch'in dynasty (255–209 B.C.), which unified China in 221 B.C., brought the state of Yen firmly under their control. The wars of this period in China undoubtedly led to considerable immigration into eastern Manchuria and northern Korea, while the Ch'in court sent large numbers of military and administrative officials into the Liaotung area, bringing direct Chinese influence into the northeast in some force. The Ch'in sword dated 222 B.C. mentioned earlier, which was found in the P'yŏngyang area, attests to the contact with Ch'in.

WIMAN CHOSŎN

In 195 B.C., shortly after the Ch'in dynasty was replaced in China by the Former Han dynasty (206 B.C.–A.D. 9), Lu Kuan,* the king of Yen, revolted against the Han and allied with their enemies the Hsiung-nu. At this time there existed in northeastern Korea a state called Chosŏn. It is said that when Lu Kuan revolted, many fled from his lands. Among these was a certain Wiman (c. Wei-man), who is said to have gone east with 1,000 followers and submitted to King Chun, the ruler of Chosŏn. Wiman was settled on the Chosŏn border with his followers, far from the Chosŏn capital, and given the task of frontier defense. Gathering more refugees under him, Wiman proceeded to the Chosŏn capital under the pretext of guarding the monarch against a Chinese invasion. With his forces in the city Wiman seized the throne.

There is a story which has every appearance of being a later fabrication that King Chun fled southward with several thousand followers, where he

*Korean, Chinese, and Japanese names are in traditional order, with the family name given first.

conquered a portion of the Mahan tribal area and proclaimed himself king of the Korean Han tribes.

The state of Chosŏn is assumed to have had its capital, Wanggŏm, in the area of modern P'yŏngyang, the ancient cultural center of the Korean peninsula; archaeological evidence shows this area to have been in the late dolmen stage in the third century B.C. Present also were the requirements for the construction of the dolmen, namely, considerable engineering skill and command of a sizable labor force.

THE CHINESE COMMANDERIES

In 141 B.C. a young man known to posterity as Wu Ti (the Martial Emperor) ascended the throne of Han China. His determination to end the continued threat of invasion by the northern tribal peoples, particularly the Hsiung-nu, was to change the course of life for the peoples on the peninsula. As an adjunct to their military efforts, the Han Chinese also searched for allies in the west and in the northeast and, in 121 B.C., secured the submission of Nam-nyŏ (c. Nan-lu), the chieftain of the Yemaek people. He permitted the establishment of Changhae commandery on Yemaek territory along the upper reaches of the Yalu River. An overextension without Chinese forces nearby to back it up, the base was closed after only 6 years. Yet it indicated the Chinese interest in the area and was a presage of future events.

In the spring of 109 B.C., an incident occurred which was to precipitate the Chinese conquest of northern Korea. A Chinese envoy, a certain She Ho, was sent by Han Emperor Wu Ti to Chosŏn to bring the area under Chinese influence and thereby secure China's northeastern flank. She Ho failed in his mission, and on his return he killed his Korean escort, apparently including the Chosŏn premier, at the border and reported that he had killed a Korean general. When as a reward for his bravery She Ho was appointed commander in chief of the eastern sector of Liaotung, Chosŏn dispatched forces to kill him in revenge. The Chinese response came in the autumn of the same year, when a large Chinese army was dispatched from Liaotung and a small naval force sent across the Gulf of P'ohai against Chosŏn. Despite several initial setbacks, for which the Chinese naval commander was beheaded in the marketplace, the Chinese forces finally surrounded Wanggŏm, the Chosŏn capital, the following year. During the siege the ruler of Chosŏn, Ugŏ, the grandson of Wiman, was assassinated, and Chosŏn fell in the summer of 108 B.C. To secure the area, the Chinese established three commanderies in Korea, viz., Nangnang (c. Lo-lang), Imdun (c. Lin-t'un), and Chinbŏn (c. Chen-fan). The following year, 107 B.C., a fourth commandery, Hyŏnt'o (c. Hsüan-t'u), was established on Okchŏ territory in the Korean northeast.

The hub of the Chinese administration in Korea was at Nangnang, which controlled the northwest portion of the Korean peninsula. While the exact boundaries are still disputed, it appears that the commandery of Chinbŏn covered the area from Chabi Pass, in modern Hwanghae Province, south to the Han River, while Imdun in the east incorporated the modern South Hamgyŏng Province. Each commandery was subdivided into administrative districts where small towns developed, all tied together through an administrative structure to Nangnang, then to the governor of Yu-chou in Liaotung, and finally back to the central government in China.

Nangnang was the great center of Chinese culture in Korea, a center which endured 400 years. Here on the southern bank of the broad Taedong River, a walled city was constructed. Buildings went up introducing new architectural concepts to the peninsula, and streets paved with brick were laid out for the canopied chariots of the wealthy and the powerful. Officials followed the military and were in turn followed by waves of colonists: artisans, craftsmen, merchants, and farmers. The high culture of Han China blossomed at Nangnang on a hundred branches. Iron and bronze items manufactured ran from military weapons to chariot fittings and agricultural tools. Delicate goldwork inlaid with semiprecious stones and superb lacquerware items were imported from China, and textiles and ceramic wares of many varieties were produced locally. Nangnang was an important trade center, and local products were not overlooked. The small horse common to northern Korea was secured through the tribute trade with the Yemaek. They became a famous Nangnang export, even being used in the palace by a dowager empress for her personal cart. Equally important were the new concepts and techniques in art, in philosophy, and in government which the Chinese brought with them. A local tribute system was instituted both with those tribal peoples directly under Chinese administration and with the Korean Han tribes who inhabited the southern portion of the peninsula.

The effect of the establishment of the Chinese commanderies in Korea was, of course, enormous, extending throughout the peninsula and across the Straits of Korea to the Japanese state of Wa, whose first recorded envoys came to Nangnang in A.D. 57. The establishment of the commanderies, like all colonial efforts, was certainly not undertaken for the benefit of the peoples on the peninsula. However, the model it provided for the Korean tribal peoples in the fields of government organization and administration, in technology and the arts, was a major stimulus in their development.

The growth of bureaucracy is attested by the thousands of tombs of lower officials found in the vicinity of Nangnang. The census of A.D. 2 covering Nangnang with its twenty-five subordinate districts and Hyŏnt'u with three subordinate districts reveals a population of some 350,000. A census conducted in A.D. 140 for the same area shows a population of some 225,000 persons. The decrease in population has been attributed to the continual warfare in the area and to some extent to the large-scale migration from North China toward new lands in the south.

The establishment of the Chinese commanderies in Korea faced the opposition of the local people from the beginning. The two commanderies of Chinbŏn and Imdun were abolished in 82 B.C., and the remnants of their administrative functions were turned over to the authorities in Nangnang. By 75 B.C. local opposition had forced the removal of the administration (and the designation) of Hyŏnt'u commandery westward into Manchuria.

During the Wang Mang interregnum (A.D. 8–23) and the troubles attendant upon the rise of the Later Han dynasty (A.D. 23–220), the opportunity was seized by a certain Wang Cho (c. Wang T'iao) in Nangnang to revolt in an attempt at independence from the Later Han. The rebellion was crushed in A.D. 30, at which time the administration of outlying districts was turned over to native leaders, and Chinese administrative officials were withdrawn from these local areas.

THE SAM HAN

In the southern portion of the peninsula below the Chinese Han commanderies were the Sam Han or Three Korean Han tribes. This Han $\left[\,韓\,\right]$ is a different character from Han $\left[\,漢\,\right]$ China. The precise geographic area held by each of these tribal groups is still debated but appears to have been generally as follows: In the southwestern portion of the peninsula was Mahan and in the Naktong delta area was P'yŏnhan. Occupying the rest of the Naktong pocket and possibly a portion of the valley of the Han as well was Chinhan, which by A.D. 44 had become tributary to Nangnang. In the Chinese-instituted tribute system, the tribal chieftains were given seals and clothing to correspond to the titles and offices awarded them by the Chinese as well as a variety of Chinese products in exchange for peaceful relations and local products which were presented in the form of tribute. Early records give us a brief description of these people in the southern part of the peninsula.

Mahan The fifty-five Mahan tribes, of whom the Mokchi were dominant until the rise of Paekche, lived in the southwestern part of the Korean peninsula in scattered communities of round earthen huts entered through a door in the top. An agricultural people, they had two chief sacrificial ceremonies to the spirits, one in the spring after the fields were planted and a harvest festival in the autumn. Both celebrations featured singing and dancing. Each village had its own "priest" who sacrificed to the spirits of heaven. They also had a shrine, called a *sodo*, constructed of great timbers from which were hung bells. The *sodo* was apparently also a sanctuary where persons could seek safe refuge. Although the Mahan are not pictured as an advanced people in the Chinese records—for example, we are informed that they did not use horses nor value gold—they were the most numerous of the Korean Han peoples.

Chinhan The twelve Chinhan tribes occupied the majority of the upper Naktong area. It is related that the Chinhan elders considered themselves to be descendants of refugees from the Chinese state of Ch'in (255–205 B.C.). They lived in walled cities, in wooden stockades, and in small villages each with its own chieftain. An agricultural people occupying a fertile area, they practiced sericulture and used oxen and horse carts. Their most famed product was iron, which was used in the markets as currency and which formed the basis for a brisk trade with the other Han tribes, the Yemaek, and the Japanese Wa. They are noted to have had a lute resembling the Chinese five-stringed instrument and to have been fond of drinking, dancing, and singing. Large feathers were buried with the dead to help them fly away. Among the tribes of the Chinhan were the *Saro*, who by the fourth century developed into the state later known as Silla.

Pyŏnhan The Pyŏnhan were a group of people who lived along the lower reaches of the Naktong River. They lived in close contact with the Chinhan, and their dwellings and dress were the same, but the speech and customs of the Pyŏnhan were different. The Pyŏnhan did not unite into a strong tribal alliance but emerged as a group of small, semiautonomous communities recognizing the most powerful of their number as leader. This group of states, the Kaya League, had strong ties with the Japanese Wa tribe. The early route used by the Wa envoys to the Chinese Han commanderies was via the island of Tsushima and the Kaya League. It is clear from archaeological findings that there existed as early as the first century B.C. a strong maritime trade in this area. There is some evidence to suggest that the Pyŏnhan people were related to the Koguryŏ people and formed part of a southward movement of peoples, some of whom crossed to the Japanese island, i.e., northern Kyūshū and southwestern Honshū, to form a major segment of the Japanese tribal groups.

On the large island of T'amna (i.e., Cheju), south of the peninsula, lived a cattle- and swine-breeding people who are said to have spoken a language different from that of the Korean Han people, with whom they had established maritime trade contacts. Chinese records relate that they were comparatively short in stature, wore leather clothing, and shaved their heads, in contrast to the Korean Han people. The little kingdom of T'amna was tributary to Paekche until the fall of the latter state to Silla in 660.

THE RISE OF KOGURYŎ

The strong thrust of the Chinese into eastern Manchuria and northern Korea apparently had a unifying effect on many of the tribal peoples in the area, while the subsequent weakening of Chinese power in the area enabled the potential for strong alliances to emerge. By the first century Koguryŏ, a tribal alliance, had emerged in the mountainous uplands of southeastern Manchuria.

Koguryŏ occupied an area along a tributary to the Yalu, northwest of Paektu Mountain between the Puyŏ to the north and the Yemaek and Chosŏn to the south. They regarded themselves as a branch of the Puyŏ people. Their language and customs were, it is related, similar, although the Chinese chroniclers were quick to add that they differed from the relatively peaceful Puyŏ not only in dress, but in their emotional and volatile temperament as well. The early references to Koguryŏ reveal a people who were fierce fighters given to warfare. They lived in a mountainous area ill-suited for agriculture and apparently turned their hunting activities into a professional military way of life. This in turn requires discipline and order on the one hand, while it also may indicate the basic structure upon which the society emerged. A third century description shows Koguryŏ as an alliance of five tribes, viz., the Yŏn, Chŏl, Sun, Kwan, and Kye. The Yŏn tribe held power and furnished kings for a period and then were replaced by the Kye tribe, who evidently allied with the Chŏl tribe, a chief source of brides for the Koguryŏ kings. The dominance of these two tribes provided a strong centralizing force and marked a political turning point from the centripetal tendencies of an alliance of five tribes. Under the king were ten classes of officials who coordinated all national activities and implemented all policies. Tribal leaders were apparently semiautonomous in their own areas and had their own civil and military officials. The tribal leaders themselves were on the highest councils of the central government and apparently they actually implemented policy in their own areas to a large extent. As the nation flourished the officials became a wealthy and powerful leisure class, dressing in silks and brocades with silver and gold ornaments. The Koguryŏ made their sacrifices to heaven in the tenth lunar month, at which time they also sacrificed to spirits in a great cave located in the eastern part of their country. They erected ancestral temples and an altar to the spirits of earth and grain. Shamanism-animism was the religious force. There were shrines to the mythical founder Chumong (= Tongmyŏng) in the capital as well as in some cities (see Appendix 2: "Foundation Myths"). The Koguryŏ kings would sacrifice at this shrine when they ascended the throne. The mother of Tongmyŏng, i.e., the daughter of the river god, was also worshipped, and there were molded clay and carved wooden images of her. Sacrifices to the

Tung Shou, last ruler of Nangnang, is shown seated in an ox-drawn chariot escorted by soldiers and musicians. Figure dated A.D. 357.

mountains and streams were made, and the function of the shamaness was important.

When Wang Mang instituted his new dynasty in China in A.D. 9, both Puyŏ and Koguryŏ sent envoys to the Chinese court and in A.D. 12 were ordered to mobilize forces against the Hsiung-nu, China's greatest enemy. The Koguryŏ refusal led to yet another flurry of conflict in the northeast. Koguryŏ had moved into the power vacuum occasioned by the Chinese Han withdrawal from the northeast to make the Okchŏ a subordinate tributary state. The Chinese system of using local officials for collection of taxes was reinstated, and Okchŏ revenues which had previously gone to Puyŏ and the Hyŏnt'u commandery now went to Koguryŏ. These products included sable furs, salt, fish and other marine products, and beautiful girls sent to the court as slaves and concubines.

Puyŏ maintained friendly relations with China, and as Koguryŏ strength increased, China used Puyŏ as an ally to check Koguryŏ, Yemaek, and Hsien-pi incursions in the Liaotung area, a situation which continued through most of the second century. By the last years of the reign of Emperor Ling (r. A.D. 168–188) of the Later Han dynasty, the Chinese colonies in Korea were at a low ebb, and local administration had become impossible. The chaotic conditions led many to flee south to the adjacent lands of the Korean Han tribes.

THE KINGDOM OF YEN

In the early years of the third century, the Later Han began to fall apart to give way to China's Three Kingdoms, viz., the Wei, the Shu-Han, and the Wu. In southern Manchuria, Kong-son Kang (c. Kung-sun K'ang), of a family active for generations as military commanders in the Liaotung area, inherited the position of Liaotung prefect in A.D. 204 from his father, who had already made Liaotung an autonomous area under his control. Kang extended this control into the Korean northwest over the commandery of Nangnang. To strengthen the position of Nangnang, he set up the commandery of Taebang south of Nangnang in the general area where the old commandery of Chinbŏn had been. After Kang's death his son Yŏn held power. At this time, two of China's Three Kingdoms, Wu and Wei, were periodically at war with each other. When a Wei campaign in Liaotung was unsuccessful in 232, the state of Wu quickly sent envoys to seek allies against the Wei. They recognized Kong-son Yŏn as the new ruler of Yen, while their envoys to Koguryŏ attempted to flatter that ruler with the title of *shan-yü*, the traditional title of the powerful chieftains of the Hsiung-nu. The relations of Kong-son Yŏn and Koguryŏ with the Wei and their allies the Puyŏ were strained at the time, but they were persuaded that rather than seek support from the distant state of Wu to kill the Wu envoys and send them to the Wei court as a gesture of good will. Wei then recognized Kong-son Yŏn by enfeoffing him as duke of Nangnang. Shortly after this in 237, Yŏn felt strong enough to challenge the Wei again and proclaimed himself the king of Yen. The Wei response to the potential threat indicated by this declaration of strength and independence was immediate. In the autumn of 238, the brilliant strategist General Ssu-ma I pushed into Liaotung and with the aid of Koguryŏ troops captured Kong-son Yŏn and beheaded him. This brought Liaotung, Nangnang, and Taebang under Wei control. It also brought the Wei into direct contact with Koguryŏ.

THE WEI CAMPAIGNS

Koguryŏ at this time had its capital at Kungnae-sŏng in the modern T'onggang (c. T'ung-chiang) area. It had gradually grown stronger through a combination of conquests and alliances with tribal groups in the northeast but was no match for the Wei and their Puyŏ allies. In 209 Koguryŏ constructed a new capital, Hwando-sŏng (probably near modern T'ung-kou), south along the Yalu river, probably as a result of the constant threat on the northern and western borders from the Puyŏ, Yen, and Wei.

Supported by her ally Puyŏ, Wei launched an attack against Koguryŏ led by General Kuan-ch'iu Chien, prefect of Yu-chou, in 244 as a reprisal for a Koguryŏ raid on Liaotung. The Wei army took the Koguryŏ capital and forced the Koguryŏ king to flee to the east coast for safety. The same campaign secured the submission of the Yemaek. A second Wei campaign against Koguryŏ in 259, however, was defeated, and Wei itself soon fell to the Western Chin (265–316), who reunified China.

THE RISE OF PAEKCHE

About this time a second Korean kingdom, Paekche, appeared in the southwestern portion of the Korean peninsula. Paekche occupied the area south of the Han River, with the capital at Hansŏng (modern Kwangju). Paekche was one of the fifty-four tribes of Mahan, whose lands lay south of the commandery of Taebang. The royal clan of Paekche was the Puyŏ— the same name as the tribe—and they considered themselves to be related to the Koguryŏ-Puyŏ peoples, with whom they shared a similar mythological founding ancestor in Tongmyŏng. Based upon this, it has been speculated that the Paekche royal family was a group of Puyŏ peoples who migrated southward after the defeat of Puyŏ by the Mu-jung tribe of the Hsien-pi in 285, settled in the valley of the Han River, and gradually gained dominance over the tribes in the Korean southwest; the view is also advanced that they were descendants of Chosŏn's King Chun.

There is little doubt that Taebang and Nangnang influenced the emergence of the state of Paekche both through trade and commerce and by their very existence, which provided a strong reason for tribal unity. Yet this tendency toward unity occasioned by a common threat was diverted by the Chinese-instituted tribute system, which, in a diplomatic divide-and-rule maneuver, tended to make unification impossible by treating each of the local chieftains as equal authorities while posing a distinct military threat against any unification attempts.

STRUGGLES FOR CONTROL OF THE NORTH

In China the Chin had inherited the mantel of the Wei in the north and with it control of Liaotung, Nangnang, and Taebang. And while they maintained Puyŏ as an ally, they faced aggressive enemies in Manchuria, particularly the Mu-jung tribe of the Hsien-pi, who had moved eastward out of Mongolia and thence southward to seize Liao-ssu, the area west of the Liao River, from the Chinese. This invasion severed the overland communications route between the state of Chin and their holdings in northwestern Korea. This eastward movement brought the Mu-jung to the northern frontiers of China and into direct conflict with Koguryŏ, whom they quickly endeavored to make a subordinate tributary state. The situation in Manchuria and northern Korea became one of intense intratribal conflict and warfare between the tribal people and the Chin Chinese. The Puyŏ, already weakened by a revolt of the I-lou in the period 220–226 brought about by taxes imposed on them by the Puyŏ, survived a Mu-jung invasion in 285 only with Chin assistance. Koguryŏ raids upon the now isolated Chin holdings in Manchuria and northwestern Korea, in time, led to the fall of Nangnang to Koguryŏ. Taebang, under periodic attacks by Paekche for years, was absorbed by that state after the fall of Nangnang to Koguryŏ. This brought Paekche into control of a key economic area, the valleys of the Han and Imjin Rivers, which were to be the center of a violent struggle for primacy on the peninsula for centuries and which would be held by each of the Korean kingdoms at the height of their power. North of the Chabi Pass were the lands of Koguryŏ.

By 316, the Chinese had, under attack from both the Mu-jung and Koguryŏ, withdrawn from southern Manchuria. The Western Chin had fled south to the Yangtze River area, from which time it is known as the Eastern Chin (317–420). North China was divided between minor states, the so-called Sixteen Kingdoms. By the first quarter of the fourth century the Mu-jung tribe had established themselves as the state of Former Yen (319–396) in southern Manchuria.

THE TRANSITION ON THE PENINSULA

In the southeastern part of the Korean peninsula, a third Korean kingdom, Silla, had emerged in the Naktong area. During this early period the people on the peninsula went through several stages of transition. The first was from a mode of living either removed from or only partially dependent upon agriculture to a completely sedentary society with all of the pertinent social, economic, and political implications. A sedentary population is, for example, easy to control for purposes of taxation and corvée and military service, conducive to the utilization of large numbers of captives and to the emergence of social distinctions and caste formation, and, finally, conducive to the provision of leisure for the elite classes, which is a requirement for learning and the development of thought.

A second stage of transition was brought about by the influx of a metal culture which, in Korea, entered during the transition stage toward a sedentary agricultural society. Both of these factors influenced the development of the early Korean-Manchurian states. The technology of the metal culture remained dominant for two millennia until the entrance of Western technology, while the predominantly agricultural pattern of life has only begun to change in this century.

In this early period manpower was the crucial factor of wealth. Land was plentiful and capital needs were few. Thus a primary objective of warfare during this period was the capture of peoples rather than the seizure of land. Thus we see people included as an item of ransom; Paekche, for example, gave 1,000 households for the return of her capital when it was captured by Koguryŏ. The conquest of settled areas, apart from lands seized to provide pasturage, had the requirements of defense and administration. It is little wonder that slavery arose from such conditions. Social controls developed to ensure that captive people remained in service positions and that political and economic power remained in the hands of the elite.

The role of foreign intervention in the development of the Korean kingdoms has parallels today as does the Chinese utilization of the tribute system. The political-religious role of the ruler is another interesting factor, but one of which we know very little. Apparently there was a trend toward more emphasis upon the political role and actual control of the state apparatus by the monarch. Yet the political and religious roles of kings never really separated completely, as the religious element was apparently used to reinforce the monarch's political position. In Koguryŏ, the monarchs were initially chosen by a meeting of clan or tribal leaders. Later two clans managed to rise to dominance. These were the clan which furnished the kings and the clan which furnished the consorts. It is possible that in the transition from a nomadic tribal society—in which there is a felt element of equality—toward a sedentary agricultural society—where political and economic difference are more markedly apparent—may have been a factor in the trend toward more political control by the early rulers of the Korean states. After its introduction, Buddhism may have aided in the process. The tedious wars as well as the manner in which they were carried out tell us something about this period. The concept of firm national boundaries was certainly lacking—the frontiers were the furthest outpost, and conditions might and usually did change swiftly—suggesting a period when rulers were ever watchful for opportunities to fulfill their own ambitions and on guard against foreign and internal threats. Stability required a strong state capable of enforcing restraint and the observation of general boundary areas. The state which played this role was China. One of the interesting questions of Korean history is the extent to which China served to stabilize the kingdoms on the peninsula.

4
The Three Kingdoms

The emergence of the southern Korean states of Paekche, Silla, and the Kaya League and the southward expansion of Koguryŏ began a contention for primacy on the peninsula which was to last for $2\frac{1}{2}$ centuries. The principal geographic area contested was the fertile plain of the valleys of the Han and Imjin Rivers, an area occupied by Paekche, Koguryŏ, and Silla in turn. The continued warfare among these states, now allies, now bitter enemies, led to a search for military support abroad in China and in Japan. One result was the strengthening of a process of Sinification, a second was the transmission of Buddhism. The development of native institutions was simultaneously underway, and linked with changes on the peninsula were dynastic changes in China.

PAEKCHE

In the southwest Paekche had absorbed Taebang and successfully expanded her borders northward to the Chabi Pass during the last half of the fourth century, which was a period of repeated warfare between Paekche and Koguryŏ. Threatened by Koguryŏ to the north, Paekche secured her claim to the valleys of the Han and Imjin with an attack on P'yŏngyang in 371, during which the Koguryŏ monarch was killed. The Paekche expansion was carried out by King Kunsogo (r. 346–375), a strong ruler who searched abroad for allies and established relations with the Chinese state of Eastern Chin in South China. It is believed that he may have been largely responsible for initiating a reorganization of the Paekche government structure into a bureaucracy along Chinese lines, at least in outward form. Paekche's sixteen official court grades were distinguished by the color of their court dress. The premier and the five chief officials beneath him wore purple robes and ceremonial caps ornamented with silver flowers, the next five grades of officials wore dark red robes, while the lowest officers at court wore robes of green. Under the premier, who was in charge of state affairs, were five ministers, viz., the Minister of Royal Security, who was in charge of the

Chronological Overview

Date	China	Manchuria	North Korea	Southwest Korea	Southeast Korea
440	North and South Dynasties				Kaya
562					
581	Sui	Koguryŏ		Paekche	
618	T'ang				Silla
660					
668					
		Unsettled Condition			
713		P'o-hai			

palace guards; the Minister of War, who was in charge of national defense; the Minister of Finance, who was responsible for the treasury and the granaries; the Minister of Rites, who was charged with all ceremonies, and the Minister of Justice, whose area was crime and punishment.

KOGURYŎ

In Manchuria, the Mu-jung state of Former Yen began a short-lived expansion in 342 with an invasion of Koguryŏ. Its troops sacked and fired the Koguryŏ capital, took thousands of prisoners including the Koguryŏ queen dowager, and scattered the tomb of the king's father, taking the bones for ransom. The ransom was finally paid for the bones of this illustrious royal ancestor in the form of tribute and hostages in 355. No sooner was this threat to Koguryŏ ended in 370, when the state of Former Yen fell to the Chinese state of Ch'in, than Koguryŏ suffered a severe defeat at the hands of Paekche forces. The death in battle of the Koguryŏ ruler in 371 brought King Sosurim to the throne (r. 371–384), the first of a series of powerful Koguryŏ kings. He established peaceful relations with the Former Ch'in (351–394), and in 372, the second year of his reign, Buddhism is said to have entered Koguryŏ from that state. It is believed that King Sosurim was active in the reorganization of the Koguryŏ military system, which had failed against the Mu-jung and Paekche invasions. This internal reorganization provided the foundation for a period of expansion, and in 391 Koguryŏ's mighty conqueror King Kwanggaet'o (r. 391–413) took the throne. In the 15 years of his reign, he brought the area of Manchuria east of the Liao River firmly under Koguryŏ control, conquered the fierce I-lou in the northeast, and began to roll Paekche out of the valley of the Han. The memorial stele at the Koguryŏ capital of Kungnae-sŏng, erected the year after his death by his son, King Changsu (r. 413–491), tabulates his conquests: 64 walled cities and 1,400 villages.

SILLA

A strong ruler had also ascended the throne of Silla, King Naemul (r. 356–402), from whose reign the Silla rulers used the title *marip kan* (supreme khan). This ruler is generally accepted by historians as being the first historic king of Silla, while the monarchs who are recorded as having preceded him are suspected of being the inventions of Silla historians. As in the case of Koguryŏ and of Paekche, a loose tribal-clan alliance developed into a more centralized tribal-clan structure through the maintenance of power by two of the more powerful clan groups, the Kim clan—which furnished the line of rulers—and the Pak clan—which produced the monarchs' consorts. Tradition would also include the Sŏk clan for the early period, but this is speculative.

The Kim clan exercised a monopoly on the throne of Silla, marrying other Kims, except for brief periods when they married Pak consorts during 500–576 and during the reign of three Pak monarchs in the period 912–927 in the final days of late Silla.

The assertions of strength by Paekche led Silla to ally with Koguryŏ. This alliance required Silla to assume a tributary status to Koguryŏ, to whom she sent hostages. It was to prove a valuable alliance to Silla in many ways. Silla envoys were sent to the court of the Former Ch'in via the Koguryŏ land route. Internally, the Kim and Pak clans had the backing of Koguryŏ in their positions, while externally the alliance served to check Paekche.

THE KAYA LEAGUE

The relationship between the "state" of Wa (Yamato) in Japan and the Kaya states which formed from Pyŏnhan in the lower Naktong delta of Korea is not entirely clear. However, there is little doubt that the relationship was an ancient one dating from the prehistoric period and which involved considerable interchange between the people of the Kaya League and the inhabitants of southern Japan and the islands of Tsushima in the Korea Straits. The Kaya area had its own distinct culture, and Kaya pottery formed the basis both for the Japanese Sue ware and for the early Silla pottery. Kaya was also a stop on the route the Wa took to the Chinese commandery of Nangnang. There were six of the Kaya states in the League: Kŭmgwan Kaya—located at the modern Kimhae, several miles up the Naktong River, on a broad flood plain—was the principal member of the Kaya League until 532. At this time leadership passed to Greater Kaya, known in Japanese records as Mimana, where it remained until 562. The other Kaya states were Ara Kaya, which was conquered by Silla in 536, Koryŏng Kaya, Sŏngsang Kaya, and Lesser Kaya. Pressed by the rise of

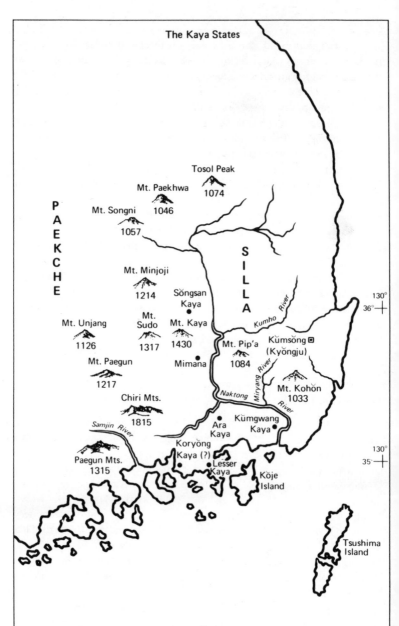

The Kaya States

PAEKCHE

SILLA

Tosol Peak
1074

Mt. Paekhwa
1046

Mt. Songni
1057

Mt. Minjoji
1214

Sŏngsan
Kaya

Kumho River

Mt. Unjang
1126

Mt. Sudo
1317

Mt. Kaya
1430

Mt. Pip'a
1084

Kŭmsŏng
(Kyŏngju)

Mt. Paegun
1217

Mimana

Miryang River

Mt. Kohŏn
1033

Chiri Mts.
1815

Naktong River

Samjin River

Kŭmgwang
Kaya

Paegun Mts.
1315

Koryŏng
Kaya (?)

Ara
Kaya

Lesser
Kaya

Kŏje
Island

130°
36°

130°
35°

Tsushima
Island

Note: Precise boundaries are unknown; probably they were the Naktong River to the east and the mountains to the west.

Silla and Paekche, the Kaya League turned to its traditional relationship with the Japanese, principally the Wa, who had formed a strong unified state in southern Japan, from whom they requested military aid. This led to the dispatch of Wa troops to the Kaya League. The price of this military assistance was, apparently, acceptance of a tributary relationship on the part of the Kaya League. Another view of this relationship, drawn from early Japanese records such as the *Nihon shoki* (720), is that Mimana was a military base established by conquest by the Japanese, who then ruled the Kaya states through a military government.

SILLA-WA-KAYA RELATIONS

In the year 399, a strong offensive in which the Wa soldiers formed a major contingent was launched against Silla. Silla's alliance with Koguryŏ again proved useful, and a Koguryŏ force of mounted and foot soldiers was rushed south to relieve the siege of the Silla capital. The defeat of the Kaya-Wa forces is recorded on the stele of Koguryŏ's King Kwanggaet'o. Although the Wa maintained their relationship with the Kaya League, they were to find an even greater source of Sinified culture in a new relationship with Paekche.

In 402, Silla concluded a peace with the Wa. Prince Misahun was then sent to Japan as a hostage. This may have been an act of revenge by the Silla monarch, who, as Prince Silsŏng, had been sent as hostage to Koguryŏ by Prince Misahun's father. Despite the peace, Silla-Wa relations were never friendly, due no doubt in part to the Wa-Kaya alliance.

PAEKCHE-JAPANESE RELATIONS

Paekche responded to the threat of the Koguryŏ-Silla alliance by searching for allies in the state of Liu Sung (420–479) in South China, with the northern or T'opa Wei (386–535) in North China, and with Japan. It is related that in 384, a dozen years after Buddhism entered Koguryŏ from the state of Former Ch'in, it entered Paekche from the southern Chinese state of Eastern Chin, with the arrival of the monk Marananda. The following year two monasteries were constructed and ten bonzes were assigned to them. Relations were opened around the middle of the fourth century. A pact of friendship was concluded with the Japanese state of Wa in 397, and Crown Prince Chŏn was sent to Japan as a hostage. This instituted a brisk period of trade conveyed by envoys between the two countries.

The Japanese motive for relations with Paekche appears to have stemmed from a desire to continue the trade pattern previously established with the Chinese commanderies in the Korean northwest. Only two early missions to

Nangnang from Wa, one in A.D. 57 and one in A.D. 107 are listed in the Han dynasty records, while four embassies from Wa are recorded as having arrived in the Chinese commanderies in the 10-year period 238–248 alone. The new trade route between Paekche and Wa apparently included the kingdom of T'amna (Cheju Island), then tributary to Paekche, the Kaya League, and the islands of Tsushima.

THE DECLINE OF PAEKCHE

In 405 upon the death of the Paekche monarch, one of his younger brothers proclaimed himself king. The news reached Japan, where the Wa furnished an armed escort to take Prince Chŏn back to Paekche. There, with the aid of the Hae clan, who furnished the Paekche royal consorts, he was able to secure the throne. Almost a century later, the Hae clan had the Paekche king murdered during a hunting trip and appointed itself the power behind the throne, since the crown prince was then a lad of only thirteen. This was quickly contested by the Chin clan, and a clash of clan troops decided in their favor. The young prince died suddenly in his second year on the throne, and the Chin clan then became the de facto power in Paekche. The new monarch, King Tongsong, furthered peaceful relations with Silla by taking the daughter of a Silla noble in marriage. These were golden years for Paekche, but they were to be few, for in 427 Koguryŏ's King Changsu moved the Koguryŏ capital from Kungnae-sŏng in the Yalu River area of Manchuria to the plains of P'yŏngyang, a move of great political significance. The ominous military implications of the move were all too apparent. An alliance was drawn up between Paekche and Silla against this new threat, which was to last 120 years. Both parties honored the alliance and aided each other with military forces. Silla did so in 474 when Koguryŏ troops advanced into the valley of the Han. Unfortunately the Paekche capital of Hansŏng fell, and Paekche withdrew southward to a new capital at Ungjin (mod. Kongju). In 538, they would pull back a little further to the town of Sabi (mod. Puyŏ).

KOGURYŎ: THE GREAT PERIOD

Koguryŏ, now in possession of the fertile valley of the Han, turned her attention northward, and in 494 brought the Puyŏ people under the Koguryŏ mantle. Koguryŏ had reached her greatest period. In addition to the national capital at P'yŏngyang, there were two subordinate capitals, the old capital of Kungnae-sŏng and the captured Paekche capital, Hansŏng. Koguryŏ was now a mighty state which controlled all of Manchuria east of the Liao River and the northern half of the Korean peninsula. A wall fresco in the

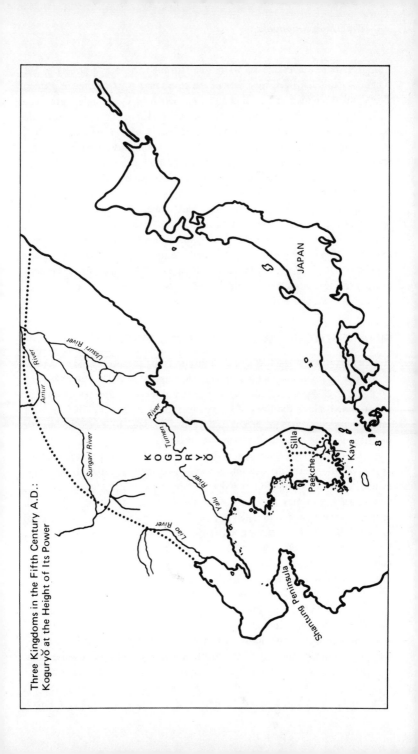

Three Kingdoms in the Fifth Century A.D.:
Koguryŏ at the Height of Its Power

Amur River

Ussuri River

Sungari River

KOGURYŎ

Tumen River

Yalu River

Liao River

Shantung Peninsula

Paekche

Silla

Kaya

JAPAN

Tomb of the Twin Pillars shows us that through the broad streets of the Koguryŏ capital strolled members of the elite families, the ladies in pleated skirts and three-quarter-length coats, their hair held by a single cloth hairband and their cheeks decorated with a large round spot of rouge, who would pause to chat with upper-class men, unmindful of the armored soldier, pennant flying from his lance, prancing his armored horse past a creaking, square, canopy-covered cart drawn by a lone bullock.·

One of the reasons for the Koguryŏ successes was a professional military class which was catered to by the society. The years of fighting in the mountains and rolling plains of Manchuria had welded this military class into legions of experienced veterans, and its mounted units gave it great tactical mobility. Supporting this military structure were the peasants, who paid their annual taxes in grain and cloth, and the nomad tribes, who paid taxes once every 3 years. According to the *History of Sui* (*Sui shu*) a seventh century Chinese work, the Koguryŏ land tax was uniformly set at 5 bolts of homespun cloth and 5 Korean bushels of grain.

SILLA INSTITUTIONS: THE BONE-RANK SYSTEM

In Silla, there was a further redefining and reorientation of old structures to meet new conditions and demands in the reign of the Silla monarch King Pŏphŭng (r. 514–540). A bureaucratic system of seventeen ranks of officials was adopted, along the lines of Chinese practices, as was the distinction of rank by purple, crimson, green, and yellow officials' robes (520), but the distinctively Silla bone-rank system was retained.

The bone-rank system was a hereditary caste system determined by ancestry, with society divided into several castes or bone-ranks. It has some similarities with Mongolian practices. There were five categories of elite, commoners (who may also have been divided into categories), and pariah groups of slaves and criminals. The highest caste levels were the *sŏnggol* (sacred bone), which incorporated the royal family, and the *chin'gol* (true bone), which included cadet branches of the royal family, the families of the consorts of the monarch, and the powerful elite families. One entered a bone-rank at birth and there, presumably, one remained, one's life regulated by the system, which limited the official grade attainable, the degree of luxury of personal dress, the size of residence, the decoration of saddles and chariots, etc. The *chin'gol* monopolized the post of general and the five highest civil posts. Similar monopolies appear to have been held by the other bone-ranks. To put it another way, any of the five bone-ranks could hold lower grades, but each bone-rank had a grade ceiling beyond which its members could not advance. The restrictions of the bone-rank system were undoubtedly a stimulus to the many talented persons who fled Silla for China or Japan.

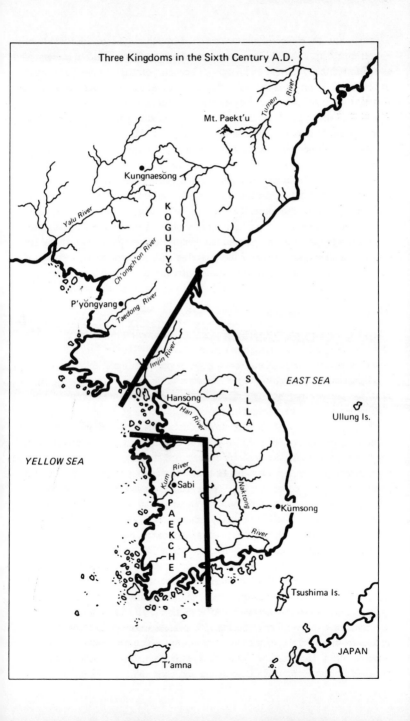

Three Kingdoms in the Sixth Century A.D.

Entry into the *sŏnggol* could be obtained by marriage into the royal family, and entry into the *chin'gol* was commonly given recognized leaders who submitted their territory and people to be incorporated into the Silla domains. The recognition of submitting leaders was a rather widespread practice which secured lands and peoples through nonmilitary means. The view has been advanced that the bone-rank system emerged in this form to ensure tribal-clan leaders of positions of power during the process of change to a central bureaucratic system, although the bone-rank system certainly had ancient precedents probably linked to shamanism.

The use of Chinese surnames appears to be closely related to the Silla bone-rank system. Members of the royal clan or those given similar status appear to have monopolized the surname Kim, written with a Chinese character whose meaning is "gold" or "metal." The Pak clan which furnished consorts to the royal line undoubtedly enjoyed a comparable position. There is one instance on record of the offspring of a *chin'gol* being degraded one bone-rank, but the reasons for this unprecedented action are unfortunately not given. Commoners, it appears, had only given names but no family names.

SILLA CULTURE AND ART

A major source of our knowledge of pre-Buddhistic Silla are the early Silla subterranean tombs, which became obscured with the passage of time and so escaped the looting suffered by the more prominent tumuli of the late Silla period. The items found in these tombs reveal a golden, glittering culture. The large-scale use of gold for crowns, bracelets, finger rings, earrings, belt buckles, pendants, and even bowls is impressive, as is their interment. The crowns, which suggest stylized antlers, are made of sheet gold to which hundreds of small gold spangles and comma-shaped jade ornaments are attached with gold wire. The crowns usually have spangled gold pendants hanging down each side terminating in a large comma-shaped jade ornament. The golden belts with their many pendants of gold, imported blue glass, and jade must have symbolized the powers of the monarch who wore them. The glass and tremendous quantities of jade are evidence of a brisk trade possibly based on the export of iron, for which this area was known. Earrings of gold tubing likewise had gold pendants attached by gold wire and were decorated by the technique of gold granulation. Earrings of a similar type seem to have been known in Han times, and in Rome, but the Silla earrings are much more elaborately decorated. In one Silla tomb believed to date from about the fifth century was found the oldest mask extant on the peninsula, a lacquered wooden mask with glass eyes which had blue irises painted on them and which were rimmed with gold.

THE INTRODUCTION OF BUDDHISM TO SILLA

Buddhism is related to have been introduced to Silla by two monks from Koguryŏ during the latter half of the fifth century. They are said to have begun proselytizing but without significant effect. Buddhism did not begin to flourish in Silla until the sixth century reign of King Pŏphŭng. During the reign of this monarch, whose canonized title *Pŏphŭng* means "Ascendancy of the Dharma (Buddhist Law)," Buddhism became the sanctioned state religion of Silla.

The acceptance of Buddhism as the state religion, traditionally dated 527, apparently began with a conflict between King Pŏphŭng, a convert to Buddhism, and the majority of the Silla elite, who opposed state support of the religion. The resolution of the conflict occurred with the execution in 527 of Ich'adon, a young official of elite descent who supported the monarch's position on Buddhism. Ich'adon's martyrdom, said to have been a voluntary act of faith, sparked religious tales of miracles which supposedly occurred at the time. Both King Pŏphŭng and his successor took Buddhist "temple names," while their queens later became nuns. There are some indications that King Pŏphŭng and his successor tried to strengthen the authority of the monarch through adoption of Buddhism. State support of the new religion had been accepted, and in 551 the Koguryŏ monk Hyeyong was made the first head of the Buddhist monkhood in Silla. This turning point marked the commencement of Silla monks going to China. State patronage, chiefly that of the royal clan at first, ushered in a period of monastery construction and the development of associated arts. The foundation had been set for a brilliant cultural efflorescence dominated by Buddhism in the late Silla period.

THE SILLA EXPANSION

In 532, Silla annexed Kŭmgwan Kaya, making inroads on the Kaya League, which a few years earlier (512) had lost some territory to Paekche. The last ruler of Kŭmgwan Kaya abdicated and was given the status of *chin'gol* and his former territory as an appanage.

Silla's great period of expansion, which was to end in the unification of the southern portion of the peninsula, began in the reign of King Chinhŭng (r. 540–576). The first step was a joint military venture with Paekche in 551 which, because of internal conflicts in Koguryŏ, succeeded in taking the valleys of the Hàn and Imjin Rivers. Then the 120-year alliance with Paekche ended abruptly as Silla occupied the entire area. Paekche's King Sŏng (r. 523–553), whose reign had been particularly bright until this point, was so furious that he personally led an expedition against Silla. Paekche's hopes dissolved with his death in the confusion of a night battle.

King Chinhŭng's conquest of the Han-Imjin River area gave Silla several important assets: a large settled population in a rich agricultural area which would provide taxes, corvée labor, and military service; a gateway to China with the newly acquired ports on the Yellow Sea; and technological gains such as the local iron industry. The conquests also provided a temporary answer to the problem of troublesome members of the powerful clans and relatives of the queen's clan. In 558, King Chinhŭng moved them into the area of the new conquests by the simple expedient of awarding them fiefs and possibly positions there. In 562, he conquered Greater Kaya, and northward he advanced to the lands of the Okcho. To commemorate the new conquests, four memorial stele, the so-called hunting monuments, were erected to mark the new borders.

A partial answer to the reasons for Silla's success was undoubtedly in the continued development of her military institutions. The Silla military system was in a continual state of expansion through the sixth century. Central to this system were the Oath Banners established in 583. Each unit was identified by an individual banner with different color fringes for each unit, a system used by the Manchu armies eleven centuries later. After the unification these banner armies were expanded to nine "oath banners," and while the original units were composed entirely of men of Silla, the majority of the new units were composed of the conquered peoples of Paekche and Koguryŏ. The formation of armies from captives was common through north Asia, particularly so among nomadic people. The development of specialized fighting units, such as armored troops, catapult teams, ladder units, teams for breaching city walls, composite bow units, and crossbow units is noteworthy.

THE HWARANG AND THE SILLA SPIRIT

There also emerged an elite paramilitary youth corps, the *hwarang*, whose origins may trace to a tribal manhood ceremony. The *hwarang* were, simply put, the sons of the Silla elite who were given austere military training involving archery and horsemanship and who made pilgrimages to sacred mountains, apparently as some sort of religious ordeal. Each *hwarang* led a group of subordinates whose numbers purportedly went as high as one thousand men. Although they were probably an ancient institution, the *hwarang* appear in the records about the same time as Buddhism emerged as the state religion. Indeed, the *hwarang* became closely related with the Maitreya (the Buddha of the Future) to the extent that they seem to have been a Maitreya cult.

In the lost *Silla kukki* (Records of Silla) was a passage which has led to charges of effeminacy. The passage, quoted in a later work, said: "They selected handsome sons of the elite and adorned them with powder and rouge. They call them *hwarang*. The people all revere and serve them." On similar grounds, American Indian warriors might also be charged with effeminacy.

The *hwarang* are reminiscent of the elite Ottoman Janissaries as instituted by Suleman the Magnificent, who were youths between the ages of eight and twenty but selected from peasant families and trained for posts in the government and the military. The *hwarang* were the sons of the Silla elite, and the seeds of their later degeneration in the leisure of decades of peace which followed the wars of unification were planted from the beginning.

During the wars of unification, however, the *hwarang* participated in battle, where they fought fiercely in the vanguard. Kim Taemun, an eighth-century Silla historian noted in his *Hwarang segi*, "Sagacious councillors and loyal ministers follow [this institution] and flower. Good generals and brave soldiers are produced by reason of [this institution]."

The ideal of the *hwarang* is illustrated by the popular story of Kwanch'ang, the *hwarang* son of General P'umil, who died in the wars of unification. Kwanch'ang, who was about sixteen at the time, was captured during a battle with Paekche forces but released because of his age. He returned to the fray a second time and was again captured and this time beheaded. When his horse returned to the Silla lines with the boy's head tied to the saddle, "P'umil grasped his son's head and wiped off the blood with his sleeve. 'My son's face is as when he was alive,' he said, 'He was able to die in the service of the king. There is nothing to regret.' " The story became the basis for the popular Korean sword dance of later days.

This martial spirit of Silla is revealed in the five precepts for secular life given to two young men in 602 by the Buddhist monk Wŏn'gwang (d. 640) upon his return from Sui China.

1. Serve your lord with loyalty.
2. Serve your parents with filial piety.
3. Use good faith in communication with friends.
4. Face battle without retreating.
5. When taking life, be selective.

The first three of these precepts are Confucian, the fourth is probably universal, and the last, which refers to religious taboos on fasting and the prohibition on taking life, is Buddhist. In addition to giving us a view of the spirit of the times, these precepts illustrate the early uses of Confucian and Buddhist doctrine in Silla.

PAEKCHE REORGANIZATION

In the western part of the Korean peninsula, Paekche had moved her capital to Sabi, where it was to remain until her fall. At the same time, a new designation was taken for the state, Southern Puyŏ (538). An attempt was made at this point to solve the problem of governmental organization which had rendered Paekche vulnerable in the past. Paekche had the early advantage of being adjacent to the Chinese commanderies of Nangnang and, later, Taebang. This produced a wealth of Chinese products via the tribute system. The tribute system, however, worked against Paekche centralization efforts as each local chieftain was given a title and a seal of authority by the Chinese. This partially accounts for the relatively late unification of Mahan by Paekche which appears to have occurred only after the Chinese commanderies had been cut off from China proper and were simultaneously under attack by Koguryŏ.

The Paekche defeat by Silla in 551 underscored the need for reorganization into a more centralized and efficient system of government which was more critical at this point since Paekche had lost the advantages of a large population and the fertile valley of the Han. After the move to Sabi, the nation was divided administratively into five areas each with a principal walled city where the official-in-charge resided with a thousand-man garrison under him. These areas were further subdivided into districts, with a military officer in charge of each district. The Paekche capital was similarly divided into five districts each with its own garrison of soldiers. This reorganization along more military lines was in response to the professional military of Koguryŏ and of Silla.

But Paekche had a critical internal weakness, and that was in her elite structure. In addition to the Puyŏ royal clan, Paekche had seven other prominent clans, viz., the Chin, Hae, Kuk, Mok, Yŏn, Paek, and Hyŏp clans. The seizure of power by the Chin clan was challenged first by the Hae and later by the Paek clan, an indication that there was as much division as unity within the Paekche elite structure. The division of the country into twenty-two fiefs assigned to royal kinsmen and members of the elite may have been an attempt to solve this problem.

SUI-KOGURYŎ WARS

On the continent, Sui (589–618) had risen to unify a China divided for centuries among contending states, a factor which had contributed to development on the peninsula. Sui faced strong Turkish forces in the north as well as a hostile Koguryŏ. A Turkish attack against Sui in 597, was followed by a Koguryŏ attack west of the Liao River the following year and a brief Sui counterattack. Sui accepted a Koguryŏ apology, but the discovery of a Koguryŏ envoy in the camp of the Turkish Khan in 607 revived Chinese fears of a strong alliance of northern peoples. This precipitated the first of a series of Sui campaigns against Koguryŏ. A Sui naval force set out but was compelled to return because of rough weather on the Yellow Sea, while an army proceeding against the Liaotung area was forced to withdraw after being decimated by hunger, disease, and natural disasters. A second attempt on a grander scale was begun in 612, when Sui Emperor Yang raised a force said to have numbered over a million men, which, even if reduced in magnitude to the more believable figure of 100,000, was a sizable army for the period. This campaign, in which the armies of the western Turks participated, had a particularly disastrous ending, and the loss of life was extreme. The expedition undertaken against Koguryŏ in 613 also ended in failure, and the armies were recalled because of uprisings at home in China. The last Sui campaign against Koguryŏ opened in 614, and the Sui armies managed to lay siege to the Koguryŏ capital of P'yŏngyang. The armies were recalled, however, in the autumn of that year after Koguryŏ envoys arrived in the Sui camp with pledges of submission. The cost of the Korean expeditions is often cited as a primary reason for the fall of the Sui dynasty, which was succeeded by the brilliant T'ang dynasty (618–905).

KOGURYŎ-T'ANG RELATIONS AND THE RISE OF YŎN'GAE SOMUN

Koguryŏ had established tribute relations with the Chinese states in the third century, and from the fourth to the seventh centuries Koguryŏ monarchs had accepted patents of investiture from the many contending Chinese states. They had successfully managed to avoid sending royal hostages or royal daughters in marriage, although both were strongly demanded by the Northern Wei. To offset their refusal, Koguryŏ doubled the tribute submitted to that state. Relations were also established with Japan, and until the Koguryŏ move to P'yŏngyang in the fifth century, Silla sent both tribute and hostages to Koguryŏ.

Koguryŏ's relations with T'ang opened on a friendly note. Koguryŏ sent back thousands of Chinese soldiers taken prisoner in the Sui campaigns, and the Koguryŏ monarch accepted investiture and the T'ang calendar symbolizing acceptance of a tributary status. The Koguryŏ heir apparent was sent to the T'ang capital to enter the academy. The T'ang authorities even attempted to mediate the continuing disputes between Koguryŏ, Silla, and Paekche.

In 631, T'ang envoys arrived in Koguryŏ to inter the bones of Chinese soldiers killed in the Sui expeditions, the wars with Silla erupted again, and

Koguryŏ completed construction of a long wall on her border with China. The fortified wall stretched from Puyŏ-sŏng in the north down to the sea and took 16 years to complete. The long wars with Sui and the strain imposed by the construction of the long wall led to unrest in Koguryŏ and to a change in leadership. In 642, Yŏn'gae Somun, a member of the Ch'ŏn clan of the Sun tribe, used his clan troops to take the throne. It is related that he first killed all the high ministers at a banquet. He then murdered the king and put a member of a cadet branch of the royal family on the throne. Yŏn'gae Somun was then the de facto power in Koguryŏ.

THE PAEKCHE-SILLA WAR

Paekche had used this period of respite to build for an attack on Silla which began in the mid-seventh century and pushed boldly into the Naktong River area. Silla General Kim Yusin would soon force Paekche out of the Naktong pocket, but at this time it was considered a national crisis. Silla quickly requested aid from Koguryŏ, who demanded return of the valley of the Han River as the price of assistance.

At this time Silla was sending hostages to the T'ang court as a tribute state. An important mission led by Prince Kim Ch'unch'u paved the way for an embassy sent by Silla Queen Chindŏk in 650. This embassy carried an appeal for aid, "Ode to Peace," written, in the form of a Chinese poem (*ku-shih*), on silk said to have been woven by the queen herself. The appeal was directed primarily against the state of Paekche, although the Silla authorities continued to send requests to T'ang for aid against both Paekche and Koguryŏ. In time these appeals would find a response.

SILLA GOVERNMENTAL STRUCTURE

In Silla the process of Sinification continued, evidenced by the adoption of T'ang court dress in 649 and in changes in the bureaucratic system. By 651, on the eve of the wars of unification, the Silla government system had taken shape through a process of growth over the preceding century and a half. While the model for the bureaucratic structure was Chinese, T'ang China being a particular influence, the operation of the parts was distinctly controlled by Silla. The political position of the Silla monarch had been strengthened to the point that his political role now overshadowed whatever former religious role he may have had. It is also clear that the emulation of the Chinese pattern as well as the acceptance of Buddhism strengthened the position of the monarch and the central government at the expense of the tribal-clan groups and the individual shamanist-animist deities. By 651, the form of the Silla government structure had been cast along the lines of the

Chinese "six boards," with subordinate departments and offices which would be increased and expanded after unification. The main features of the higher echelons of the Silla government structure are outlined below.

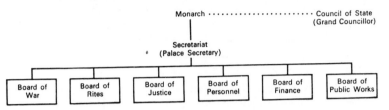

The "grand councillor" was the head of the Council of State, which had developed from the *hwabaek* council of the elite. The *hwabaek* council was an ancient Silla institution which seems to have resembled the Mongolian *quriltai*. When an important state matter, such as the selection of a new monarch, was to be decided, the highest members of the elite met at one of Silla's sacred sites to discuss and decide the matter. Unanimity was required in all decisions.

The Secretariat was not initially a policy body, but an administrative agency assisting the monarch. In time the "palace secretary," who headed the Secretariat, became, by virtue of his intermediary position between the monarch and the operational level of the six boards, a powerful official second only to the grand councillor. During this particular period the Office of Foreign Affairs, which had been chiefly concerned with relations with the states of Wa and Kaya earlier, had high status due to the importance of relations with T'ang China.

Silla adopted the Chinese province (*chu*), district (*kun*), and county (*hyŏn*) administrative systems in 505. The constant warfare ensured the dominance of military commanders in the provinces, which would expand to nine after unification. Regional military forces were stationed in garrisons in the provinces and also functioned as a constabulary force to ensure the maintenance of order and the fulfillment of government demands, e.g., taxes, levies, corvée labor, and military service. An Office of Ships was established in 583, meeting demands for defense against the Wa, who raided by ship, as well as for shipping to make the hazardous voyages to China. This action may have instituted a maritime tradition as well, for Silla ships soon came to have a virtual monopoly on maritime trade and passage between China, Japan, and Korea.

The basic institutional foundations established prior to the unification would be developed and expanded in the years to follow, while the pattern of the Chinese bureaucratic structure would be followed by every succeeding Korean state.

T'ANG-KOGURYŎ WARS: THE EARLY CAMPAIGNS

Turkish forces to the northwest of China had held the attention of T'ang, preventing her from doing more than attempting to mediate a peace between the three warring states on the peninsula. Silla continued to seek aid from T'ang. With the defeat of the Turks in 628, T'ang reconsidered the Silla appeals and responded. There were several reasons for the Chinese response beyond T'ang claims to the Liaotung area. Koguryŏ had blocked the overland routes for tribute missions from Paekche and Silla, had continued the wars on the peninsula—particularly against Silla, whose rulers had made a special effort to win Chinese friendship—had held a T'ang envoy captive, had erected a defensive wall along its eastern border, and presented a definite military threat which, when other measures failed, would be resolved by force. Moreover, in the eyes of the Chinese court, T'ang would be morally correct and gain the support of Heaven, since the previous Koguryŏ ruler had been murdered. Further, in Silla, T'ang had a proven military ally. Although there were many setbacks and victory seemed elusive, the T'ang-Silla alliance would, in time, prove successful. Factors contributing to the eventual T'ang victory were the large-scale utilization of non-Chinese people, such as the Ch'i-tan, Hsi, and Silla armies, and the careful planning and organization which preceded the expedition. Shipwrights were recruited from South China, the taxes of entire provinces were set aside, stores were transported to advance bases, and great expenditures were put into construction of the machines of war necessary to conquer the Koguryŏ walled cities, many of which were strategically located on practically inaccessible mountain summits. The T'ang campaigns against Koguryŏ were one of the greatest coordinated and planned military endeavors the Chinese had ever undertaken. Suggestions for the pacification of Koguryŏ by diplomacy or by Sinification were brushed aside in favor of conquest.

The first T'ang offensive against Koguryŏ began in 645, with a large army advancing into Liaotung and a naval force of almost equal proportion embarking from the Shantung port of Tung-lai aboard 500 ships. Initially successful, the T'ang armies, with non-Chinese troops in the vanguard, overran several Koguryŏ cities until they reached the small walled city of Ansi-sŏng. There, an unsuccessful 60-day siege exhausted the T'ang forces. With winter setting in, they withdrew, taking thousands of prisoners back to China. A second T'ang invasion in the period 658–659 also ended in failure.

THE FALL OF PAEKCHE

The Silla request for aid against Paekche led the T'ang commanders to consider flanking Koguryŏ by first conquering Paekche. In this undertaking, which opened in 660, T'ang threw more Chinese forces into the battle, drawing troops from sixty-seven districts. Uigur troops were added to the non-Chinese armies already involved. In the spring a massive force of thirty-five armies advanced by land and by sea. One T'ang army, under General Su Ting-fang, fresh from victories over the Turks in 657, crossed the Yellow Sea and landed at the mouth of the Kŭm River. From the southeast came an army under Silla's great General Kim Yusin which proceeded via the mountain pass east of the modern city of Taejŏn in a joint attack on Paekche. Upon the fall of the Paekche capital of Sabi, Paekche King Ŭija (r. 641–660) fled to Ungjin and there surrendered. Chinese commanders with troops were placed in five governorships to administer the former territory of Paekche. King Ŭija, the Paekche royal family, ninety-three ministers, and several thousand prisoners were shipped to China. The main body of the T'ang forces under Su Ting-fang again took ship and, sailing northward along the coast, landed near the mouth of the Taedong River. They tried a direct attack against the Koguryŏ capital but were forced to withdraw without a victory after encountering a fierce blizzard. They then withdrew south where bypassed Paekche forces had begun a restoration movement.

THE PAEKCHE RESTORATION MOVEMENT

The Paekche restoration movement was led by Poksin, a nephew of the Paekche king sent to T'ang as a hostage in 627, and the Buddhist monk To-ch'im. Their forces were strong enough to retake several cities. Paekche Prince P'ung, who had been in Wa as a hostage, returned home and was proclaimed king. A crisis in leadership occurred to weaken the restoration movement when Poksin killed the monk To-ch'im and was in turn killed by Prince P'ung. Prince P'ung then sent envoys to Koguryŏ and to the Wa, seeking troops to fight the T'ang-Silla invaders. One of his brothers, Prince Yung, who had been captured by the T'ang forces and sent to the T'ang capital, returned as a guide for the T'ang-Silla warships and supply ships. This T'ang naval force was en route from the Ungjin River to join the land forces near the mouth of the Kŭm River when they unexpectedly encountered Wa naval forces at the mouth of the river, where they had planned to disembark the T'ang troops. The Silla-T'ang forces emerged with a great victory and claimed some 400 Wa ships sunk in the engagement. It would be almost a 1,000 years before the Japanese would return to Korea in force, while the loss of the reinforcements meant it was only a matter of time until the Paekche restoration movement ended, which it did with the capture of Prince P'ung's main base in 663.

THE FALL OF KOGURYŎ

As Paekche fell, a leadership crisis was occurring in Koguryŏ. Yŏn'gae Somun had died in the summer of 666, and a dispute arose among his three sons. The eldest, Namsaeng, had fled from his brothers and had taken refuge at the old Koguryŏ capital of Kungnae-sŏng. He then sought to return to power by submitting to the T'ang authorities. T'ang Emperor Kao-tsung appointed him commissioner-general of Liaotung and pacification commissioner of P'yŏngyang. It was a windfall for the T'ang court. The work of collecting stores for another expedition against Koguryŏ commenced.

In 667, T'ang General Li Chi led the opening thrust, while forces under General Hsüeh Jen-kuei swept eastward, catching a large Koguryŏ force on the flank and inflicting a severe defeat. Despite the loss of their supply ships in the north in the Yalu River estuary, the remainder of the Chinese naval forces continued south along the Korean coast and arrived downstream from P'yŏngyang. There they were joined by a Silla force under General Kim Inmun. General Kim had served in the T'ang palace guards as a Silla hostage and was a good choice for the assignment. The T'ang-Silla forces settled down to a month long siege of the capital. Then, as the winter of 668 set in, the city surrendered, and it was suddenly all over. Koguryŏ had sustained massive Chinese invasions for some 70 years, a military record no Korean state would ever match. The monarch, King Pojang, was sent to China as were the two sons of Yŏn'gae Somun. The T'ang records relate that at the time of her fall, Koguryŏ had 176 walled cities and a population of 697,000 families. Converted at the usual rate of five persons per family, this would be a population of 3,485,000. P'yŏngyang was practically destroyed in the siege, and with it were lost the Koguryŏ records, while the city itself would not again be a major center until the tenth century.

For T'ang China the defeat of Koguryŏ was an immense victory, a victory so magnificent that the Chinese historians depicted it in the grandiloquent sweep of a mighty crusade imperially sanctioned and led, while they raised T'ang Emperor T'ai-tsung to the heroic proportions appropriate to a legend.

KOREAN COMMUNITIES IN CHINA AND JAPAN

Some sizable Korean communities were established along the China coast at this time when some 28,000 Koguryŏ families were moved and resettled in areas south of the Huai River. There was apparently also a large-scale immigration to Japan about this time. The Japanese register of influential families, the *Shinsen shōji roku* of 815, lists about 400 Korean families who had settled in Japan. Koguryŏ immigrants to Japan, among other things, probably influenced the development of performing arts in Japan. The *Nihon gakusho* mentions the titles of twenty-four dance performances of Koguryŏ origin. In an entry in the *Nihon shogi* dated 612, a Paekche immigrant to Japan, a certain Mimaji, is credited with introducing the *gigaku* type of performing arts to Japan, which probably included the "lion dance." Undoubtedly immigrants from the Korean states who settled in Japan played an important role in this early period. Traditionally, the Paekche scholar Wang-in (j. Ōnin), who is related to have brought a copy of the *Thousand Character Classic* to Japan, is credited with introducing the study of Chinese characters to Japan.

THE T'ANG-SILLA CONFLICT

The fall of Koguryŏ brought T'ang and Silla into conflict even as Koguryŏ remnants under An Sung, a de classé son of the last Koguryŏ king, fought on. Following the fall of Paekche and Koguryŏ, T'ang endeavored to establish administrative control over the peninsula. Five governorships were established in the lands of the former kingdom of Paekche, and Prince Yung was placed at Ungjin nominally in charge of administering this territory, although real control was in the hands of the Chinese military commander.

An attempt was made to include Silla as well, and the Silla capital was designated Kyerim Governorship with Silla's King Munmu (r. 661–680) munificently appointed "governor" of his kingdom. The Silla monarch was also forced by the Chinese commander Liu Jen-kuei to meet Prince Yung at Ungjin. A white horse was sacrificed, and a covenant of peace dictated by Liu was signed and the document stored in Silla's ancestral temple.

In Koguryŏ, T'ang established nine military governorships with a military governor-general who was to have complete charge over affairs in the peninsula. General Liu Jen-kuei was placed in charge and stationed in P'yŏngyang with an army of 20,000 soldiers.

The Silla reaction to the T'ang attempt to translate their gains into permanent holdings was to aid the Koguryŏ resistance movement, and they quickly recognized An Sung as king of Koguryŏ. When An was defeated and fled to Silla with his followers, he was settled in conquered Paekche lands and awarded *chin'gol* status. In the south Silla began to move militarily against the T'ang forces in the former Paekche lands. T'ang countered, using primarily Paekche forces. For T'ang, the attempt to control the entire peninsula without more men was highly unrealistic. By 671 Silla had occupied Sabi the former Paekche capital and by 676 she had taken the Taedong River area. T'ang moved their military governor back into Manchuria.

LESSER KOGURYŎ

King Pojang, the last Koguryŏ monarch, was enfeoffed as king of Chosŏn in 677 by T'ang and sent to the Liaotung area to rule the Koguryŏ peoples moved into that area, with de facto control resting with the T'ang military governors. While this monarch was soon removed after an attempted revolt, his position was passed along to his descendants. The area, which grew independent under his son Tongmu, is sometimes known as Lesser Koguryŏ. Other areas of eastern and northern Manchuria, largely bypassed in the T'ang military campaigns, had also retained a large degree of independence.

PARHAE (c. P'o-hai)

In 696, a Ch'i-tan revolt involving Malgal people erupted in Ying-chou, a city west of the Liao River. Leadership of the revolt was seized by Tae Choyŏng a Malgal and former Koguryŏ general, who had been resettled with his followers in the Ying-chou area by the Chinese. Tae Choyŏng led his forces northeast while T'ang and Ch'i-tan forces fought in the Ying-chou area. He was successful in reuniting the former Koguryŏ peoples and in defeating a T'ang army sent against him. Further T'ang military moves against Tae were blocked by the rise of Turkish peoples who had obtained the submission of the Ch'i-tan, Hsi, and other tribal peoples north of China.

T'ang Empress Wu, recognizing the *fait accompli*, turned to diplomacy and enfeoffed Tae Choyŏng as duke of Chin in 698, and in 713 T'ang Emperor Hsüan-tsung invested him as king of Parhae.

The Manchurian-Korean state of Parhae was based upon the foundations welded together by Koguryŏ, and, indeed, in a missive to Japan they described themselves as having recovered the former territories of Koguryŏ and as possessing the surviving customs of the Puyŏ. The leadership element of Parhae was drawn from the Malgal people who had been one of the components of Koguryŏ.

Initial relations with T'ang involved Chinese attempts to implement the old policy of playing off the barbarians against themselves. T'ang was successful in detaching the Blackwater Malgal tribes from the Parhae alliance in 722 by awarding the chieftain a prefectural post. His followers were then organized into a border army. Further Chinese ploys involving an attempted assassination of the Parhae ruler led to a Parhae naval raid on the busy T'ang seaport of Teng-chou on the northern side of the Shantung peninsula in 732. A joint T'ang-Silla expedition was launched against Parhae the following year in retaliation. The Silla part in the campaign was a complete disaster. Deep snow drifts had made the northern mountain roads impassable. Caught in the icy blizzards in an area where the temperatures plummet to −45 degrees, far from the plains of the Naktong, over half of the Silla soldiers perished. A major battle was never joined. The Silla participation in this tragic adventure had only one favorable aspect and that was formal T'ang recognition of Silla's claim to the conquered territory south of the Taedong River.

A few years later Parhae took advantage of the rebellion of An Lu-shan which ravaged China to gain control of the Liaotung area and absorb Lesser Koguryŏ.

The capital of Parhae, modelled after the T'ang capital of Ch'ang-an, was in the Amur region. Four regional capitals were established and five roads pushed out through Parhae's fifteen provincial departments for trade and communications. The Parhae government administration was a replica of the T'ang system, with the added flavor that the six government boards were each named for a principal Confucian virtue, e.g., the Board of Good Faith was concerned with public works, while the ministry charged with taxes and general matters of finance was called the Board of Benevolence. T'ang influence pervaded the arts as well, as evidenced by Buddhist stone sculpture, while Parhae artisans became famous in T'ang for the manufacture of a purple porcelaneous ware.

Although a brisk trade was carried on with T'ang, with Japan, and to some extent with the Turkish peoples, there appears to have been very little contact with Silla. Yet, the Manchurian-Korean state of Parhae, which endured until 926, stabilized the area north of Silla. Silla itself now occupied the Korean peninsula south of the 39th parallel. A sparkling new era was about to open on the peninsula.

BUDDHISM AND THE ARTS: KOGURYŎ

Buddhism is traditionally said to have entered Koguryŏ in 372, when the ruler of the Former Ch'in (351–394) sent the monk Sundo with Buddhist texts and images. Several years later a second monk, Ado, arrived, and two monasteries were constructed for these monks. A decade later in 382 a decree was promulgated commending veneration and belief in Buddhism as a means of securing blessings. There is a record of several monasteries being built in P'yŏngyang, while an inscribed fragment of a gilt bronze statue of Maitreya dated 396 has been found in the area.

Koguryŏ monks began going to China for study and returning to propagate the faith. Mahāyāna Buddhism predominated. By the sixth century the Samnon (c. San-lun) or Mādhyamika school, which maintained reality to be beyond human conception, hence phenomenal existence unreal, had developed in Koguryŏ. The Nirvāṇa and Sarvastivāda schools also appear to have emerged in Koguryŏ in this period. Yet despite the enthusiastic support of many monarchs, Buddhism apparently never became the dominant force in Koguryŏ. One reason may have been the influence of native beliefs and of Taoism, which are seen expressed in wall paintings in Koguryŏ tombs. Taoism was revived in 624, following its revival in China, when the T'ang Emperor Kao-tsu sent a Taoist priest to Koguryŏ with Taoist texts and statues of Taoist divinities. The priest gave lectures on the philosophy of Lao-tzu attended by the Koguryŏ ruler and his ministers. This resulted in a number of conversions to Taoism, among which was that of Yŏn'gae Somun, who became the de facto power in Koguryŏ in 642. In 643, following a Koguryŏ request, T'ang T'ai-tsung sent the Taoist priest Shu-ta and seven others with copies of the *Tao-te-ching*, and upon their arrival in Koguryŏ Buddhist monasteries were expropriated for them.

The opposition of Taoism may, together with missionary zeal and the continuous warfare, partly account for the many Koguryŏ Buddhist monks who left the country. Some of the more famous include Hyeja, who went to Japan in 594 to become Buddhist tutor to Prince Shōtoku, and Hyegwan, who went to Japan in 625 to develop the Samnon (j. Sanron) school. Koguryŏ influence was particularly strong in Silla, where a Koguryŏ monk became, in 551, the first head of the Buddhist establishment in Silla.

Accompanying Buddhism was the general influence of Chinese literature. In the same year that Buddhism entered Koguryŏ, an academy was established for the sons of the Koguryŏ elite. In 600, a scholar of the academy, Yi Munjin, was ordered to summarize the *Ancient History* into a five-volume *New Collection*. The titles of other Koguryŏ works, including the *Koryŏ kukki*—apparently a national history, which is mentioned in the late ninth-century Japanese bibliography *Nihon genzaisho mokuroku*—and the hundred-volume *Yugi*—apparently an encyclopedic collection—reflect the development of learning. Provincial schools called *kyŏngdang* were later established, and it is believed that the general curriculum included the Chinese classics and the military arts.

Some fourteen kinds of reed, stringed, and percussion instruments are known to have been used in Koguryŏ from the shell trumpet to the pipa of central Asia. The seven-stringed zither brought in from Eastern Chin was developed into the *kŏmun'go*, still one of the most popular of Korean instruments. With music went the dance, and Koguryŏ dancers in their long-sleeved gowns, singers, and musicians are depicted in many of the wall paintings of Koguryŏ tombs.

Tomb construction shows a rapid development of architecture. The larger of the early step-pyramid tombs measure as much as 200 feet square at the base, and the construction implies considerable engineering skill. The stone chambers of the later tumuli, with their wall paintings, are square constructions with vaulted corbel ceilings, and some of the late tombs include stone supporting columns.

But it is to the realm of painting that our attention is drawn, specifically to the wall paintings in the Koguryŏ tumuli tombs at T'ung-kuo, in the Chi-an district of Manchuria, and the tombs in the area of P'yŏngyang. The strong line and use of color are noticeable, while style and subject matter show Chinese influences dating from Han to the Six Dynasties.

An example from one of the Wu-kuai-fen group of tomb paintings is an excellent illustration. Every inch of the tomb except the floor was decorated with bright reds, greens, whites, blacks, and golds. The main chamber was decorated in bands on the corbels reflecting the construction. On the ceiling itself was a huge intertwined dragon. In the first band were four deities, semihuman figures with faces like terrible masks and limbs with claws; this band was bordered by an alternating flame and lotus petal design. The second band, more narrow, contained a fantastic knotted and interwoven series of dragons like a long snake, and one panel shows two-winged men putting spokes in a wheel. A third band, also narrow, contained a series of smaller paintings of the four deities associated with the cardinal points of the compass (black warrior, red bird, green dragon, white tiger) and two females mounted on a dragon playing musical instruments. Other tombs contain hunting or battle scenes, scenes apparently depicting beliefs of the times, and realistic genre scenes of daily life of members of the elite. The general arrangement is one of the real world depicted in the genre scenes and the other world depicted in the scenes of demigods and spirits. The domed ceilings are often decorated with the stars and constellations found in this latitude. What appear to be Taoist influences in subject matter are strong.

Ceramic figures of Buddhas and Bodhisattvas found at old monastery sites and tomb ware shows similar influences from early Han, such as ceramic ovens and house models, while bronze images often reflect Northern Wei styles. The surface of some terra cotta iconographic figures show traces of having been painted white and red. Some survivals of older forms may be seen in the characteristic four "lugs" of Koguryŏ pots.

Lacquerware was another craft carried on in Koguryŏ. Lacquered wooden coffins show a use of black lacquer on which red and white flower designs were painted.

Ornamental bricks and roofing tiles in which the lotus flower was a favorite design also show Six Dynasties influence.

The Koguryŏ conquest of the Chinese commanderies in the fourth century provided artisans and industry which formed the basis for many of the subsequent artistic developments in Koguryŏ. To this foundation were added additional imports, particularly Buddhist iconography, as well as native skills and motifs.

BUDDHISM AND THE ARTS: PAEKCHE

According to traditional accounts, in 384, a dozen years after it had entered Koguryŏ, Buddhism was brought to Paekche by the monk Marananda from the state of Eastern Chin in South China. Buddhism appears to have had a greater influence in Paekche than in Koguryŏ, and it developed in Paekche much earlier than it did in Silla. It had reached a high point in the sixth century during the reign of King Sŏng (r. 523–553). The monk Kyŏmik, in 536, is said to have brought back Sanskrit texts of the Vinăya school, which emphasizes monastic discipline, and to have translated them with some twenty-eight assistants. In 541, an envoy was sent to Liang to fetch the *Nirvăna sūtra* and other texts as well as to request artisans and painters and Confucian scholars conversant with the *Book of Odes*. Buddhism appears to have been transmitted to Japan from Paekche during the reign of King Sŏng; the date is traditionally given as 552.

The Samnon school also flourished in Paekche, and several Paekche monks went to Japan to propagate the doctrines of that school. Buddhism was enthusiastically supported by the Paekche royal clan, and one monarch in the late sixth century, King Pŏp, prohibited the killing of all living things and ordered the release of all privately owned hunting birds and the burning of all fishing and hunting gear. It comes as little surprise to learn that he occupied the throne for only 5 months.

The Buddhist art which accompanied the doctrine became the dominant force in Paekche art. Paekche had strong ties with many of the southern Chinese states, such as the Liang, as well as with states such as the Northern Wei, and the gilt bronze Bodhisattvas and Buddhas which remain reflect their influence in sculptural patterns and reveal a deep religious feeling often sensually expressed. Many of the Paekche Buddhist figures have thin, elongated bodies suggesting a spirituality reminiscent of figures in some paintings by El Greco. The source of this inspiration has been suggested as the Lung-men cave figures of the late Northern Wei and Paekche figures do have the same mysterious smile.

For the better examples of Paekche art we must look to Japan. The great wooden *Kudara (Paekche) Kannon* at Hōryū-ji is believed either to be a Paekche product or to have been executed in Japan by Paekche artisans. Many early Japanese monasteries are also believed to have been constructed following Paekche examples.

5
Late
Silla

The unification of the greater portion of the Korean peninsula under Silla in the early eighth century was the beginning of the history of Korea in the grand sense, as distinct from the history of the elements of which it was composed. In eastern Manchuria and northern Korea the state of Parhae had risen from the former Koguryŏ peoples, but unlike Koguryŏ its relations with Silla were apparently peaceful. An exception was the disastrous T'ang-Silla expedition against Parhae in 733. Silla's relations with Japan underwent a change following the removal of Japanese influence from the peninsula. There were some raids by Japanese during this period: one force of 300 ships is recorded as having attacked Silla in 746. Silla pirates made occasional raids on Tsushima and the Japanese coast; yet relations, although cool, continued, and a pact of amity was finally concluded in 803. One of the reasons behind the Japanese desire for friendship with Silla was the latter's control over the maritime trade route to China. Silla's usual hostility to the Japanese made shipwreck on the Korean coast something to be dreaded.

But it was to the continent that Silla looked, for there T'ang China, the greatest state in the world, held sway. Silla princes were sent to the Chinese capital as hostages, and there they served in the palace guards. Students and monks from Silla flocked to Ch'ang-an, the cosmopolitan capital of T'ang, and they brought back influences which, in the century of peace then opening, were to result in a burst of cultural brilliance. Of the fifty or so Buddhist monks known to have gone to China, fully 90 percent went after the Silla unification. The number of students who went to China to study in the National Academy at Ch'ang-an is unknown, but judging from the return of 105 students in the single year 844 alone, several thousand must have gone. Many Koreans also entered the service of the Chinese government. One of these was Ko Sŏnji (c. Kao Hsien-chih), who routed the Tibetan forces blocking the lofty passes over the Pamirs in 747 to temporarily secure the Chinese trade route to Iran. Four years later Ko made an ill-advised attack on Tashkent and was defeated at the battle of the Talas River in the summer of 751 by the combined forces of the prince of Tashkent and the prince's Arab neighbors. Ko's defeat meant the withdrawal of Chinese influence from

Chronological Overview

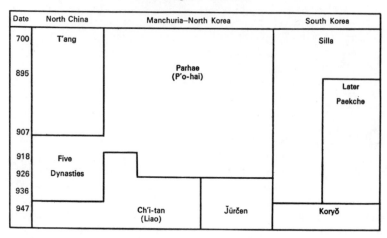

the area and its replacement by Arab influence. The closing of this important overland trade route stimulated Arab merchant voyages to South China. The closing of the overland route through Manchuria had a similar impact on Silla and led to the rapid growth of Korean maritime activity in the Yellow Sea.

Internally the process of Sinification continued, Buddhism flourished, and Confucianism slowly developed. This was also a period of enormous construction, with the building of palaces and royal parks with lakes, botanical gardens, and rare plants and animals. Great monasteries and walled cities also rose throughout the peninsula.

EXPANSION OF GOVERNMENT

The growth and development of the governmental structure followed the lines laid out in the reorganization of 651. Hundreds of departments and offices were established. Offices subordinate to the Board of Rites, for example, included the National Academy, Office of Sacrifices, Department of Monasteries, Office of Music, Office of Astronomy, the School of Medicine, probably the Office of Clepsyedras (water clocks), Office of Mathematics, and Office of Translation as well. The development of such offices reflected not only the tremendous organizational tendency of Silla society but the development and growth of technology and the specialization of knowledge. The renewed interest Buddhism had kindled in medicine, astronomy, and other subjects in T'ang was soon transmitted to Silla. Chamsŏngdae, an observatory still standing on the Kyŏngju plain, was built in 640, and in 692 the monk Tojŭng brought back star charts from T'ang. Medicine occupied an important position in Buddhist activities, and the establishment of the government School of Medicine probably reflects this concern. At this school, which had a pharmacy attached, medical texts from China were used, including the ancient Chinese medical work *Su-wen-ching*; the *Mo-ching*, a work on blood vessels; the Chin dynasty work on cauterization *Chia-i-ching*; the *Materia Medica Classic*, and works such as the *Ming-t'ang-ching* and *Chen-ching* on acupuncture. Needless to say the development of these governmental offices had its corollary in an increase of bureaucrats to fill them. There had already appeared under Chinese influence a marked separation between the high-status occupations which required literacy and those technical and artistic skills which did not. This distinction would be further emphasized in succeeding periods.

REGIONAL ADMINISTRATION

The Silla regional administrative system had grown from three provinces (*chu*) prior to the unification to nine by 685. Each province was divided into a number of districts (*kun*) and each district into a number of counties (*hyŏn*). Beneath the county level were subcounties (*hyang* and *pugok*). The chief officials in the provinces, districts, and counties were appointed by the central government. The villages were under the administration of a locally selected village chief. Representatives of strong local families gained positions in this regional administrative structure as local officials.

Silla Regional Administration

Provinces	9	Governor
Districts	100+	Prefect
Counties	300+	Magistrate
Villages	?	Village Chief

Five regional centers were designated subordinate capitals and were under the jurisdiction of an administrator who was ranked only by provincial governors.

There is some evidence of a hostage system (*sangsuri*), which required representatives of powerful regional families to do service in government bureaus in the capital. There may have existed a number of restricted subcounties (*pugok*) in each province where members of outcaste groups labored producing goods for the government. Unfortunately the evidence seems inconclusive, although such outcaste communities did exist later in the Koryŏ period.

The extent to which the central government of Silla actually controlled affairs in the countryside and the extent to which Chinese institutions such as the district (*kun*) and county (*hyŏn*) system were actually implemented are also unclear. They may have amounted to little more than confirming the authority of local leaders in the beginning, just as the award of appanages (*sigŭp*) apparently was used to confirm existing authority. I believe that we can assume with some certainty that while the centralizing process may not have been fully complete, it was well under way and was reinforced by military units stationed throughout the nation.

THE LAND SYSTEM

While the concept of state ownership of land may have existed in Silla, it did not prevail, for lands accumulated by powerful families and great monasteries tended to remain private possessions. Private gifts of land to monasteries themselves indicate a trend toward the concept of private ownership. The elite received appanages which included the land and everyone and everything on it. The amount of the appanage was commonly expressed in terms of the number of households residing there and ranged from small ones of 100 households to one recorded appanage of 2,000 households. Salary appanages (*nogŭp*) and stipend appanages (*kwallyojŏn*) were assigned to support the expenses of government officials. During and immediately following the wars of unification, grants of prisoners of war and slaves were made to members of the elite, who were also given lands as pasturages for horses.

It has been said that from 733, the Silla land system closely followed the Chinese equal-field (*chün-t'ien*) system, which had been reinstituted in T'ang China during the late seventh century. In this system peasants were assigned land returnable to the state at the death of the holder. The state then collected taxes and did its utmost to prevent the lands from becoming tax-exempt private holdings. Unfortunately the evidence appears to be contradictory, but it does suggest that the land system changed considerably during the late Silla period.

Buddhist monasteries were holders of large tracts of land, and one entire county was set aside by the state to provide stipends for students in the National Academy. The royal household was the largest landholder. Gifts of land were often given as rewards for distinguished service. The peasants were apparently tied to the land and subject to the head tax paid in grain, the household tax paid in regional specialities, and occasional levies as well. They were also subject to military service and to the corvée, which was, for large projects such as the construction of defense works, often a nationwide labor draft involving thousands of men. The lowest authority standing between the peasants of a village and the government officials was apparently either the village chief or the local clan head. The village chief or clan head was apparently responsible for the village or community meeting its taxes and levies. The basic unit of taxation during the late Silla period seems to have been the village, although there is a notice that households were divided into nine tax categories at one time.

The registers of four villages located near the Silla regional capital of Sŏwŏn, near the modern Ch'ŏngju, which are believed to date from 755, give a clearer view of the village structure. The purpose of these registers, which were brought up to date every 3 years, was taxation and service. Taking into account the notice in the records that land was first distributed by the state to peasants in 723, the possibility arises that direct taxation of the peasants

Data from Four Silla Village Registers, A.D. 755

(Chiefly after Hatada Takashi, *Reikishigaku Kenkyu*, no. 12)

	Village A	Village B	Village C	Village D	Total
1. *Households*	10	15	8	10	43
2. *Population*					
Male adults (16–59)	28 (1)*	27 (4)	16 (0)	15 (2)	86 (7)
Female adults	35 (5)	42 (3)	14	31 (4)	122 (12)
Children (4–15)	39 (2)	26	18	31 (3)	114 (5)
Infants (under 4)	31 (1)	15	17	20	83 (1)
Aged (over 60)	3	5	1	2	11
Total	136 (9)	115 (7)	66 (0)	99 (9)	416 (25)
3. *Increase/Decrease Past 3 Years*					
a. Households	−1	0 (+1, −1)	+1	−2	−2
b. Population					
Left village	12	3?	4	26?	48
Died	10	?	6	21	37
Sold	1	0	0	0	1
Born	13	6	5	7	31
New arrivals/returnees	2	7	7	4	20
4. *Livestock*					
Horses (± last 3 years)	23 (+1)	18	4	10	55 (+1)
Oxen (± last 3 years)	18 (+1)	12	10 (+5)	5	45 (+6)
5. *Fields*					
Paddy fields†	94 (8) 9‡	60 (3)	68 (3)	26 (3)	248 (17)9‡
Dry fields	62	119	58	76 (1)	315
Hemp fields	1	?	1?	1	3
6. *Orchards*					
Mulberry trees	1004	1280	730	1235	4249
Pine-nut trees	120	6?	19‡	68	194+19‡
Walnut trees	102	71	107	48	328

*(Slaves) not included in primary figures.
†Rounded in Korean acres (*kyol*). Figures in parentheses represent government land.
‡Cultivated for the village chief.

by the government did not begin until the eighth century and that this was a new land system designed to break the regional autonomy of local clans and to strengthen the central government.

THE TRIBUTE SYSTEM

International relations between China and Korea were developed through what is generally called the *tribute system*, since it included exchanges of goods on the governmental level. It should be noted that political considerations were often involved and that the economic aspect was often of secondary consideration. Again, there were certain ceremonial obligations which in themselves were a manifestation of what might be called the Chinese world view, and a failure to observe this protocol could be taken as a premeditated insult. The system, something like an open recognition of the balance of power, was paternalistic in nature. Silla recognized China as the paramount power, and her embassies paid ceremonial obeisance to the Chinese court and to Chinese envoys to Silla. Some of the appurtenances of the system were the use of a political rhetoric incorporating the idea of a superior-inferior relationship, the use of the calendar and reign titles or era names of the "superior" state, and the submission of tribute by the inferior state. For their tribute the inferior state's envoys were benevolently rewarded with "gifts." Although decisions for a course of action were based upon practical estimates of the results of such action, the rhetorical phrases in which they were clothed were also important, since they reflected the attitude of the state concerned. The states peripheral to China adopted this system of diplomacy in varying degrees: in the case of Korea it was adopted rather completely.

Concomitant with the tribute trade carried on by official embassies was private trade carried on by individual members of the embassies. This private trade usually took place at monasteries and towns where members of the embassy lodged en route to the Chinese capital. Official trade with Japan was handled through the Dazaifu, a Japanese government office located in northern Kyūshū concerned with foreign affairs and national defense, and the Japan Bureau of the central Silla government. Having a position in an embassy was immensely profitable, and as a consequence embassies were normally large. One Japanese embassy to Silla is recorded as having 204 members, and there is a record of a Chinese embassy arriving in the Silla capital with over 500 members in its party. As it was customary for the host nation to pay all the expenses of a foreign embassy as long as it was within its borders, these embassies were a considerable drain on state revenues, since they usually stayed for many months because of the difficulty of transportation back to their own country.

INTERNATIONAL TRADE

In addition to official trade, considerable private trade developed with China and Tsushima and the lords of coastal provinces in western Japan. This export trade, together with increased demands by the Silla elite, stimulated the rapid development of manufacturing. Individual offices established and controlled by the central government existed for the production of high-quality textiles, mats, felt, hides, furs, desks and tables, wooden items, horse and chariot equipment, leather shoes, drums, pottery and roof tiles, items of gold and silver, clothing, tents and banners, lacquerware, weapons and metalwork, ships and paintings.

Silla goldsmiths and silversmiths had apparently reached a high degree of skill in their art. Finely crafted weapons decorated with gold and silver and elaborately engraved with hunting falcons and hawks, gold and silver arrowheads and arrow cases, silver needlecases engraved with flowers or other decoration, and small bells of gold and silver were all important Silla exports to China. During the Sung period basins of gold and silver were commonly known as "Silla," and copper basins were called "copper Silla." High-quality textiles, particularly embroidery, were second in importance. Other standard Silla exports to China included horses (obtained in trade from the northern tribesmen), hunting birds and dogs, several medicinal items of which ginseng was most highly valued, gold and silver bullion, and furs. Many of these items were previously imported by Silla, which attests to the development reached in metalworking and textile manufacturing.

The artisans in charge of production appear to have been a socially mixed group of commoners and outcastes. The latter may have represented former Koguryŏ and Paekche artisans captured during the wars of unification. Imports from Japan were chiefly luxury items, such as pearls, fans, and screens, while exports to Japan included surplus goods from the China trade as well as domestically produced goods. Imports from T'ang China included robes and caps for court use, a variety of textiles, tea, weapons, numerous speciality items and curiosities such as parrots or other rare birds, and above all books.

Undoubtedly many of these items must have found their way into the four large government-regulated markets in the Silla capital and thence into the regional markets held periodically in the countryside. Chinese coins of the T'ang period found around the Silla capital of Kŭmsŏng suggest that such coinage as was used was entirely Chinese, while other traditional mediums of exchange probably included raw metals, viz., iron, silver, and gold, as well as grain and homespun fabrics.

International letters of credit existed for travelling monks and students, one having been issued to travellers to T'ang in 869 in the amount of 300

Korean ounces (*yang*) of silver. Korean ships dominated the maritime trade in the Yellow Sea and handled the majority of the trade and passenger traffic between Japan, Korea, and North China. Korean ships were regular callers at the ports of North China, and large Korean communities developed at such principal coastal cities as the Shantung port of Teng-chou and the commercial cities of Lien-shui and Ch'u-chou on the Huai River. Korean vessels also went south to Yang-chou, but maritime trade in the south was largely in the hands of the Arabs. It was probably from Arab encounters with Koreans in these ports that Arab geographers such as Ibn Khordaheb (mid-ninth century) and Masudi (mid-tenth century) heard reports of the salubrious climate and fertile fields of *al Sila*, a land where gold was said to be in abundance.

THE SILLA CAPITAL

The vast wealth accrued by the members of the royal family and the powerful elite families was poured out in lavish personal expenditures and in the construction of great private mansions, imposing Buddhist monasteries, sumptuous royal palaces, and government offices. The thirteenth century *Samguk yusa*, a work more noted as literature than history, gives the population of the Silla capital during its "great period"—by which we might understand the mid-eighth century—as 178,936 households, which would be something like 895,000 persons. The same source relates that at this time there were thirty-five immense private estates in the capital. The monarch had four major palaces, one for each season of the year. Government service offices existed for the repair and maintenance of palaces and government buildings, city walls, bridges, parks, and royal graves. And on the mountains flanking this rich capital on the broad and fertile Kyŏngju plain were the vast monasteries.

THE EDUCATIONAL SYSTEM

The National Academy, established in 651 and strengthened in 682, provided a formal structure for the development of Confucianism. It had received an initial stimulus in 640 when Silla sent students to the T'ang academy, where T'ang T'ai-tsung had assembled noted Confucian scholars. The Silla academy was under the jurisdiction of the Board of Rites, and instruction was carried out by scholars and their assistants. There were three levels of study, and the texts were all in Chinese, a foreign language. The lowest level read the *Classic of Filial Piety* and part of the *Book of Rites*, the second level added the *Analects*, while the highest level added one other text: the *Wen Hsüan* (Anthology of Literature), the *Tso chuan*, or the complete *Book of Rites*. The basic curriculum of the Silla academy appears to have been practically the same as that of the Japanese academy later established in Nara. Students, who were between the ages of fifteen and thirty, received stipends by holding official rank up to grade 12 and were allowed 9 years to successfully complete their studies. Talented individuals were allowed to remain longer, leaving school with official rank at grade 10. Texts beyond the three-level curriculum included the *Book of History*, *Book of Poetry*, *Book of Changes*, the three histories, viz., *Shih chih*, *Han shu*, and the *Hou Han shu*, and the writings of the Hundred Schools.

In 717 an embassy returning from T'ang brought back portraits of Confucius, the ten Confucian sages, and seventy-two Confucian disciples, which were placed in the academy and which must have given it something of a shrine-like atmosphere. In 788 the first government service examinations were held. Given the strong caste and clan structure of Silla society at this time, it is difficult to judge to what extent these examinations were more than pro forma exercises in institutional chinoiserie and to what extent they were useful in promoting changes such as channeling competition for bureaucratic posts or consolidating the position of the ruler.

The Confucianism of the late Silla period seems to have been a hard-headed practical matter concerned with literacy and literature and with affairs of state. It was devoid of the enervating orthodoxy and metaphysical bent which it was later to acquire at the hands of the Sung philosophers. Its concern with this world complemented Buddhist otherworldliness, and men could and did study both. While the study and practice of Confucianism may have been restricted primarily to the ranks of the educated elite at that time, the doctrine itself was to have rather far-reaching effects upon all of Korean society in time.

Confucianism provided certain basic ideals of government centered on the conduct of men in their relationship to each other. The five principal relationships were those of ruler and minister, father and son, husband and wife, brothers, and friends, which were extended and related by analogy. The position of the father, for example, as the head of the family was seen as analogous to that of the king, who was the head of the state. Unfilial conduct thus became analogous to lese majesty. The notion of filial piety must have been attractive to Korean society with its strong primary or familial relationships, since it provided moral sanction for these relationships. Confucianism further related its ideals of government to nature. Natural phenomena were seen as direct manifestations of heaven's approval or disapproval of the conduct of the ruler. Confucianism also incorporated a distinct view of the past in relation to the present. Since proper conduct was crucial, history could provide, by example, numerous learning models and could be, in this sense, a mirror for all men. Benevolence, righteousness, propriety, wisdom, and sincerity were held as ideal qualities to be cultivated through such methods as reading the classics and exemplary biographies of historic figures. There is, of course, much more to Confucianism than is summarized above. Yet I believe that we can see some of the reasons why Confucianism would have appealed to Silla authorities. Its prestige as an institution from the greatest state in the world gave it an authority useful for implementing change. Its concern for ethical relations among men and the ethical pursuit of government addressed questions that men are concerned with to this day. As Buddhism provided answers to questions regarding the individual's relationship to the universe and the future, Confucianism defined men's relations with each other and with secular authority.

Of these two traditions, Buddhism and Confucianism, which emerged in the late Silla period, the former remained dominant in the religious sector and the latter in the bureaucratic sector in remarkable harmony for half a millennium.

BUDDHISM AND THE ARTS

Buddhism was a major tradition of Korean life and a dominant feature of Korean society until its influence began to wane in the fourteenth century. It shaped and influenced men's perspectives and the institutions they built. It was a vehicle for a vast body of thought, a tremendous literature, and an art of rich splendor. It provided a major incentive for the study of Chinese characters, into which the Buddhist canon had been translated. And it brought a universalism which transcended national boundaries. Buddhism in late Silla, and most of the succeeding Koryŏ period as well, colored men's lives and thoughts in much the same manner as Christianity dominated medieval Europe. The resources of the state and the elite were poured into lavish religious projects to ensure the protection of the state and the good fortune of the individual. When relics of the Buddha were brought back from China by Silla monks, the entire capital turned out, with the monarch and the high officials of state leading the way. The splendor of the great monasteries and the ornate and colorful ceremonies were undoubtedly attractive to the Silla elite. For the people of Silla, Buddhism opened a door to a different world with its views of man and the universe, its concepts of vast and limitless time, its notions of an unending series of births and rebirths until nirvana is reached, and its great compassion. The notion that men's positions in this life were due to their activities in a former life was probably as attractive to the leaders of a society of hereditary caste groups as the promise of a better future life was to the masses. The mysticism and supernatural aura which permeated the Buddhist outlook blended well with native shamanistic elements and Taoistic practices brought in from the continent.

The monasteries were also places of refuge and succor. The compassion of the Buddhist doctrine was expressed in providing for the sick and injured, the aged and the poor, and many a ruler of the states of Korea would turn to Buddhism for solace following a personal tragedy even in later centuries when the state policy could accurately be described as anti-Buddhist. Philosophic schools emerged, and native beliefs merged with many of the popular schools of Buddhism. While the texts of both Mahāyāna and Hīnāyana Buddhism were studied by Silla monks who went to China, the doctrines of the former were always dominant in Korea. By the seventh century the development of different Mahāyāna schools had begun.

The development of these schools does not mean that the texts upon which they were based were not known or had not been discussed in Silla earlier, but rather implies the development, by some monk who is usually credited as being the Korean patriarch of a particular school, of a teacher-disciple relationship devoted to the doctrines of a particular school at a monastery where the doctrines of one school were emphasized and where the tradition continued. Most, if not all, of the Buddhist schools which emerged in China seem to have been known in Korea as well; the ones mentioned below emerged as schools in Silla.

The Vinaya, rules or discipline, school was developed by the monk Chajang (fl. mid-seventh century), who returned from T'ang in 641 with 400 cases of the Tripiṭaka, the Buddhist canon. T'ongdo-sa was built for him, not too distant from the capital, and it became the main monastery of this school.

The Nirvāṇa school was developed in the late sixth century by the Koguryŏ monk Podŏk, although the monk Wŏn'gwang had brought back the Nirvāṇa sutra to Silla from Sui China in the first half of the sixth century. The head monastery of this school was at Kyŏngbok-sa, near the town of Chŏnju in the former Paekche area, which came under Silla control after the wars of unification.

The Silla patriarch of the Hwaŏm (c. Hua-yen, j. Kegon) school was Ŭisang (625–702), who went to T'ang in 661, where he studied under Chi-yen, who became the third patriarch of the Hua-yen school in China. Ŭisang's fellow student was the noted Chinese monk Fa-tsang. Ŭisang returned to Silla in 670, and 6 years later, at the age of 55, supervised the construction of Pusŏk-sa in the Taebaek Mountains. It became the headquarters for the ten Hwaŏm monasteries in Silla. Ŭisang was one of the great Korean Buddhist teachers, with ten well-known disciples who propagated the faith in Korea. He sent yet another disciple, Simsang, to T'ang to study under his friend and classmate Fa-tsang. Simsang subsequently went to Japan, where he lectured on the Hwaŏm doctrine at Tōdai-ji monastery.

In the mid-eighth century the Pŏpsang (c. Fa-hsiang) school, a realist

Mahāyāna school, was developed by the monk Chinp'yo. The principal center of this disciplinary school was at Kŭmsan-sa.

Wŏnhyo (617–698)—ranked with Ŭisang as one of the great Buddhist figures of the period, although usually associated with the Hwaŏm school—stands apart from clear identification with a single doctrine or philosophical school. He was a voluminous reader and wrote commentaries and discourses on the texts of many Mahāyāna schools. Through these writings his influence reached Japan and China, although unlike the majority of well-known Silla monks he had never been to China. Highly honored during his own lifetime, which he spent partially at the great monastery of Punhwang-sa in the capital, Wŏnhyo was also a great popularizer of Buddhism. He returned to secular life after the birth of his son, Sŏl Chong, and travelled through the country-side popularizing Buddhism through song and dance, it is related. He is credited, along with other monks, with popularizing the Pure Land school. This school calls for the adherent merely to demonstrate his faith by repetition of the formula of faith "Namu Amidabul" to gain salvation into the Western Paradise of Amida Buddha.

Many Silla monks went to China to study, and several went beyond. In 726 Hyecho (704–?), whose travels we know through his diary found in a cave temple at Tun-huang, travelled from T'ang to India by sea and then returned to China by way of central Asia. At least seven Korean monks are known to have gone to India before Hyecho. Unfortunately, none of these distant travellers is known to have returned to Silla.

Sŏn or Zen, the meditative Dhyāna school, was developed in the early ninth century by Toŭi, who founded Porim-sa on Mount Kaji. A total of nine Zen monasteries on nine different mountains were built from the reign of King Hŏndŏk (r. 809–825) to the early years of the reign of Koryŏ T'aejo (r. 918–943). These Zen monasteries were often called the Nine Mountains, an appellation which refers to the Buddhist concept of nine concentric mountain ranges of a universe, i.e., a Buddha world.

Esoteric Buddhism with its dhāraṇī or magic incantations was strong in Silla. Equally influential was the concept of Buddhism as the protector of the state and the individual as well as the provider of good fortune. The latter is seen in the lectures held on the In-wang sutra, which supposedly ensures these blessings. Popular beliefs of the times included the notion that the existence of the nine-tiered pagoda of Hwangyong-sa in the capital ensured that the "nine tribes," i.e., all the tribes, of the peninsula would submit and bring tribute to Silla. The construction of the monastery of the Four Heavenly Kings, Sach'ŏnwang-sa, was also supposed to ensure Silla's unification of the peninsula. Under the influence of Buddhism cremation came into popularity. The remains of one Silla monarch, King Munmu, were interred in a tomb on a large rock in the Eastern Sea. This monarch was popularly believed to have been reincarnated as a dragon to protect the nation, a story which parallels the tale of a Bodhisattva who transformed himself into a dragon king. In popular Buddhism the Maitreya or Buddha of the Future occupied a particularly influential position, as did Avalokiteśvara (c. *Kuan-yin*), the latter because of its position in the Pure Land school, since Avalokiteśvara is considered an incarnation of Amida.

During the ninth century a renewed interest in theories of prognostication and divination developed in Silla, brought back by students influenced by Taoism in T'ang and reinforced by the popular beliefs of the period. It was in this atmosphere that the contemplative school of Zen developed. Buddhist monks played a major role in popularizing these theories, most of which were not entirely new to Korea. The geomantic theories of the monk Tosŏn (d. 898) were extremely popular, and a book of prophecy attributed to him was particularly influential during the Koryŏ period.

Unfortunately all too little is known of the socioeconomic role of Buddhism and the Buddhist monasteries in the life of the people of Silla, but it must have been enormous. The great monasteries in the provinces with their hundreds of resident monks and attached village communities must have been influential centers of social and economic activity. Various festivals centered at monasteries were held, such as the Lantern Festival and the Festival of the Eight Commandments (*P'algwanhoe*). The *P'algwan* Festival, first held in the sixth century to commemorate war dead, developed into a shamanistic-animistic ceremony concerned with deities of rivers and mountains rather than with Buddhism.

The patronage of Buddhism by the state and the elite ushered in a period of artistic splendor in monastery building and in the arts. Monasteries great and small crowded the capital and its environs, while hundreds of others were constructed in the mountains throughout the country. The wooden buildings with their paintings and wooden carvings disappeared centuries ago in the smoke of accidental fires or the torches of invaders, but through the more enduring forms of metal and stone we may glimpse the brilliance of this age of Buddhist art. The true greatness of Silla Buddhist art may be seen in stone sculpture and construction, and in metal casting. Records reveal that many large Buddhist figures were cast, such as the huge 16 Korean foot (*ch'ŏk*) high image of Buddha cast for Hwangyong-sa, which is said to have required 37,000 Korean pounds (*kŭn*) of copper for the image itself and 10,000 Korean grams (*pun*) of gold leaf to cover the figure. Very few of the larger figures remain, and they seem far below the artistic quality of the smaller gilt bronze figures. The casting of monastery bells reached a high point of excellence. The oldest extant Silla bell is the Sanwŏn-sa bell cast in 725, which weighs some 3,300 pounds. Three Silla bells also survived in Japan. The largest is from the former monastery of Pongdŏk-sa. Cast in 770, this huge bell stands 11 feet high, has a diameter of $7\frac{1}{2}$ feet, and weighs over 158,000 pounds. It is the second largest bell in the world, the largest being in Moscow. While the size alone is impressive, it is the quality of the bells and the delicate bas-relief design of apsaras, flowers, clouds, and flames on them that bring them into the sphere of art.

The high achievement in stone construction may be seen in two excellent and rare examples: the entrance terrace at Pulguk-sa, completed in 751, and the stone Śākyamuni or Tabo stupa at the same temple. This monastery is built on the slope of a spur of a mountain which soars high above the Kyŏngju plain to the east of the old Silla capital. Far up toward the summit and facing the East Sea on the other side of the mountain is the eighth-century man-made grotto of Sŏkkuram. Inside the grotto is an 11-foot Buddha on a lotus petal carved from a single block of granite. The figure is seated in the center of the grotto in such a position that the first rays of dawn breaking across the East Sea shine through the entranceway and illuminate the Buddha. Carved in delicate bas-relief on granite slabs set into the wall circling the Buddha are figures of Bodhisattvas, arhans, and devas which are particularly fine examples of Silla monumental art. The same idealistic and sensuous style may be seen in Buddhist figures carved on the sides of stone lanterns and stone slabs from temples no longer extant. Some of the stone lions carved in the round as supporting figures for stone lanterns or as guardian figures are of a similar style. Perhaps an inspiration for the late Silla work may be seen in the T'ang period figures at Tun-huang. They share the same naturalism and vitality and obvious Hellenistic influences, although the Silla figures seem to be more concerned with exterior ornamentation.

The style of tombs underwent a great change, with the construction of conspicuous tumuli bordered by great stone slabs on which were carved the twelve animals of the zodiac and guarded on the approach by larger-than-life figures of civil officials and military officers carved in the round. Commemorative stele of inscribed stone were mounted on enormous carved granite turtles, and the stele were topped with headstones carved in the form of two interwoven dragons.

There were other arts in Silla, to be sure, such as decorative tile, and it appears that cloisonné may have been known in Silla by the sixth or seventh century.

In 1967 a Buddhist text printed by wood block was found in the course of repairing a pagoda at Pulguk-sa. If it dates to the construction of the pagoda in 751—as is probable, since it was customary to include such items at the time—it is then the oldest extant example of printing in the world, predating the *dhāraṇi* printed in Japan in the 760s. The almost 5,000 extant Silla wood blocks attest to the flourishing printing industry on the peninsula.

The Silla pottery of the fifth to seventh centuries was based to a large extent upon prototypes made in the Kaya League. An unglazed, wheel-thrown ware, it is characterized by a general absence of design and a pierced foot or pedestal. The square or triangular holes cut, often awkwardly, in the foot remind one of similar perforations in Chinese Chou bronze vessels. The covers of many Silla vessels were decorated with small, molded marine specimens such as fish, turtles, crabs, eels, and lobster, probably reflecting major ingredients of the cooking pot. Rarely, a crude "stick drawing" of a deer, tiger, or human figure may be found on a pot. Also made in Silla were numerous molded clay figurines, including long-horned buffalo, rabbits, cows, turtles, ducks, huts and houses, mounted riders, males in double-ended boats with a single sweep oar, porters with the characteristic Korean pack-frame, and hundreds of very crude male figurines. The last may have been, judging from the number, an ingredient in shamanistic ritual, while the other figurines undoubtedly were influenced by practices of the Chinese Han colonies, where similar pottery figures were common funerary items. In the seventh to eighth centuries a stamped grey stoneware began to replace this pottery. The grey, unglazed vessels were decorated with stamped or impressed designs of stylized birds, circles, or chevrons, and it continued to be made in the early Koryŏ period. A greenish brown glazed ware appeared in the years of the Silla decline; it too continued into the Koryŏ period.

BELLES-LETTRES

Many peoples living on the periphery of China became acquainted with the Chinese system of writing and lacking a script of their own adopted the Chinese system. Some of these peoples were stimulated to utilize the phonetic and semantic values of Chinese characters to develop a system of writing the sounds of their own languages. These peoples, among whom the Koreans were probably the earliest, included the Japanese, Annamese, Jürčen, Ch'i-tan, and Hsi-hsia. The development of a means of writing the Korean language was crucial to the history of Korean literature. One of the earliest examples of this system of writing, called *hyangch'al*, is in the inscription on the so-called hunting monument of Silla's King Chinp'yŏng (r. 540–576), which means it was in use in Silla at least from the sixth century. There is some evidence that a similar system was used in Koguryŏ.

Sŏl Ch'ong (mid-eighth century), the son of the monk Wŏnhyo, has as early as the mid-tenth century been linked with the invention of this method of writing, but this is certainly in error, since *hyangch'al* was in use at least two centuries before his birth. Sŏl, one of the ten Confucian sages of Silla, is said to have used the Korean language to explain the Nine Chinese Classics in the Silla academy, and it seems likely that he also used *hyangch'al* for this purpose.

Hyangch'al was used to record the *hyangga* or Korean songs of Silla. While the titles of many of these songs remain, the texts of only a few have been passed along, viz., some fourteen in the *Samguk yusa* and a single eleven-verse cycle by the monk Kyunyŏ. The short verse written in 1120 by Koryŏ King Yejong is often included, since it was also written in *hyangch'al*.

The most widely known *hyangga* is probably the Song of Ch'ŏyong. It was incorporated in a masked performance and presented in an expanded version at court in the Koryŏ (918–1392) and early Yi (1392–1910) periods. The performance of this work, of which a summary follows, apparently had the function of protecting the state by exorcising the demon of pestilence.

Ch'ŏyong, one of the seven sons of the Dragon King of the Eastern Sea, has been given a beautiful girl to wed by the Silla monarch, who wishes to keep his services as advisor. One night when Ch'ŏyong returns late after a night of carousing in the capital, he discovers the Demon of Pestilence in bed with his wife. Ch'ŏyong then dances and sings this song to exorcise the demon:

> *Under the bright moon of the capital,*
> *'Til far in the night I sported.*
> *Returning, I see in the bed,*
> *There are four legs!*
> *Two were mine,*
> *Whose are the other two?*
> *Those originally mine have been taken;*
> *What shall I do?*

The demon then kneels before Ch'ŏyong and tells him he will never enter a gate where a likeness of Ch'ŏyong (in the form of a door placard) is displayed.

There appear to be several identifiable strata in the Ch'ŏyong and similar stories incorporating *hyangga*. The song appears to be of shamanist origins and possibly represents the oldest stratum, while those features identifiable as Buddhist or which are continental in origin, e.g., the door placard of the Ch'ŏyong story, represent later strata.

The adoption of the Chinese system of writing by the peoples of the Korean states offered many advantages in domestic and international use. The development of *hyangch'al* is something else again. It is one thing to write a few place names using Chinese characters phonetically and quite another to write complete songs in this fashion. These songs could have been written—and read much more easily—in Chinese. Why was it important to render the songs and only the songs in Korean? Like the Buddhist *dhāraṇi* or magic chants written using Chinese phonetically to render the Sanskrit original, these songs probably had a magico-religious significance and had to be written in Korean so that the incantations would not lose their power. Similarly, the *manyōgana*, a system of writing like the *hyangch'al* and which may have been stimulated by it, was used by the Japanese in recording the *norito* Shinto prayers and the *senmyō* or divine orders of the Japanese rulers, which again suggests the necessity for retention of the original *sounds* of the language.

As a repository of ancient Korean literature, the *Samguk yusa* is without equal. It was compiled in 1279 by the Zen monk Iryŏn (1206–1289) from works now lost. Its content is divided about evenly between stories concerned with (1) the states of the Korean peninsula, supernatural events surrounding famous men, and marvelous occurrences during the reign of various monarchs and (2) tales of miracles and supernatural events linked to Buddhist temples, famous Buddhist monks, and *jātaka* or Buddhist fables from India. The *Samguk yusa* bears resemblances to the eleventh-century Japanese work *Konjaku monogatari*, although the latter was written in Japanese in contrast to the Korean work which is chiefly in Chinese. Both works undoubtedly trace their origins to earlier collections of Buddhist tales. Among the Korean tales are many concerning the great hero of the wars of unification the valiant General Kim Yusin, whose life and exploits inspired many romanticized stories.

The prose literature of Silla is strongly narrative in style and is colored by the supernatural religious powers of Buddhist priests and their miracles. There are also many stories involving dragons which guide and counsel men, suggesting, with other evidence, a dragon cult of possibly pre-Buddhist origins in Silla. While it does include an occasional didactic anecdote, as in the exemplary biographies of dutiful daughters with their Confucian orientation, the literature was permeated with the fantastic, with immortals, with the supernatural revelation of dreams, with demons, with prognostications of omens, and with humans changing into animal form. In this we see the influence of the Chinese *ch'uan-ch'i* tales of the strange and unusual, which flourished in the T'ang period and which gained great popularity in Korea. Silla envoys are related to have eagerly sought the works of Chinese authors of such tales, such as Chang Tsu (657–730), on their trips to Ch'ang-an, the T'ang capital.

Many works were written and compiled during the late Silla period, and some writings of Buddhist commentators remain, but for the bulk of Silla writings we have only some intriguing titles.

Chinese influence was strong. For example, the *Wen-hsüan* (Anthology of Literature) was taught in the Korean academy. Chinese poets, such as Po Chü-i (772–846) and Tu Fu (712–770), became immensely popular in Korea and stimulated Koreans to compose works in Chinese themselves.

Koreans quickly learned to write a variety of Chinese verse forms, such as the five- and seven-word *ku-shih*, the lengthy *fu* or rhyme-prose, and parallel prose. Silla poets in the Chinese tradition, such as Kim Un'gyŏng, became popular enough in Japan—probably as representatives of Chinese rather than Korean culture—to have their works included in the tenth-century Japanese anthology *Sensai juku* of Oe Koretoki.

The best known of Silla scholars in the Chinese tradition was Ch'oe Ch'iwŏn (d. 857). He went to T'ang China when he was twelve, passed the T'ang examinations at eighteen, was given a post in the Chinese government, and remained there until he was twenty-eight. Ch'oe held a government post in Silla for some time after his return but soon resigned to wander about the country, which was then in decline, spending his final years at the monastery of Haein-sa, on Mount Kaya in the southeast. Some remnants of his poetry which show him to favor the Chinese *shih* and *fu* poetic forms survive as do several of the commemorative inscriptions he wrote for Buddhist monks. Ch'oe might be viewed as an early representative of the alienated Korean Confucian-influenced intellectual who looked across the sea to the traditions of China for inspiration and guidance.

THE PERFORMING ARTS

Although our information on the performing arts of this period is meager, we have a few records which tell us something of them and give us some insights into Silla society. Popular during the Silla and Koryŏ periods was the 3-day Festival of Wine (*T'aep'o*), a word used in the modern idiom for "wine shop." This festival was imported from T'ang China and was sometimes hosted by the monarch, the earliest recorded occasion being 615. Performances featuring dancers supported by musicians and singers were a highlight. At the Festival of Wine given by King Kyŏngdŏk in the capital in 746, a general amnesty was declared, and 150 Buddhist novices were permitted to become monks. At another festival, held in the village of Sinsin in the year 689, seven dance performances were held, four of which featured singing. The Korean dance (*saenae-mu*) presented upon this occasion, for example, featured one lute player, two dancers, and two singers. A dance with a similar title presented in 807 had four dancers in green dress, one lute player in red dress, and five singers in multicolored costume with golden cord belts and embroidered fans.

Korean performances at this time included masked performances, which are generally believed to trace their origins to central Asia and India via the various states of China; some apparently came with Buddhism. Ch'oe Ch'iwŏn's *Hyangak chabyŏng*, incorporated in the *Samguk sagi* of 1145, mentions the Lion Dance, masked performances, and juggling.

The Golden Balls

Bending his body and bracing his arms, he juggles the golden balls.
Moons wheel, stars float and fill the eyes.
Even though there were the proper officials, how could they excel this?
I know for sure that a sea of whales stops the waves.

The Mask

What man is this with the golden colored mask?
In his hand he holds the pearl whip to exorcise the ghostly spirits.
Walking quickly, then running slowly, he performs an elegant dance,
Which faintly resembles the Phoenix Dance and the spring [of the
    golden age] of [Emperor] Yao.

The Lion

From afar across ten thousand li *of shifting [desert] sands he came,*
His fur is all torn and [covered with] dust,
He shakes his head and swishes his tail mildly in benevolence and virtue.
He is braver than all other animals.

SOCIAL STRUCTURE

The organization of Silla society included the Buddhist elements, the monks and the monasteries and cloisters where they lived. In addition to the Department of Monasteries in the central government staffed by members of the elite, there were three levels of supervisory offices staffed entirely by monks. The office of National Buddhist Supervisor, first established in 551 and patterned after Chinese institutions, was staffed by one, occasionally two, eminent monks with a few assistants. They were the head of the Buddhist monkhood in Silla. Subordinate to the national office were nine provincial and eighteen district Buddhist supervisors. Among their principal duties was the regulation of novitiates to the monkhood, for which exams were held periodically. They were probably also concerned with the offices established for the construction of new monasteries. The creation of these construction offices, one at each of seven great monasteries, incorporated some danger, since construction could, theoretically, continue indefinitely. In 806 a decree prohibited further use of embroidered silks or gold and silver utensils in the monasteries. A decree issued a few years later condemning extravagance suggests fiscal troubles in the central government but was probably due as much to unsettled conditions in the country as to the extravagance in Buddhist monasteries.

All this internal development was restricted and channeled by the crucial social structure of Silla society, the *bone-rank system*. The hereditary features of this class system implied recognition of privilege on one hand even as it implied strict social control measures and restrictions on the other. Regulations covered the size of the dwellings, the number and type of gates, the size of the stable, chariot ornamentation, and clothing, including materials permitted for women's garments from the highest officials down to commoners.

THE ROYAL CASTE GROUP AND THE SILLA ELITE

The royal caste group was drawn from one bone-rank, the *sŏnggol*, which meant that, in theory, it relied upon direct descent for its existence, since cadet branches of the royal family were presumably of the *chin'gol* rank. In 653, Queen Chindŏk died without heir, and the *sŏnggol* rank was regarded as ended. Actually members of collateral branches of the royal family had held the throne before, and whatever distinction had previously existed between the *sŏnggol* and *chin'gol* ranks seems to have disappeared in practice. Kim Ch'unch'u, a member of a collateral branch of the royal clan and hence of *chin'gol* rank, was put on the throne to become King Muyŏl (r. 652–660). He was supported by General Kim Yusin, a direct descendant of the last ruler of Kŭmgwan Kaya. General Kim's younger sister, Ahae, married Kim Ch'unch'u, while Yusin married one of the daughters of Kim Ch'unch'u. At the time it must have seemed as though an important precedent had been established, for the struggles among the *chin'gol* to control the throne intensified until they literally tore the state apart.

King Muyŏl may not have set a precedent, but his son Pŏmmin who succeeded him utilized one effectively. Pŏmmin, canonized King Munmu (r. 661–680), in 674 resettled Koguryŏ peoples in the lands of the former Paekche and gave them appointments in the regional administrative system. Then he resettled members of elite families from the capital in these lands in positions of authority, following precedents set by King Chijŭng in 513 and King Chinhŭng in 558. This led to the development of an outer *chin'gol* or *oejin* class in the provinces who, in the matters of dress, dwellings, and chariots, were given the restrictions of the third bone-rank as opposed to the *chin'gol* in the capital, who were treated as members of the first bone-rank. Many of these *oejin* undoubtedly became powerful local figures, but their goals were in the capital. They were to be an ever-present element of political instability within the Silla elite.

The more powerful elite families lived in the capital as absentee landlords, which, together with the goals of the *oejin*, checked tendencies toward local autonomy as long as the central government remained strong. The great, wealthy elite families lived opulent lives in the capital with large numbers—"thousands," if we believe the records—of slaves, and they began to develop their own private armies, both to protect themselves and their holdings and to use in the frequent attempts to gain the throne. There were peasant revolts from time to time, but these appear to have occurred chiefly during the years of famine and pestilence, when doles issued from government granaries could do little to ease local conditions. In years of famine and pestilence or when order broke down, peasants would leave the land and either migrate elsewhere or turn to banditry and piracy.

STRUGGLES FOR THE THRONE

During the period 750 to 800, there were six revolts or palace coups by the elite, and in the period 800 to 890 there were fourteen. The majority involved collateral branches of the royal Kim clan and were attempts to seize the throne. The more successful were the palace coups led by the two most powerful officials: the grand councillor and the palace secretary. It comes as no surprise to find that of the last twenty monarchs of Silla, only nine died apparently natural deaths, the remainder dying violently or under suspicious circumstances.

In 822, intraclan warfare recommenced with new intensity with the revolt of Kim Hŏnch'ang, a member of the *oejin*, who was angered when his father was not made king. Kim Hŏnch'ang set up a short-lived state in west central Korea which he named Ch'angan after the T'ang capital. This base soon fell, and his son moved northward to the P'yŏngyang area, where he apparently amassed considerable power. In 826, a large corvée labor force was raised in a nationwide levy, and a 300-*li* defensive wall was built south of this area at the Taedong River.

When King Hŭngdŏk (r. 826–835) died, a struggle broke out over the throne once more. The contestants were the king's paternal cousin Kim Kyujŏng, then grand councillor, and the latter's son, Kim Cheyung. Kim Kyujŏng was supported by a group which included another of his sons, Ujing, who was a sixth-grade official, a nephew, and a certain Kim Yang. In the fighting which erupted in the palace, Kim Kyujŏng was killed, and his son gained the throne. This was King Hŭigang (r. 836–837). The group which had supported Kim Kyujŏng fled southeast with their supporters to Ch'ŏnghae in the Korean southwest, the insular stronghold of Silla's merchant general Chang Pogo.

CHANG POGO

Chang Pogo, who had a reputation as a strong swimmer, had left Silla to seek his fortune in T'ang, where he rose to the position of military officer.

He returned to Silla and in an audience with King Hŭngdŏk told of the many Koreans he had seen in China being sold as slaves. He then requested that he be given support to establish a naval base at Ch'ŏnghae, on the modern Wando Island, to prevent people living near the seacoast from being kidnapped and sold as slaves in the markets of China. Several years of poor harvests in Silla and chaotic conditions in China had led to some rather widespread famines and a sudden rise in piracy. By the middle of the ninth century, pirate raids on the coast of China and Korea had reached serious proportions. The pirates were seizing Silla ships at sea and ravaging not only the Korean and Chinese coasts but the western coast of Japan and offshore islands as well. The Silla authorities, anxious to eliminate the pirates and restore the profitable trade with China and Japan, appointed Chang Pogo commissioner of Ch'ŏnghae in 828. Chang appears to have been a native of the area, and the large number of troops he commanded may have been his own private forces rather than government forces as the records relate.

Chang's base at Ch'ŏnghae occupied a key position off the southwest coast and straddled the Korea-Japan-China trade route. Korean ships homeward bound from the Chinese ports of Ming-chou, Yang-chou, or Teng-chou crossed the Yellow Sea to the Hŭksan Islands in the southwest and then either proceeded north to ports along the island-strewn western coast of Korea or sailed eastward through the Cheju Straits toward the Korean southeast and Japan. This was the route taken by most ships, although there were also two northern routes. One of these was a coastal route around the Gulf of P'o-hai and the other was a straight run across the 110 miles of water separating the Shantung peninsula of China from Korea's Hwanghae promontory.

Chang Pogo's activities were not limited to a coastal patrol. He also engaged widely in maritime commerce himself and practically monopolized maritime trade on the Yellow Sea. His ships carried the official Korean embassies to T'ang. The Japanese monk Ennin, who went to China on one of Chang's ships, noted that Chang, a patron of Buddhism, had built the cloister Flower of the Law (*fa-hua*) on Mount Ch'ih, near the port of Teng-chou. Chang donated sufficient fields to the cloister to provide its twenty-four Korean monks and three Korean nuns with an annual income of 500 Chinese bushels of rice.

CHANG POGO AND THE SUCCESSION STRUGGLES

In his struggle for the throne King Hŭigang had been supported by Kim Myŏng, and after gaining the throne he rewarded Kim with the post of grand councillor. Kim Myŏng, as grand councillor, was now in a position to overthrow the monarch, which he did. King Hŭigang, wounded and trapped in the palace, hanged himself in despair. Kim Myŏng, later known as King Minae (r. 838), ascended the throne.

Kim Yang, who had previously supported the unsuccessful attempt to put Kim Kyujŏng on the throne, led his forces to Ch'ŏnghae garrison to join Kim Ujing. Chang Pogo was sympathetic to Kim Ujing and backed him in his bid for the throne, furnishing 5,000 of his soldiers and his ablest lieutenants. In return for Chang's support Kim Ujing seems to have contracted a marriage between either himself or his son, who would be the crown prince and the next king, and the daughter of Chang Pogo.

The joint venture was successful, and the combined forces of Kim and Chang entered the capital and killed King Minae in the western suburbs of the city. Kim Ujing was then put on the throne. This was King Sinmu (r. 839). He reigned only 3 months and died, in bed it is said, before the year was out. Before he died, he purged those who had opposed him and rewarded Chang Pogo with an appanage of 2,000 households. This monarch's son, canonized King Munsŏng (r. 839–856), bestowed more honors and titles on Chang Pogo as soon as he had taken the throne. He then proposed to take the daughter of Chang Pogo as his second wife. This caused an uproar at court. The objections offered concluded that Chang was "an islander" and that his daughter would be out of place at court. King Munsŏng followed his minister's advice and cancelled the marriage. Chang Pogo was enraged and apparently planned to revolt but was murdered by Yŏm Chang, one of his principal officers, who had turned against him. The fight was carried on by Yi Changjin, one of Chang's generals, and he was successful in holding off government forces for some time. The base at Ch'ŏnghae was finally captured and destroyed by forces led by Yŏm Chang. Some of Chang Pogo's followers fled to Japan but were pursued by Yŏm's envoys, who requested their return. The majority of the populace of Ch'ŏnghae was moved and resettled in other areas, bringing an end to Silla's maritime activities, and shipborne commerce in the northeast gradually passed into the hands of the Chinese. Official trade through the tribute system was also broken. The New History of T'ang (*Hsin T'ang shu*) remarks succinctly: "After the Hui-ch'ang era [841–847] official tribute did not again arrive."

THE DISINTEGRATION OF SILLA

The control of the central government had steadily weakened in the provinces. The fun-loving monarch King Hŏn'gang (r. 875–886) devoted more of his time to song and wine than to administration. By the reign of his daughter, Queen Chinsŏng (r. 887–897), control over the provinces had fallen apart. There had been some objection to a woman ascending the throne, and it is related that she remitted taxes for 1 year when she took the throne, but this may have been simply a reluctance to admit the impossibility of collecting them. By 890, the third year of her reign, disintegration had progressed to the point where taxes could not be collected from the provinces at all.

The breakdown in Silla was paralleled by conditions in China. T'ang was still recovering from the effects of the rebellion of An Lu-shan in 755 when the rebellion of Huang Ch'ao erupted in 878. The countryside was left in chaos, and the dynasty never fully recovered. On the peninsula large-scale forces, uniformly called "bandits" by the Silla court, dominated Silla in the areas beyond the capital province. Some of the major fighting groups which emerged during the period 890–900 were Wŏnjong in the south-central area; Yanggil in north-central Korea; Kihwŏn in south-central Korea; Kyŏnhwŏn based in the southwest; Kungye, a monk said to be an illegitimate son of Silla King Hŏnan, who had been a former lieutenant of Yanggil until he set up his own army in central Korea; Ch'ŏnggil, operating in south-central Korea; and finally a group called the Red Pantaloons, who caused widespread terror in the southeast. The breakdown of the power of the central government had left the provinces on their own, and powerful local leaders based in walled cities emerged with their own private armies. Some even sent their own embassies to China.

By 900 Kyŏnhwŏn felt strong enough to declare himself king of a state which he called Later Paekche. In 901 Kungye had consolidated his holdings in the Taedong River area and declared himself the king of a state which began by adopting Silla organizational patterns. At this time the local magistrate of the minor district of Songak went to Kungye and submitted his district for incorporation into the rebel domains. He also commended his 20-year-old son Wang Kŏn for service. Wang Kŏn, and there is some doubt that this was his real name since the characters can be interpreted to mean "the king who founded [the state]," proved himself quickly. The ensuing years found the youth continuously in the forefront of the battles against the armies of Later Paekche, now leading a naval force south along the coast, now riding to battle in the rugged mountains of south-central Korea. Soon he was the foremost general of the rebel forces under Kungye until in 918, Wang Kŏn, the founder of Koryŏ, overthrew and killed Kungye. But the wars were far from over. At this time the peninsula was dominated by three rival kingdoms: Silla, Later Paekche, and Koryŏ. These states are commonly known as the Later Three Kingdoms. Silla was apparently on the defensive most of the time, and the major fighting was between Later Paekche and Koryŏ. Pushing strongly and boldly northward, the forces of Later Paekche captured the Silla capital and placed their own candidate on the throne of Silla. A low point for Wang Kŏn's men was reached in battles with Later Paekche forces on P'algong Mountain, west of the Silla capital. The armies of Later Paekche disastrously defeated the Koryŏ armies, and Wang Kŏn barely escaped death in the field. Two of his officers, Kim Nak and Sin Sunggyŏm, sacrificed their lives so he could escape. Their deed was later eulogized by King Yejong, and a masked dance depicting their valor was popular in the early Koryŏ period.

In 935 the last king of Silla submitted to Wang Kŏn. The former Silla monarch was given the Silla capital as an appanage and a salary of 1,000 Korean bushels of rice annually. A marriage arrangement was concluded with Wang Kŏn and the Silla monarch, each marrying one of the other's daughters. In the southwest, divisions had appeared within the leadership of the forces of Later Paekche, and in 936 their armies were decisively defeated on the field of battle. After 35 years of continuous warfare Wang Kŏn, the son of a minor official and now a battle-scarred veteran, had unified the peninsula.

DISTINCTIVE FEATURES OF THE LATE SILLA PERIOD

During the late Silla period many distinctive features emerged which would reappear throughout Korean history. One was the weakness of the institution of the monarchy, for whatever divine authority the kings of early Korean states may have had, no ruler of any Korean state following the Silla unification could invoke such authority. This contrasts vividly with the divine authority claimed by the Chinese and Japanese rulers. The result was that acrimonious struggles for the throne were continuous. It seems doubtful that the rulers of any other nation have been subjected to the vicissitudes which have befallen the kings and princes of the various states of Korea. They have been murdered by all imaginable means, including the sword, poison, and drowning. They have been dethroned, kept captive, sent into exile, and upon occasion munificently permitted to take their own lives. And as plots against them were all too common, so too were purges to eliminate the suspect or the accused.

The change in the decision-making apparatus from the Hwabaek elite council to a Chinese influenced bureaucratic system may have been an element in the numerous succession disputes which began in the eighth century. Decisions taken by the Hwabaek council were made by a small group of the top elite. Six men, for example, selected Kim Ch'unch'u (King Muyŏl) to be king. Council decisions were reached only with the concurrence of each council member. This gave such decisions an authority which bureaucratic decisions could scarcely hope to match.

Further, Silla had become a sedentary agricultural state with all the attendant technological and administrative problems. It was rather natural that Silla and succeeding Korean states should seek to draw from the richer and deeper experience of a much larger sedentary agricultural state, China.

To be sure the influence of China upon Korea was not, indeed could not have been, limited to purely technological and administrative matters. It was far more pervasive and reached every facet of life. Silla shared another common feature with China, namely, these two sedentary agricultural societies faced similar problems regarding the nomadic people of Manchuria. The stability or instability of Manchuria, itself apparently related to the stability of China, was a crucial factor in relations between all succeeding states of China and Korea.

The adoption of Buddhism, Confucianism, continental technologies, and administrative systems during the Three Kingdoms and Silla periods could not but influence the development of Korean society and culture. Each of these "systems" had its own "system imperatives." Buddhism, for example, incorporated not only a cosmology and cosmogony but also functional requirements for individuals with specialized training (monks) and for monasteries and religious paraphernalia, as well as certain ritual requirements for its practitioners.

These functional needs stimulated study of the Chinese written and spoken languages. The substitution of written Chinese for the Korean language in the educational system and in government communications meant that a degree of acculturation in the direction of the Chinese pattern was unavoidable, particularly among the Korean elite. When texts written in Chinese were made the basis of the educational system, a pattern was set that would be modified but not basically changed until the modern period.

6
Early
Koryŏ

By 936, Wang Kŏn, canonized T'aejo (Grand Progenitor) in Chinese fashion as the dynastic founder, had obtained the abdication and submission of the last Silla monarch and had defeated the forces of Later Paekche in the field. His choice of the name Koryŏ, an abbreviated form of Koguryŏ, reflected his ambitions and guided many of his actions. Even as the wars of unification were in progress, he had sent his young cousin Wang Singnyŏm to push the borders north to the Ch'ŏngch'ŏn River and to rebuild and garrison the old city of P'yŏngyang.

To the northeast he sent General Yu Kŭmp'il to establish a base for future advances into the Hamhŭng plain. The tradition established during these formative years that Koryŏ was the successor of the Korean-Manchurian state of Koguryŏ, while no more than a fanciful dream at this time, meant that a continuous effort would be maintained to expand northward. Primary attention was given to the northwest, the traditional invasion route. During the third quarter of the tenth century some seven walled cities and eleven military garrisons were built in this area. It took a century more to gain a foothold on the banks of the Yalu River. The reconstruction of P'yŏngyang, abandoned since the fall of Koguryŏ in 668, was an important part of both the tradition and the preparations for expansion northward. From this time P'yŏngyang became, and in all respects remained, the second city of Korea.

Wang Kŏn devoted his own energies to establishing firm control of the south. He had been only one of a number of ambitious military men allied with Kung Ye. Most were, like himself, from powerful regional clans who had established their independence in the years of warfare which commenced in the late ninth century. The more formidable of these men, generally referred to as "lord of the city" (*sŏngju*), controlled walled cities and the surrounding countryside. Some, like the lord of Kangju, had independently established relations with states in China. These men were the greatest check on the ambitions of Wang Kŏn. When, in 918 at the age of forty-two, he ousted Kung Ye and took over the leadership, many of them turned against

Chronological Overview

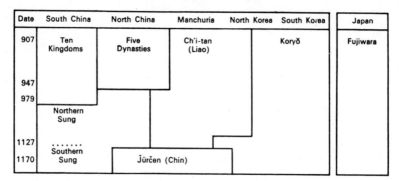

Date	South China	North China	Manchuria	North Korea	South Korea		Japan
907	Ten Kingdoms	Five Dynasties	Ch'i-tan (Liao)		Koryŏ		Fujiwara
947							
979	Northern Sung						
1127	. . . .						
1170	Southern Sung	Jürčen (Chin)					

him. These defections led Wang Kŏn, the following year, to locate his capital at his home district of Songak (Kaesŏng), between the Imjin and Yesŏng Rivers, where he could be confident of strong local support. Representatives were then sent to the more powerful provincial lords with messages of friendship and gifts in an effort to persuade them to join him. The success of this policy gave him the support he needed to reunify the peninsula.

But the independence of the strong provincial clans proved difficult to overcome. Wang Kŏn instituted several measures designed to bring these independent leaders under his control. His first effort was to strengthen the central government by incorporating into the central bureaucracy all the powerful provincial leaders and the military leaders who had served with him in the campaigns. This was done by giving titles of office, grants of land, and annual stipends to each leader. In the case of the provincial clans, however, it was limited to recognition and indorsement of their power by appointing their leaders to positions in the regional government. Theoretically, at least, this brought all land and all people under the central government, although the reality would not be realized for many decades. Actual central government control at the time was very weak. Tax collectors were sent out at harvest time, but real administrative control remained largely in the hands of the regional elite. Later, the grand title of "merit subject," which carried with it great privileges and large tracts of land, was awarded to those who had assisted in the founding of the state and those "lords of cities whose orientation has been righteous and whose return has been obedient," an action which rewarded the faithful and encouraged the hesitant.

A system of internal hostages called *kiin* was instituted to serve as a check on regional leaders. These hostages, the sons or close male relatives of the provincial leaders, were required to reside in the capital as a guarantee of the good conduct of their clans. A further measure taken by Wang Kŏn to bind the leaders of strong clans to him was marriage into their families,

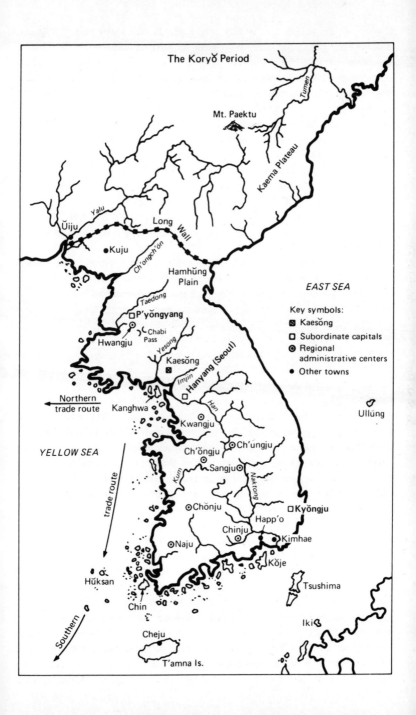

The Koryŏ Period

Mt. Paektu

Tumen

Kaema Plateau

Yalu

Ŭiju

Kuju

Long Wall

Ch'ŏngch'ŏn

Hamhŭng Plain

EAST SEA

Taedong

P'yŏngyang

Chabi Pass

Key symbols:
⊠ Kaesŏng
□ Subordinate capitals
⊙ Regional administrative centers
● Other towns

Hwangju

Yesong

Kaesŏng

Imjin

Hanyang (Seoul)

← Northern trade route

Kanghwa

Han

Ullŭng

Kwangju

YELLOW SEA

Ch'ŏngju

Ch'ungju

trade route

Sangju

Kum

Naktong

Chŏnju

Kyŏngju

Happ'o

Chinju

Kimhae

Naju

Kŏje

Hŭksan

Tsushima

Chin

Iki

Southern

Cheju

T'amna Is.

a ploy which gained him twenty-nine consorts. Although this indulgent accumulation accomplished his immediate goal, it seriously undermined the authority of the monarch. It practically ensured a violent succession dispute upon his death. More important in the centuries which followed was another result of this action. The royal caste group became related through marriage with the powerful elite families who had played important roles in the reunification or who were members of the high Silla or Parhae notables incorporated into the Koryŏ elite structure. Succeeding generations tended to intermarry. The entire Koryŏ elite group and the royal caste group became closely interrelated as cousin married cousin and half brother married half sister. Further, the close interrelationship between royal and elite clans reduced the power of the monarch, as the royal clan became merely first among equals. This in turn led to clan struggles and opened the door for attempts by the powerful clans to control the throne through their royal relatives.

Yet in his final years, Wang Kŏn could look back upon considerable achievement. He had unified the southern part of the peninsula, and the outlines of a central government based on the Silla system had been formed. It would be up to his descendants to do the rest.

THE CHALLENGE OF WANG KYU

Shortly after the death of Koryŏ T'aejo, the first of many struggles over the throne commenced. It was led by Wang Kyu, who had been a companion-in-arms of Wang Kŏn and was thus one of the revered and respected founders of the state. Wang Kyu had married two of his daughters to T'aejo and one to T'aejo's son and successor Hyejong (943–945). In preference to other royal heirs, Wang Kyu threw his considerable support behind one of the offspring of these marriages. His actions terrorized King Hyejong, who was powerless to eliminate his father's old supporter. This poor monarch was forced to live with an armed guard continually by his side during his brief reign. Upon Hyejong's death, his 23-year-old brother, canonized Chŏngjong (r. 945–949), was placed on the throne. Chŏngjong quickly appealed to his paternal uncle, General Wang Singnyŏm, who controlled P'yŏngyang. Troops were brought in from the north, and Wang Kyu was finally eliminated. The challenge of the great clans was to be a recurring theme through Korean history. Among the powerful clans in the early Koryŏ period were the Kim clan of Ansan, which was dominant during the first half of the eleventh century, and the Yi clan of Kyŏngwŏn (Inju), which succeeded it as the de facto power behind the throne from the middle of the eleventh to the mid-twelfth century.

THE BEGINNINGS OF A STRONG CENTRAL GOVERNMENT

The early Koryŏ period, until the rise of the military in the late twelfth century, was marked by the rise to prominence, power, and landed wealth of the civil officials of the central government. Their philosophy of government was largely based upon Han-T'ang Confucian principles modified by Korean views of a hierarchical society regulated by ancestry and acceptance of Buddhism and popular beliefs. Concomitant with defense efforts taken to secure the northwestern frontier had been a large military manpower build-up. The resulting large standing army under central government control provided the muscle the civil bureaucracy needed to consolidate the central government.

This process began in the reign of Kwangjong (r. 949–975), who proclaimed the new strength of the monarchy and independence of Koryŏ by adopting the title of "emperor" for the first time in Korean history, a title which would not again be used until 1897. In 956 Emperor Kwangjong instituted the Slave Investigation. The contention of this investigation was that commoners had been taken as slaves by elite families and that they should be set free. This act undercut, militarily and economically, the strength of the landed elite and provided a broader financial base for the central government by transferring people from the nontaxable slave category to the taxable category of commoner. Such a drastic policy was not without opposition, and threats against the ruler were soon reported. As a result the change was accomplished in a purge atmosphere. The palace halls resounded with accusations and incriminations as old grudges ignited and new ones were incurred. Suspects were mercilessly eliminated as the monarchy and the central bureaucracy strengthened themselves at the expense of the regional elite and the old retainers who had gained wealth and power through their merit in founding the state.

GOVERNMENT STRUCTURE

During the late Silla period the outlines of many Chinese institutions had been implemented and these institutions had been adopted by the rising state of Koryŏ. In 982 the youthful ruler of Koryŏ died at the age of twenty-two. His eldest son who by right of primogeniture should have taken the throne was then an infant barely 2 years old. Because of the boy's tender years he was temporarily by-passed in favor of a young man of a cadet branch of the royal family. This teenaged youth, canonized Sŏngjong (r. 982–997), had been strongly influenced by a group of civil officials led by the Confucianist Ch'oe Sŭngno. The orientation of King Sŏngjong is suggested by the paraphrase of a Confucian tenet attributed to him: "In general, the regulation of the state and the family requires, first of all, a fundamental principle; that fundamental principle is none other than filial piety."

The reorganization of the government structure at this time may have been partially prompted by the rise of the Ch'i-tan Liao conquerors of Manchuria and North China, who had threatened the Koryŏ frontier. Although the bureaucratic structure underwent many reorganizations in later days, the general outlines which emerged were drawn principally from the bureaucratic structure of T'ang China.

The monarch had two groups of personal advisors in the "three preceptors" (*samsa*) and the "three councillors" (*samgong*), who acted as councillors and teachers for the monarch and tutored members of the royal family. Beyond these private advisors was an elaborate bureaucratic structure.

The apex of the central government was the Central Council (*Yangbu*), where the chief officials met to deliberate national policy. The council was originally composed of the chief civil officials of the Bureau of Military Affairs (*Chungch'uwŏn*) and the Royal Chancellery (*Munhasŏng*).

The *Royal Chancellery* promulgated all orders and decrees. The chief minister of this office was probably the most important official in the land. This office had the power to comment on orders and return them to the monarch with suggested revisions. Included in the Royal Chancellery was an office charged with remonstrating to the monarch on his conduct, generally upon moral grounds.

The *Royal Secretariat* (*Chungsŏsŏng*) drafted royal decrees for the king and handled matters pertaining to the appointment and dismissal of officials. After commenting and suggesting changes to orders, the Royal Secretariat forwarded them through the monarch to the Royal Chancellery.

The *State Secretariat* (*Sangsŏsŏng*) was in charge of all government officials and passed orders down to the six ministries (Personnel, Finance, Rites, War, Justice, and Public Works) for implementation.

The *Bureau of Military Affairs* (*Chungch'uwŏn*) handled military matters including the palace guards, and the defense of the capital. It was composed, interestingly enough, of civil officials. The chief minister of this office and the chief minister of the Royal Chancellery were the principal figures in the Central Council.

The *Censorate* (*Ŏsadae*) had the independent function and responsibility of maintaining vigil over the activities of officials to prevent misconduct and misuse of state resources. The Office of Remonstrance and the Censorate exercised considerable influence through their ability to debate and block official appointments.

Koryŏ also had a number of institutes called *kam*, which included the National Academy, the Royal Library, the Office of Royal Genealogies, the

Royal Treasury, the Armory, the Board of Astronomy, and the Board of Medicine.

Serving the palace and the royal household were seven offices called *si* in charge of the collection and storage of grains from the royal estates, maintenance of chariots and horses, and preparations for banquets, sacrifices, and the like.

Administratively the nation was divided into ten provinces under the jurisdiction of civil officials and two frontier districts in the north governed by military commanders. Not until 983 had the central government felt strong enough to designate twelve provincial towns as centers of administrative regions (*mok*) and dispatch officials as governors. The regional administrators organized their districts, and in the process the higher positions formerly held by representatives of the rural elite became largely honorary in nature. Under the jurisdiction of the administrative towns were districts, and beneath them were counties, subcounties, and finally the villages.

Three alternate capitals, P'yŏngyang, Kyŏngju, and Hanyang (mod. Seoul), were designated in the provinces. Although their establishment is cloaked in geomantic theory, it reflected political recognition of the three major population centers of the nation outside of the capital of Kaesŏng. For purposes of internal and national security, five regional military centers were located in the provinces. While the primary function of the military was the maintenance of order, it also performed a wide variety of services, including manning a nationwide network of fire beacons used to signal the approach of invaders.

A system of roads was pushed out through the provinces, and a postal-relay system was established. There were twenty-two routes or circuits with over 500 post stations. At major river crossings, river ferry stations were in operation to transport relay riders and government officials. These stations were under the authority of a low-ranking official, and peasant families were assigned to man the station and cultivate the tracts of land granted each station to meet its expenses. Both the postal-relay horses and military mounts came from a number of state-operated horse ranches.

GOVERNMENT SERVICE EXAMINATIONS

One of the earliest Chinese institutions adopted was the government service examination system. It was instituted in 958 under the guidance of Shuang Chi, a member of an embassy from the state of Later Chou who had fallen ill and remained behind in Koryŏ to become a close advisor of Emperor Kwangjong. He was a natural choice to become the first head of the examinations, since he was unrelated to either the royal or elite clans.

The examinations were, in theory at any rate, open to all save the outcaste class and the offspring of Buddhist monks, whose ancestry was probably often difficult to trace. The adoption of the examination system as a basis for appointment to government office provided a way to absorb and regulate the entrance of the provincial elite into the central government. It favored the civil officials of the central bureaucracy to the disadvantage of the provincial elite and the military and was another step in the development of a managerial bureaucratic government.

Some enjoyed exemption from the examinations, such as the relatives for three generations of the five highest ranks of officials, who could obtain direct appointment to office. This was called the *Ŭm* (*yin*) privilege. Unranked, lower positions in the government could also be obtained by appointment rather than through the examinations. Entry into the principal ranks of the bureaucracy in all other cases was through the examinations.

Candidates were required to pass qualifying examinations held in the capital and in the provinces. A second examination was held for qualified candidates at the National Academy. In each case the number of successful candidates appears to have been limited; provinces, for example, had quotas based upon population. Those candidates who succeeded in the first two examinations went on to the National Examinations.

The system, as instituted in 958, provided for three main classes of examinations: *composition*, with emphasis upon belles-lettres; *exposition* of topics selected from the Chinese classics; and *occupational examinations* in such subjects as law, astronomy, mathematics, and prophetic theory. The greatest prestige was attached to the examinations in composition, which led to the degree of *chinsa*, and the recipients of the coveted red diploma received the highest positions. This emphasis was naturally reflected in the educational system and in literature. It has been estimated that over a period of some 425 years, the Koryŏ government examinations were held 252 times with 6,718 successful candidates. For every student who succeeded in *exposition* a dozen passed in *composition*. The government examination system, although it would be changed considerably through the centuries, remained a basic institution of all governments on the peninsula. And, while it was perhaps never entirely free from manipulation, the system did produce large numbers of officials whose initial appointment to office was based primarily upon their success in the examinations.

EDUCATION

The Koryŏ educational system provides a clear look at the influence of the Koryŏ considerations of ancestry on an institution. The National Academy established in 992 contained three divisions for the study of similar subjects, chiefly literature and the classics. Descendants of officials of the highest three grades went to the first division, relatives of officials of the fourth and fifth grades attended the second division, and descendants of officials of grades six and seven were enrolled in the third division. Descendants of all ranked or unranked lower officials and commoners could enter any of the occupational divisions of the academy but were ineligible to attend any of the higher divisions.

Academies and libraries were built in Kaesŏng and in P'yŏngyang, and regional schools were developed in the major administrative towns, while demands from the regional elite led to the assignment of instructors in the Chinese classics and in medicine to the major provincial centers.

The development of the educational system and the government service examination system to which it was preparatory led, in time, to the growth of private academies, the first of which was established by the Confucian scholar Ch'oe Ch'ung (984–1068) following his retirement from official life. Ch'oe's academy had nine courses of study, and in the hot months of summer teachers and students adjourned to the cool tranquility of a mountain monastery for study. Many of the private academies, and there were over a dozen in the capital alone, were founded by retired heads of the government service examination system, which gave them considerable prestige.

The success of the private academies served to illuminate weaknesses in the National Academy and led to its reorganization in the early twelfth century. A new seven-course curriculum, largely copied from the private academy founded by Ch'oe Ch'ung, was instituted, while learned scholars were appointed as instructors to raise the prestige of the National Academy. Students attending the National Academy—which was now something like a university, with its six colleges—were aided by the interest return on loans from an investment fund with the appealing name Treasury for Nourishing Wisdom, established by the state for that purpose. Three of the colleges were devoted to the same general subjects but admitted students according to the rank and grade of their sponsoring relatives. The other colleges taught law, mathematics, and office administration, which included writing styles, documentary forms, and reporting procedures.

The Koryŏ educational system was highly specialized in its complete orientation toward preparation for the government service examinations and appointment to government service, which remained the ultimate source of wealth and power, the lone road to achievement and reward. Its content was often revised, but its goals never shifted.

The most notable feature of the educational system was that all books were and had been since the Silla period in a foreign language: Chinese.

ECONOMIC STRUCTURE

Since the Silla unification land had been a primary factor of wealth. The land system of Koryŏ, which had similarities to the system of T'ang

China, centered upon the concept that land would be granted to individuals and returned to the state after their death. The intent was to provide a permanent and theoretically inexhaustible fiscal foundation for the state with all lands owned and managed by the central government. Although private acquisition of land was prohibited by law it flourished in practice. Tracts of land were allotted to government officials and to all government offices, including schools, postal-relay stations, river ferry stations, hostels, and military families for support and maintenance. Royal estates met the expenses of the royal caste group and provided for palace upkeep. Categories of land which either had the character of or were in fact private lands freely bought, sold, and traded included lands granted to officials of the first five ranks and monastery lands. Lands granted for the support of military families and to members of the provincial elite for the support of regional offices became private lands, as their descendants inherited both the father's occupation and his lands.

Taxes, which provided the actual financial foundation of the state, fell into the following categories:

1. *Land tax*. This was collected from all lands except monastery holdings and lands assigned to military families. Three different tax rates based upon assessed productivity were applied.
2. *Household tax*. This was paid in regional products other than grain and computed on the basis of the number of taxable adults in the household.
3. *Corvée service*. Male commoners between the ages of sixteen and fifty-nine were simply levied when and where needed for public works projects, such as irrigation, maintenance of city walls, and road building.
4. *Levies*. These were imposed to meet some particular requirement.
5. *Regional tribute*. This consisted of stipulated annual amounts of speciality products from each area, which were used by the central government offices. Cheju Island, for example, was noted for its regional tribute in high-quality ramie cloth.

Government manufactories (*so*) existed in the capital and in the provinces. Some nine bureaus in the capital were given the responsibility for all state production and construction. The regional manufactories were engaged chiefly in the production of raw materials and unfinished products, such as gold, silver, iron, thread, silks, paper, ornamental titles, charcoal, salt, ink, and ceramics, while state farms raised grain, fruit, and spices such as ginger and sesame. It is believed that these manufactories were operated using chiefly workers from the outcaste groups but that skilled artisans and technicians of the commoner class were employed in many of the manufactories in the capital. It is also believed that the outcastes in the regional manufactories did not have the right of free movement outside of their communities. Similarly restricted communities were the *pugok* and *hyang*, whose inhabitants apparently engaged principally in agriculture. While the people in some of these restricted communities may have been criminals engaged in production under state supervision, in others they seem to have been largely immigrants and persons taken captive in the wars who were resettled throughout the country.

Excluding the monasteries, which were large land holders, land ownership in Koryŏ increasingly became synonymous with government position. Peasants could not own land. Rather they went with the land and had the obligation, not the right, of cultivation and service.

Large grain storage facilities were built in the provinces for the collection and storage of grain at harvest time. One of these depots was on the coast north of the capital, two were situated on the Han River, and ten others were located along the southern coast. A maritime transport service was established to transport grain shipments from these regional collection points to the capital. Among the granaries in the capital were the Righteous Granary and the Ever-Normal Granary. Both were utilized to stabilize market prices, and they purchased or sold grain, salt, and cloth in the major markets as prices rose or fell. The Righteous Granary also served as a grain reserve for military and relief purposes. During years of crop failure seed grain was distributed for repayment following the next harvest.

SOCIAL STRUCTURE

The emergence of powerful regional clans during the ninth century had broken the back of the Silla bone-rank system. The institution of the civil service system and the rise of the new elite, most of whom were by Silla standards of humble origin, ensured that it would never revive. Yet the concept of social distinction by birth prevailed in Koryŏ, one's position in the hierarchy of social classes being overwhelmingly based upon ancestry. The following groups can be distinguished during the Koryŏ period:

1. *Royal caste group* who were senior members of the collateral branches of the royal clan and were usually granted patents of nobility as dukes, marquises, or earls and provided with annual allowances which reinforced the distinction.

2. *Yangban*, i.e., civil and military officials.

3. *Namban* or palace functionaries, who were restricted to the lower official ranks.

4. *Hyangni* (regional clerks) and unranked lower echelon government officials.

5. *Commoners*, often called *yangmin* (the "good people") chiefly peasants and fishermen.

6. *Outcastes* included those working in occupations which were thought defiling because of Buddhist religious restrictions, such as the butchering and processing of animals. Occupations which required mobility, such as peddlers, seamen, hunters, travelling entertainers including *kisaeng* (dancing girls), and slaves, whether owned by the state or by private individuals, were also in the outcaste category.

Slaves and outcastes were not afforded the honor of surnames, nor were they allowed to ride horses. One of the requirements for the government service examinations was proof of the absence of outcaste relationship for eight generations. One of the more interesting of Koryŏ laws held that the social class of a child followed that of the mother. These measures helped to keep the elite ranks closed.

CHANGES IN MANCHURIA

As these internal developments occurred, vast changes were taking place in China and Manchuria. The Ch'i-tan people swept across Manchuria and conquered Parhae, whose capital in the Amur River region fell in 926. In 947 the Ch'i-tan proclaimed the formation of the Liao Empire, which would soon hold North China and Manchuria. Parhae refugees moved southward. Thousands entered Koryŏ by foot and by ship, including members of the Parhae royal family, officials, artisans, and peasants. This great influx of refugees from the chaos in the Manchurian cauldron continued through the tenth century. Some Jürčen tribal people formerly members of the state of Parhae moved southward into the Tumen River area and the Hamhŭng plain in the Korean northeast. Other Jürčen tribes moved into the Yalu River area, where they formed the short-lived state of Chŏngan. These events prompted major Koryŏ efforts in military preparations, particularly in the northwest.

Koryŏ had brief relations with the states of the Five Dynasties in North China and the Ten Kingdoms in South China. With the rise of the state of Sung in the mid-tenth century, relations were established with that nation which were later to stimulate an era of great commercial and cultural activity.

Until the late tenth century the energies of the Ch'i-tan Liao were spent on the conquest of North China and internal quarrels over the throne, so that little notice was given to the tiny state of Chŏngan or to Koryŏ, both of whom had established profitable trade relations with Sung China.

THE LIAO INVASIONS

When the Liao monarch Sheng-tsung (983–1031) took the throne, he initiated a military campaign against the Sung which would in time bring that state to its knees. Determined to stop the continual flow of military mounts to the Sung from the hostile Jürčen state of Chŏngan and from Koryŏ, he directed a brief campaign against both of them. In 993 Liao forces crossed the Yalu to conquer the Yalu River Jürčen and to reverse the position of Koryŏ. Koryŏ forces stopped the Liao advance at the Ch'ŏngch'ŏn River, and negotiations were begun. The Liao demands included Koryŏ acknowledgement of a tributary status to Liao, payment of a set annual tribute, and cessation of relations with Sung. Koryŏ had little alternative and submitted, receiving recognition of her claims to lands in the lower Yalu River area.

With peace concluded in 994, prisoners were exchanged, Koryŏ moved into the lower Yalu region, a monopoly market for trade was established at the Liao city (mod. Ŭiju) on the southern banks of the Yalu, and twenty Koryŏ students were sent to the Liao court to learn its script, language, and customs. In the probable knowledge that they would fail, an embassy was sent to Sung, then on the defensive, to request military aid against the Liao. When the request was refused, Koryŏ felt justified in severing official relations, which they had agreed to do in the peace negotiations with Liao.

In 1005 the Liao gained a great victory over the Sung and were free to look into the matter of Koryŏ once more. In 1009 an internal incident in Koryŏ prompted a second Liao invasion. The event that precipitated Liao intervention was a struggle over the throne. King Mokchong (r. 997–1009) had taken the Koryŏ throne as a lad of seventeen, and de facto control was exercised by the queen dowager. The queen dowager had a son by a paramour, and he maneuvered to have Mokchong abdicate and his son made king. Mokchong and his supporters appealed to General Kang Cho, the military commander of P'yŏngyang, for support. General Kang brought his troops into the capital and eliminated not only the queen dowager and her clique, but Mokchong as well. Then, with the apparent approval of the Koryŏ military and the powerful Kim clan of Ansan, a young lad claimed as the last surviving direct descendant of the founder of the dynasty was put on the throne. This was Hyŏnjong (r. 1010–1031). Thus Kang Cho was placed at the pinnacle of power.

Fresh from victories over the Sung, Liao used these internal difficulties as a pretext for its second invasion of Koryŏ. Liao grievances included private Koryŏ trade with Sung and the Koryŏ efforts to bring the Jürčen tribes of the northeast under its control which had resulted in a massacre of some ninety-five members of a Jürčen embassy whom the Liao authorities considered their subjects.

The Liao offensive opened in the winter of 1010 when the highly mobile Liao cavalry could cross the frozen Yalu. In a rapid sweep southward the Koryŏ armies were smashed, and Kang Cho himself was captured and killed. In the first month of 1011 the Liao forces captured, sacked, and burned the

Koryŏ capital. The Koryŏ court, which had fled to the south, quickly yielded up the officials responsible for the massacre of the Jürčen envoys and sued for peace. After demanding that the Koryŏ monarch present himself at the Liao court, the Liao armies withdrew northward across the Yalu.

The Liao maintained a foothold on the Koryŏ side of the Yalu by holding two cities there, and a bridge was built using the large islands in the river to advantage. Skirmishing continued in the northwest until the third and final Liao invasion, which lasted through the late winter of 1018 and into the early months of the following year. Severe defeats inflicted by ambushes laid by the Koryŏ General Kang Kamch'an at the strategic northwestern town of Kuju forced the Liao armies to withdraw after heavy losses. A peace was finally concluded in 1022 which reinstituted Koryŏ's tributary status to Liao. Formal relations with the Sung were, for all practical purposes, severed.

Official northern Sung-Koryŏ relations had been opened by Koryŏ initiative in 962 and ended by Koryŏ initiative in 1030. There is little doubt that a primary incentive for such relations was the Korean hope of Sung intervention against the Liao, while a primary motive for the invasion by the Liao was to prevent a Sung-Koryŏ military alliance.

Despite the severance of official relations, Sung merchant ships were frequent callers, and so there was no lack of commodities flowing in from the continent. The merchants also used to secretly exchange official messages between the two courts at times. Official relations between the two nations would again be opened, but the next time it would be by Sung initiative.

In an apparent move to encourage better relations with Liao, the Koryŏ monarch Hyŏnjong had a false report of his death sent to the Liao court with a request for the investiture of his son, King Tŏkchong, (r. 1031–1034), who did not actually take the throne until some 9 years later. Liao settled Koryŏ prisoners taken in the wars in small communities on the dry plains of Jehol, while Koryŏ settled Liao prisoners in small "Ch'i-tan communities" on the peninsula.

Immediately following the peace arrangements with Liao, the Koryŏ court raised a corvée force said to have numbered 304,000 to reconstruct the capital, a task which was completed in 1029. Then, as an added precaution against both the Liao and the Jürčen, who alternately traded with and raided Koryŏ, a long wall linking fourteen walled towns was constructed across the northern border. The wall, begun in 1033 and completed in 1044, began near the mouth of the Yalu, bulged northward through the mountains, and then ran southeast, with its eastern terminus near the modern town of Ch'ŏngpy'ŏng on the East Sea. The two centuries which followed, while they could hardly be called peaceful, were without serious foreign incursion.

MARITIME TRADE: THE GREAT COMMERCIAL ERA

Government regulated markets were held periodically in the northwest to trade with the Liao and in the northeast to trade with the Jürčen tribes. A brisk trade developed with Fujiwara Japan, being particularly active in the late eleventh century.

The tribute system itself had generated a considerable exchange of goods between the Koryǒ authorities and the courts of Sung and Liao. But the great bulk of Koryǒ's international trade was carried in ships owned by wealthy merchants of Sung China. Ports of South China, such as Kuang-chou, Ch'üan-chou, Hang-chou and Ming-chou, were busy centers of the south Asian maritime trade, which was chiefly in the hands of Arab merchants. The Sung-Koryǒ and the Koryǒ-Japan maritime trade were northern links in this vast commercial network. Maritime trade in the

Sung Merchant Vessels Arriving in Koryǒ, 1011-1278

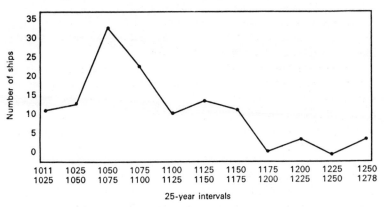

Source: After W. E. Henthorn, Korea: The Mongol Invasions.

northeast previously monopolized by Silla was now dominated by Sung merchants. In the 260 years over which this trade extended, it has been estimated that a minimum of 5,000 Sung merchants visited Koryǒ on some 120 voyages. No less than 1,670 arrived in the period 1046 to 1070 alone. A few Koryǒ ships were also engaged in trading activities principally at the North China port of Teng-chou; after the Sung were pushed out of North China in 1127 by the Chin, all maritime trade emanated from ports in South China.

With a favorable wind the Korean Hŭksan Islands were about a 3-week voyage from the southern port of Ming-chou. The ships then had a short

6-day sail along the Korean coast, where the merchants would frequently stop at the official inns maintained for their convenience. At major stops such as the Hŭksan Islands, Buddhist temples were maintained for voyagers to pray for a safe crossing, while beacon fires spotted on mountain summits along the coast guided ships toward the anchorage up the Yesŏng River. After resting a few days at the inn, merchants proceeded some 40 li over the hills to the Koryŏ capital of Kaesŏng. At least two Arab merchant ships managed to make the sea voyage north to Koryŏ in the early eleventh century, with cargoes of medicines, incense, perfumes, and curiosities such as betel nut. Writing in the period when this trade had reached a low point— and there were probably many ships never reported in the records—the great Koryŏ scholar and poet Yi Kyubo (1168–1241) wrote of the view from a tower at the anchorage.

> The tide floods, the tide ebbs,
> Stem to stern ships come and go.
> At dawn they sail from below the watchtower
> And before noon their oars dip into the
> Heaven of the Southern Barbarians [i.e., South Seas].*

The bulk of this trade appears to have been controlled by the court. Hsü Ching, a member of a Sung Embassy which arrived in Koryŏ in 1123, observed in his report of the trip (Hsüan-ho feng-shih Kao-li t'u-ching):

> It is a tradition in Koryŏ that upon the arrival of every embassy the people assemble and there is a great market. Hundreds of commodities are displayed. The red lacquerware and silks both show a regard for elegance as do the utensils of gold and silver. All items are from the royal household.

Principal Koryŏ exports to Sung were large quantities of raw copper, gold and silver utensils, ginseng, pine nuts, a variety of silks (gauze, damask, chiffon), fine ramie cloth, numerous kinds of paper, ink, felt, otter furs, horses, and surplus products such as folding fans and swords from the trade with Japan. Luxury items such as carriages elaborately decorated with mother-of-pearl inlay work were standard inclusions in the official tribute trade.

Koryŏ imports included copper cash—until Sung merchants were forbidden to carry it to Koryŏ in the late twelfth century—tea, lacquerware, books, and ingredients for dyes, cosmetics, and medicines. Sung official embassy "gifts"—the counterpart of the Koryŏ embassy tribute—also

*From Tongguk Yi Sangguk Chip of Yi Kyubo.

usually included ornate and fancy clothing for the Koryŏ ruler and high court officials.

The effect of this commercial activity and the cultural, intellectual, technological, and religious currents it generated were absolutely enormous and extended to every phase of life.

A second official phase of Koryŏ-Sung relations began in 1068 when they were reestablished by the initiative of the Sung authorities, who were interested in obtaining military support from Koryŏ against the rising Chin in North China. After the Chin drove the Sung from North China in 1127, official relations with Koryŏ were again broken.

LIFE IN THE CAPITAL

By the early eleventh century Koryŏ was reported to have had a population of some 2.1 million, a figure which has been interpreted to mean the capital district alone rather than the entire country. If this interpretation is correct, then it would appear that the total population could hardly have been less than 5 or 6 million. The *History of Koryŏ* relates that there were 238,938 adult males (ages fifteen to sixty) in the capital and some 8,450 artisans.

Construction of palaces and government buildings at the capital of Kaesŏng began in 919. Like the majority of major Korean walled cities, Kaesŏng was strongly influenced by Chinese prototypes. The principal orientation of the city was toward the main palaces located in the northern portion of the city. The location of the site for the palace was made only after careful deliberation and the conclusion that such a site would be auspicious for geomantic reasons. Some of the requirements for a favorable location included a mountain immediately backing the palace site with slopes extending in protective fashion east and west; to the south a river was required to ward off the undesirable influences of fire from that direction. The principal gate to the walled palace area was located in the south. A second major orientation was toward the four major gates in the city wall, and roads from these gates intersected the city to form the principal crossroads. Here at the gate, where country met the city, markets developed. A government-regulated bazaar also existed for the exchange and sale of goods.

In the capital of Kaesŏng lived the wealthy and powerful elite families. Through the three great streets of the city walked Buddhist monks chanting aloud for the protection of the state from texts carried before them on multicolored platforms. White was a favored color for clothing, although women wore veils of black gauze.

The great Buddhist holidays—such as the Lantern Festival—which were opened by the king burning incense at the monastery of Pongun-sa, had the atmosphere of commercial festivals. There were large parades with masked performers and decorative floats. At night the roads would be lit with lanterns from the city out to the large Buddhist monasteries. Gifts of fruit and wine were exchanged, and people celebrated with singing and dancing. At times, court musicians and court dancing troupes would perform, prayers were held for the prosperity of the monarch and the state, and dancing troupes would spell out short slogans such as "long live the king" and "great peace on earth." Commercial activity at these times was very much in evidence and was especially associated with two of these festivals. The Festival of the Myriad Buddhas (*Manburhoe*), a continuation of the Maitreya cult of Silla, was one of these until it was finally prohibited, apparently because of its commercial activities. The other was the Festival of Eight Commandments (*P'algwan-hoe*) held first in P'yŏngyang, where it was also called the Festival of Eastern Brilliance (*Tongmyŏng-hoe*). It was held a second time in Kaesŏng a month after the P'yŏngyang festival.

In the Koryŏ capital hostels were maintained for foreign merchants and embassies from China, Japan, and Manchuria. The larger cities—such as the capital of Kaesŏng, P'yŏngyang, and Hanyang—had permanent shops in a marketplace apparently resembling a bazaar, which included wine shops, restaurants, and tea houses. In 1208 the bazaar in the capital was enlarged and extended from Kwanghwamun, the principal gate of the city, to the crossroads. Grain storage facilities were constructed near Kwanghwamun, and over 1,000 shops or stalls are said to have existed in the expanded market area. Surplus products were released by the government on the market. The market was strictly regulated by a government bureau which regulated weights and measures and collected fees and taxes from the merchants. The bulk of commercial activity was transacted on set market days in large cleared market areas. On market day or when a foreign ship or embassy arrived, merchants would set up their shops on the market grounds in the manner of a market fair. Peddlers and travelling merchants going from market to market in the countryside were the principal distributors of goods outside of the major cities.

COMMERCIAL ACTIVITIES OF THE ELITE

The royal caste group, the elite, and the Buddhist monasteries were all deeply engaged in moneylending, which they did by means of two instruments for this purpose: the *Po* (Treasury) and the *Changsaenggo* (Long Life Storehouse). While both were used in lending cash or grain at interest, the *Po*, believed to trace its origins to the Silla period, was usually established to achieve a specific goal, such as assistance to students, relief of the poor, monastery construction, copying of sutras, or support of the two medical clinics in the capital. The *Changsaenggo* seems to have been purely usurious in nature and to have been widely used by Buddhist monasteries, which had become the possessors of large land holdings. Monastery-controlled lands scattered in parcels located some distance from the monasteries have been found with stone markers indicating that the harvests of these separate fields were consigned to the Long Life Storehouses as a result of court decisions.

Buddhist monasteries had large numbers of slaves who worked their lands and who engaged in the production of wine, vermicelli, and tea. Monks regularly engaged in merchandising. Periodic decrees prohibiting commercial activities of this sort proved difficult if not impossible to effect. Monasteries used some of their wealth for building small Buddhist hostels for travellers and for the construction of monasteries whose primary function was relief of the poor, the aged, the homeless, and the ill.

COINAGE

Concomitant with increased commercial activity, various Koryŏ monarchs attempted to encourage the development of coinage to replace the use of cloth and grains as mediums of exchange. The earliest record of coins minted in Korea was an issue made of iron struck in 995. King Mokchong continued this effort, and in 1002 he ordered all wine shops, tea houses, and restaurants to use coins. In the late eleventh century, following a visit to Sung China, the Buddhist monk Ŭich'ŏn urged his elder brother King Sukchong (r. 1082–1096) to encourage the use of coins. A mint was established in 1097, and a variety of coins was cast and put into circulation. In 1102 a smaller coin, the *Haedong t'ongbo* (Circulating Treasure of Korea), was cast in 15,000 strings of 1,000 coins each and paid out to officials and soldiers to stimulate circulation. Private wine shops and restaurants in the capital were encouraged to use coins, and allotments of grain were given to the major administrative cities to establish wine shops and restaurants with the idea that their existence would stimulate the use of coinage. The only coins which appear to have had a long circulation were made of silver, first cast in 1102, which were used principally by the elite because of their great value; they weighed one Korean pound (*kŭn*) and were worth as much as 100 Korean yards of homespun or 30 Korean bushels (*sŏk*) of rice. These coins, called *unbyŏng* (silver-urn), are said to have been cast in the shape of the peninsula. Issues of the silver-urn coins were also struck in 1331 and 1340. Counterfeiting, the lack of a continued policy for minting coins, and other factors led to a general return to cloth and grains as basic mediums of exchange. Coins of the various states in China also circulated in Korea. Yüan paper notes circulated in Koryŏ in the late thirteenth century, and in the late Koryŏ period paper notes were issued for the first time by the Korean authorities.

BUDDHIST ACTIVITIES

Immensely influenced by the far-flung contacts with the other states of Asia were the Buddhist monks. The leadership of the Buddhist establishment in Koryŏ was an extension of the royal caste group and the elite and was drawn largely from the younger sons of these groups. Many monasteries were built for these sons by their powerful kinsmen, which partially accounts for the thousands of monasteries and shrines scattered throughout Koryŏ, seventy of which were clustered in and about the capital of Kaesŏng.

Through a multitude of economic activities and patronage, the monasteries prospered and grew. And like the rest of Koryŏ society, the monkhood of the two great divisions of Koryŏ Buddhism, instructional (Kyo) and meditative (Zen), was organized into a hierarchy of ranks entered by examination held at monasteries in the capital. From the top of the six ranks Kyo and Zen advisors were selected as national Buddhist leaders.

The finest example of royal and elite offspring who entered the monkhood was Ŭich'ŏn (1055–1101), fourth son of King Munjong, whose mother was of the powerful Kyŏngwŏn Yi clan. It was probably for Ŭich'ŏn and his two younger brothers in the monkhood that King Munjong began construction of the great monastery of Hŭngwang-sa in the capital in 1056, a project which lasted 12 years. On the monastery grounds was the famous gold and silver hall, decorated with gold outside and silver inside. Ŭich'ŏn, principally a follower of the *Hwaŏm* (*Hua-yen*) school, has been credited with making the first significant contribution to Buddhism in the Koryŏ period when he formed the *Ch'ŏndae* (*T'ien-t'ai*) school in Korea. Following a 14-month visit to Sung in 1085 to 1086, Ŭich'ŏn took charge of the Hwaŏm monastery Hŭngwang-sa and instituted studies of the Ch'ŏndae teachings. His purpose was to unify the Kyo and Zen schools through the Ch'ŏndae school. Since his father was followed on the throne by his elder brother, Ŭich'ŏn was able to simply order talented Zen monks to enter the Ch'ŏndae school, whose main monastery, Kukch'ŏng-sa, was constructed in 1097.

The national crisis brought about by the Ch'i-tan Liao invasions in the early eleventh century brought about more state regulation of Buddhist activities through the establishment of central offices staffed by monks. Such matters as clothing, issuance of travel certificates, and approval of applications to enter the monkhood came under supervision.

The monasteries acted as havens for the younger sons of poor families. This, together with the fact that the Koryŏ monks were as noted for their offspring as for their celibacy, swelled the ranks of the monkhood. Finally, n 1059, a law was promulgated to curtail this drain from the tax registers which stated: "in families with three sons, [only] one son shall be allowed to shave his head and become a monk at age fifteen." An effort, highly unsuccessful, was also made to stop the monasteries from brewing liquors.

The monkhood was a national institution. In times of peace its members prayed for the welfare of the state and its rulers. Every third year, in a gesture of national almsgiving, maigre feasts were given for the monks throughout the country by the state. In more troubled days armies of monks served the state and fought in every war waged on the peninsula until recent times.

INTELLECTUAL OUTLOOK

Although they were certainly more international in outlook than their secular colleagues, Buddhist intellectuals shared with them the general belief that Buddhism, Confucianism, Taoism, and native beliefs were complementary and not basically in opposition. Ŭich'ŏn's explanation of these diverse beliefs as manifestations or parts of a single faith is reminiscent of the outlook of Wŏnhyo of Silla, whose works so impressed Ŭich'ŏn that he sent copies of them to Sung and to Liao.

The eminent Koryŏ Confucian scholar Ch'oe Sŭngno (927–989) expressed it this way in 982:

> *Carrying out the teachings of Buddha*
> *Is the basis for cultivation of the self.*
> *Carrying out the teachings of Confucius*
> *Is the source for regulating the state.*
> *Cultivation of the self is necessary for the future world;*
> *Ruling the state for affairs of the present.*

Emphasis upon filial piety continued to be strong, and it was encouraged by the state through such acts as the erection of a memorial stone in North Kyŏngsang Province in 1182 to honor a certain Son Siyang for his filial piety. One extreme was certainly reached by the scholar Ch'ae Ch'ungsun in 1022 when he wrote an inscription for a stele to be erected at a Buddhist monastery that Buddhism and Confucianism emanate from a single principle: filial piety.

A hierarchical view of society prevailed in early Koryŏ, one's role dictated largely by birth. Increasingly this was expressed in Confucian terms of opposition between the "superior man" and the "mean man", and, in time, the attributes of the superior man came to be associated with learning of a particular type, namely, Confucianism.

There is little question that Buddhism was a dominant influence upon early Koryŏ society and even the most ardent of court Confucianists generally were sympathetic with its teachings. The ameliorating influence of Buddhism is reflected in the almost total abandonment of capital punishment. An exception was made in the case of treason, but even then the condemned were seldom simply executed, but bound and thrown in the river to drown, perhaps in the thought that it was the river that was executing the sentence.

BELLES-LETTRES

Six Dynasties and T'ang literary influences from Silla continued into the Koryŏ period. Undoubtedly known since late Silla times were works like the *Shan-hai-ching*, a collection of fantastic tales of distant lands and their weird inhabitants, and the *Sou-shen-chi*, an anthology of supernatural stories and marvels. In 1101, the encyclopedic literary collection *T'ai-p'ing kuang-chi* was introduced from Sung. The Koryŏ prose tales of miracles and incredible happenings were essentially a continuation of the literary traditions of late Silla carried forward by the absorption of the Silla literati into the Koryŏ elite structure. One of the earliest Koryŏ products in this tradition was the *Suijŏn*, a mid-eleventh century work attributed to Pak Illyang (1047–1096), written under the influence of stories such as Chang Tsu's *Yu-hsien-k'u*, which were popular in the late Silla period.

By the early Koryŏ period there had emerged the view of a scholar-official as one who could produce Chinese verse with skill upon demand, and this had the rather natural result that Chinese verse was widely written. It was also a major part of the government service examinations. The early Yi dynasty literatus Sŏ Kŏjŏng considered the *fu* (prose poems), *t'zu* (lyrics), and antithetical style of the period 950–1050 as the high point for these forms. A stimulus for composition of verse in Chinese was provided by a requirement set forth in 995 for all lower ranking civil officials to submit each month a poetic composition in the short *shih* form or the lengthy *fu* form based upon topics selected by the scholars of the Hallin Academy. The influence of Sung, T'ang, and earlier Chinese poets is discernible. And, as might be expected, the Zen influence is distinctly noticeable in much of the Sino-Korean verse of the Koryŏ period.

The writing of Korean verse or songs in *hyangch'al* apparently continued during the early Koryŏ period, but, as mentioned earlier, only a single eleven cycle, contained in the *Kyunnyŏjŏn* from the tenth century, and a lone verse in memory of Generals Sin Sunggyŏm and Kim Nak composed by King Yejong, remain. A handful of poems is about all that has survived from the early Koryŏ period.

Following a large, politically motivated gift of musical instruments and texts from the Sung emperor in 1114, the Koryŏ court adopted Sung music at court. Thousands of books entered the country during this period in the traditional categories of commentaries on the classics, belles-lettres, and histories and in the separate categories of medicine and Buddhist texts. The Korean fondness for books was known in China, and in 1091 the Chinese authorities sent to Koryŏ a long list of titles of Chinese books no longer extant on the continent, and the Koryŏ authorities were able to supply copies of many of them.

Many new texts were compiled in Koryŏ during this period, among which were works relating to national history. The new interest enkindled in Korean history led to the compilation of Veritable Records (*Sillok*) for the reign of each monarch, beginning in the reign of King Hyŏnjong (r. 1010–1031). This interest culminated in the compilation of the earliest Korean dynastic history, *Samguk sagi* (History of the Three Kingdoms), compiled by Kim Pusik in 1145.

SCULPTURE AND METAL CASTING

A notable feature of the Koryŏ period is the increased secularization of art, yet a major if not dominant role was still played by Buddhism both inspirationally and as patron of those arts intimately associated with the monasteries.

The growth of the Zen school, which deemphasized religious statuary, led to a decline in sculpture. The stone work of the monasteries loses the simple directness and firm line of the Silla period and becomes more ornate, a trend already evident in late Silla. There is more elaboration and variety expressed in slight alterations of form as a realistic naturalism gives way to an almost gothic severity. Stone stupas are often richly decorated with bas-relief, at times very intricately so, which contrasts greatly with the Silla forms.

The stern, severe Koryŏ form is apparent in metal figures of Buddha, increasingly cast of iron, with their stylized robes. It is also noted in the Koryŏ bells. Not all the Koryŏ bells equalled the Silla bells in quality, as the following poetic Zen inscription by the Confucian Kim Pusik for the Hŭngch'ŏn-sa bell indicates:

> *The God of Fire fanned the flames.*
> *The God of Wind made a great stir.*
> *But only metal as mute as leather*
> *Could produce this beautiful bell*
> *And sentence it to a lonely silence.*
> *Strike it and, peacefully, mildly,*
> *It fills the cloudless sky*
> *With its soundless voice.*

CERAMICS

Both the gray stoneware and the greenish brown glazed late Silla ware continued into the early Koryŏ period. Considered to be one of the highest peaks of artistic expression in the Koryŏ period is the Koryŏ celadon. This is a ware with a greenish glaze. An inscription on an early vessel of this type reveals it was made for T'aejo's shrine by one Ch'oe Kirhoe in 993. The Koryŏ celadon was based upon Sung prototypes, but it soon became distinctive in color—particularly the famed kingfisher shade—by design, and by variety of shapes. The earlier undecorated celadon gave way to designs utilizing several techniques. In the eleventh to twelfth centuries bas-relief designs, chiefly floral, were molded or stamped. Then in the twelfth to thirteenth centuries an inlay technique using black and white clays to fill in an incised design was practiced. A continuity in decoration may be seen in the use of inlaid designs similar to the geometric designs of the stamped Silla ware.

Modelling reflects T'ang pottery influences in the many plant and animal shapes of vessels, including monkeys, parrots, lions, dragons, fish, gourds or melons, bamboo, flowers, and foliage. Ceramic items include cups, dishes, teapots, vases, incense burners, pillows, roof tiles, and brush holders. Tea drinking, popularized by Buddhist monks, who introduced it to the Koryŏ elite, was an important incentive to ceramic production and helps to account for the dozens of kilns scattered chiefly through central and south Korea.

MEDICINE

Korean interest in medicine had not diminished since the Silla period, and the inclusion of medicine as a subject of study in the school system aided in stimulating activities in this area. The illness of King Munjong— he apparently suffered from an arthritic condition—was another factor. Texts of medicine were compiled by provincial officials and forwarded to the capital. Physicians and over a hundred basic components for the preparation of medications were sent by the Sung court in 1075. A request was also made to Japan in 1080 for physicians, but the Japanese court fearing that failure by the physicians might lead to adverse relations between the two nations cancelled the mission. In the mid-thirteenth century the same bureau which was carving the second set of woodblocks for the Buddhist Tripiṭaka published the oldest extant native Korean *materia medica* or herbal, the *Hyangyak kugŭppang*. The continued interest in medicine was promoted by Buddhist beliefs, since healing represented by the Buddha of Medicine, was an important element of Buddhist practice and proselytizing. Drawing from Chinese practices, Korean physicians now began to compile their own works and to include herbs and medicines common to the peninsula.

PRINTING

Printing with wood blocks or xylographs, practiced since the Silla period, was revived on a large scale during the Koryŏ period. The stimulus for state activity in this field was increased internal demand created by the enlargement of the National Academy, the establishment of regional schools, the growth of the academy at P'yŏngyang, the purchase of thousands of texts from Sung China, and the increased concern with historiography which led to the compilation of official histories, and finally the production of works by Korean authors. Sung editions of classics, commentaries, histories, mathematics, medicine, and particularly those texts necessary for the Koryŏ examination system were reprinted in Kaesŏng for schools in the capital, in P'yŏngyang, and in the major regional centers. Many found their way to Japan.

Buddhist monks were extremely active in printing and publishing projects. Ŭich'ŏn, for example, established a compilation and printing office at Hŭngwang-sa which published the Tripiṭaka Continued (*Sokchanggyŏng*), a vast undertaking of several thousand volumes including the writings of Koryŏ, Chinese, and Ch'i-tan monks. Ŭich'ŏn also made a contribution to Buddhism in China when he took with him on a voyage to Sung several thousand volumes of works which had been lost in China. The ease of international contacts permitted a widespread exchange of Buddhist texts with Sung, Liao, and Japan.

The largest undertakings in wood block printing were Buddhist enterprises accomplished with state patronage. The most outstanding were the two carvings of the complete Buddhist canon, the Tripiṭaka. The first carving was undertaken as an act of faith to gain the protection of the Buddhas against the Ch'i-tan invasions in the eleventh century. These wood blocks were destroyed in the Mongol invasion of 1232. A second undertaking was completed in 1251 after 16 years of effort. These 81,137 woodblocks are today stored in the monastery of Haein-sa on Mount Kaya, west of the city of Taegu.

During the eleventh century experiments were being carried out with movable wooden and clay type in Sung China. This may have influenced Korean experiments in this direction. At any rate, in 1234 movable iron type was cast on Kanghwa Island and used to print the 50-volume (*kwŏn*) *Sangjŏng kogŭm yemun*, a work on ceremony and propriety compiled by Ch'oe Yunŭi (1102–1162). This was the first known use of movable metallic type in the world, preceding its use in the late Yüan period in China and 200 years ahead of its use in Europe. By 1392, a Book Bureau in charge of fonts of movable iron type and book printing had become a standard government office. The development and use of movable metallic type was continued through the Yi period. Many fonts were cast and thousands of books printed. Printing also stimulated developments in paper making, and Koryŏ became famed for the quality and variety of its paper.

KORYŎ-CHIN RELATIONS

In the twelfth century a period of unrest in Manchuria culminated with the replacement of the Liao dynasty by the Jürčen peoples who founded the Chin dynasty. In 1115 Chin forces defeated a Liao army in a crucial battle in the Sungari River region and then came southward to engage the Liao garrisons on the Koryŏ side of the Yalu River.

Koryŏ had made a brief attempt to take advantage of the situation in Manchuria in a bit of military adventurism aimed at securing the Hamhŭng plain. The Koryŏ general Yun Kwan was successful in his campaign of 1107 and built nine walled garrison towns in the northeast to hold the lands gained. The rise of the Chin dynasty, however, checked this expansion and forced Koryŏ to withdraw its forces from the northeast. By 1116 Koryŏ had acknowledged their tributary status to the Chin empire. In 1127 the Chin had driven the Sung south of the Yangtze River, after which time the latter is known as the Southern Sung. Since Koryŏ relations with Sung had been terminated by the latter, they did not become a *casus belli* between Koryŏ and Chin. Koryŏ relations with Chin were peaceful, but internal strife more than offset this as the structure of Koryŏ society began to tear apart.

THE REVOLT OF YI CHAGYŎM

Since the early days of the dynasty the great clans residing in the capital had been the major influence behind the throne. These clans maintained their power by providing wives and consorts to the Koryŏ monarchs and maneuvering the offspring of these marriages on and off the throne. Marriages between clans provided further alliances. In some periods an uneasy balance of power seems to have existed, while at other times a single clan held sway for generations. From 1010 the Kim clan of Ansan remained dominant until its fall in 1046 to the Yi clan of Kyŏngwŏn (Inju). These clans accumulated large-scale agricultural holdings in the countryside, which supported their luxurious life in the capital. They also had large numbers of slaves and servants, many of whom apparently functioned as quasi-military retainers. When the great power struggles erupted among these clans, bloody and violent battles raged through the capital, destroying palace buildings and sections of the city.

In 1126 a power struggle was precipitated by the Yi clan of Kyŏngwŏn when the clan head, Yi Chagyŏm, attempted to seize the throne. The reigning monarch, King Injong (r. 1123–1146), had been put on the throne at the age of thirteen and was just seventeen at this point. Yi Chagyŏm, his father-in-law, apparently encouraged by a prevalent prophecy which implied the dynasty was coming to an end, came to believe that he was destined to replace King Injong. Bulling his way into de facto power, Yi ruthlessly eliminated the opposition groups. In the attendant strife the palace buildings were burned and the city thrown into chaos. Yi quickly placed six of his sons in top government posts, but he was assassinated before he could carry out his plan to take the throne himself. His death meant the fall of the Kyŏngwŏn Yi clan, whose members were rounded up and exiled. It also signalled the opening of a new struggle for influence at court.

MYOCH'ŎNG'S REBELLION

Shortly after the fall of the Kyŏngwŏn Yi clan and during the period when the Koryŏ court was still debating future relations with the rising Jürčen Chin dynasty, two dominant groups expressing widely divergent views on both internal and external affairs emerged. One of these was the P'yŏngyang group, fiercely "nationalistic" in character, which stressed faith in the popular views of the times. These popular beliefs were a mixture of animism-shamanism, Buddhism, Taoism, and geomancy.

The leader of this group was the Buddhist monk Myoch'ŏng, who was a follower of the mystic notions attributed to the late Silla monk Tosŏn. Myoch'ŏng had great popularity in P'yŏngyang and a considerable reputation in *ŭm-yang* (*yin-yang*) theory among officials at court. Various members of the P'yŏngyang elite, including the talented and respected man of letters Chŏng Chisang, supported Myoch'ŏng's views at court. Myoch'ŏng and his followers advocated a declaration of Koryŏ independence by use of the title "emperor" then used by the Sung, Chin, and Japanese rulers in preference to the lesser title of "king" used by the Koryŏ ruler. They also strongly urged that an alliance be made with China for a joint military campaign against the Jürčen Chin masters of Manchuria.

A central argument which they advanced was their claim that Kaesŏng had lost its geomantic virtue, while P'yŏngyang was geomantically a favored location. There was a danger of the king being injured by fire in Kaesŏng, they added, and urged the capital be transferred to P'yŏngyang. They were backed by some precedent, since several Koryŏ monarchs, including the dynastic founder, had considered moving the capital to P'yŏngyang. And the palace buildings had been burned in the revolt of Yi Chagyŏm a few years earlier. Considering the popular tradition that Koryŏ was the successor to Koguryŏ, it may be assumed that the appeal of these views was powerful.

King Injong was apparently strongly influenced by Myoch'ŏng, and a detached palace and several temples and shrines to deities of popular beliefs were constructed in P'yŏngyang and its environs. Inside the palace grounds at P'yŏngyang was the Shrine of Eight Sages, a pantheon of deities which included Korean mountain spirits and Buddhist divinities. King Injong himself paid several extended visits to the city and saw several of these shrines.

Opposing these views were a Confucian-oriented group of the Kaesŏng elite whose chief spokesman was the historian Kim Pusik. Peaceful relations with the Chin were an unavoidable necessity, they argued, and pointed to the tragic experiences the states of China had faced in military campaigns against the northern people. At the same time they ridiculed the geomantic theories advanced by Myoch'ŏng. King Injong gradually sided with their views.

In 1135, Myoch'ŏng and his followers led a revolt and attempted to set up an independent state at P'yŏngyang. Their archenemy Kim Pusik was appointed as one of the military commanders sent to crush the rebellion, which took almost a year to quell. The failure of the revolt placed the Confucian civil bureaucracy, whose top ranks were drawn primarily from the Kaesŏng elite, in absolute power around the monarch.

THE REIGN OF ŬIJONG

Little politico-economic distinction had existed in the earlier years of the dynasty between the civil and military officials, but the steady growth of the power of the civil bureaucracy had led to a marked separation in status, power, and privilege. The decline of the military reached a climax in the reign of Ŭijong (r. 1140–1170). Many tales are told of the grand and luxurious life of the court under this monarch. Eunuchs and diviners gained the monarch's favor and grew powerful. There was endless feasting with higher civil officials in the palace and in the royal botanical and zoological gardens, with their exotic plant and animal life and their elaborate buildings which even included a pavilion roofed with celadon tiles. The military officials were, it is related, constantly humiliated by the civil officials. One luckless general is said to have had his beard set on fire in sport by some bureaucrats. Perhaps more crucial to the military was the continued decrease of allotments of land and the loss of power in decision making. The dissatisfaction of the military was only the surface of an iceberg of discontent built of centuries of political, social, and economic discrimination and oppression, which extended to every level of society and which had manifested itself sporadically in riot and revolt throughout the land. Now an even more threatening storm cloud was already on the horizon.

7
Late
Koryŏ

In 1170 while King Ŭijong was absent from the capital, General Chŏng Chungbu gathered his colleagues and began a revolt. Instructions were given to their men to kill all the civil officials. Ŭijong was deposed, and his younger brother Myŏngjong (r. 1170–1197) was placed on the throne. Later, following an abortive attempt to restore Ŭijong, who had been in exile on Kŏje Island, Chŏng had him killed. Two of Chŏng's men visited the ex-monarch, got him drunk, then rolled him up in a mat and drowned him. This action triggered a series of false reports to the Chin court, to which Koryŏ was then tributary, to cover up the real situation. The seizure of power by the military began a century of rule by military overlords.

Koryŏ Military Rulers

1170–1179	Chŏng Chungbu	
1179–1183	Kyŏng Taesung	
1183–1196	Yi Ŭimin	
1196–1258	Ch'oe clan	
	Ch'oe Ch'unghŏn	1196–1218
	Ch'oe U	1218–1249
	Ch'oe Hang	1249–1256
	Ch'oe Ŭi	1256–1258
1258–1268	Kim Chun	
1268–1270	Im clan	
	Im Yŏn	1268–1270
	Im Yumu	1270

The competition among the military leaders led to the rapid development of private armies. A quarter of a century of social chaos and struggles finally ended in consolidation of power under the Ch'oe clan, who were the de facto rulers of Koryŏ for four generations. During this period the monarchs were largely in the position of figureheads. Ch'oe Ch'unghŏn himself deposed three monarchs and placed four on the throne. Initially control of affairs of state were handled by the generals through the Military Council (*Chungbang*). In 1225 Ch'oe U shifted civil affairs to a Civil Council (*Chŏngbang*) run by a staff of administrators from Ch'oe's residence. The monarch and the machinery of the central government still remained, but they were operated by the Military and Civil Councils.

Chronological Overview

Date	South China	North China	Manchuria	North Korea	South Korea	Japan
1170	Southern Sung	Jürčen (Chin)		Koryŏ (Military Rulers)		
1185						Kamakura Shoguns
1234					••••••••••••••••••••••	
1259						
1271						
1279						
1336		MONGOL (YÜAN)				
1350				••••••••••••••••••••••		
1368	Ming		Jürčen	Yi Dynasty		Ashikaga Bakufu
1392						

PEASANT AND SLAVE UPRISINGS

The military period opened a Pandora's box of social discontent. The purges of the civil officials and the widespread fighting stimulated revolts by peasants, slaves, monks, outcastes, and provincial military garrisons. Natural disasters intensified the situation. In 1173 drought and epidemic led to reports of cannibalism in portions of the country. A Silla restoration movement erupted in the Kyŏngju area, and a Paekche restoration movement grew in the southwest. Many of the literati fled to the provinces to escape the purges, and there they formed small wine-and-verse associations.

The removal of the core of the civil bureaucracy created a need for new talent and removed the obstacle of ancestry from the path of social mobility. At the same time, bribery and sale of official posts became rampant. In 1178 some 990 officials were dismissed for alleged malfeasance.

The social unrest had caused many peasants to leave the land and turn to banditry on a large scale. Military men in the provinces rose to contest the new military rulers in the capital. The most severe challenge was the opposition offered by General Cho Wichong in the northwest.

Cho held the area north of the Chabi Pass and had even sent envoys to the Chin court with an offer to submit the area in return for support against the usurpers. The area was brought back under central control only after some 22 months of intense fighting and a lengthy siege of Cho's main base at P'yŏngyang.

The demands of the times created considerable social mobility, and men of humble origins came into power. Representative of the newcomers was the military ruler Yi Ŭimin, whose father had been a salt merchant. Another was Kim Hŭije, a merchant sailor from Kunsan Island who rose to become a general. There were even a few like P'yŏngyang, a slave, who acquired enough money while managing one of his owner's estates to purchase his freedom. He then bought an appointment as an eighth-rank military officer, but unfortunately in later dealings he met an untimely end.

These individual examples of social mobility led to the unprecedented realization by some that there was indeed a possibility of breaking the bonds of class and caste. For the first time in Korean history an attempt was made by members of a caste group to join in a concerted action under their own leadership to gain freedom and abolish the distinction and existence of caste.

In 1198 the private slave Manjŏk and five others assembled government and private slaves while gathering firewood on North Mountain, outside of Kaesŏng. Manjŏk told the group:

> Since [the military revolt of] 1170, many of the crimson and purple [robed officials] of the nation have arisen from the slave [ranks]. Are these generals and ministers [of] seeded [lineage]? When the time comes, then [all] can become [officials]. Can it be that we [alone] are to toil, sinew and bone beneath the whip?

All the slaves agreed with him. They cut several thousand pieces of yellow paper in the form of the character *chŏng* (T-shaped) as badges of recognition. This character was probably chosen since it was also used to indicate a free commoner. Manjŏk then outlined their plan:

> We will simultaneously assemble [in the area] from the verandah of Hŭngguk-sa monastery to the polo grounds. When we make a loud clamor then the eunuchs inside the palace will surely follow us. The government slaves will kill those inside the palace and my followers will rise in the city. Ch'oe Ch'unghŏn must be killed first and then each of us will slay his master and burn the slave registers. When we eliminate outcastes from the San Han [i.e., Korea] then we will all be able to become nobles and ministers.

At the set time only a few hundred gathered, and fearing their numbers were insufficient, they agreed to meet at the monastery of Poje-sa at a later date. A private slave, however, disclosed the scheme to his master, who promptly informed the military ruler. Manjŏk and a hundred others were arrested and executed. The informant was rewarded with eighty pieces of silver and his freedom. Some years later another group of private slaves was discovered practicing battle tactics in the wooded areas of the eastern suburbs, where they were supposedly gathering firewood. Some fifty were executed.

With the failure of these attempts, the massive door of social oppression weighted with the traditions of centuries rolled back and extinguished the small flicker of hope which had been kindled. There were other slave revolts to be sure, but none for over 700 years which had the elimination of caste as an objective.

Ch'oe Ch'unghŏn used a dual policy to regain social stability. While revolts were quickly and harshly suppressed, he abolished many of the restricted *pugok* and *hyang* areas and had them designated as counties in the regular administrative system. The outcastes in these areas were then legally considered to have the status of commoners. Yet these restricted areas survived in part into the early Yi dynasty.

BUDDHIST OPPOSITION TO THE MILITARY RULERS

The military takeover was violently opposed by the Buddhist leadership, and in the spring of 1174 some 2,000 monks from monasteries around the capital attempted to storm the east gate of the city but were driven off. A similar incident occurred in 1217 when monks from the great monasteries around the capital were called up to fight an invasion in the north. They used the occasion to attack the capital in an attempt to overthrow the Ch'oe clan. In the fighting some 800 monks were killed by the house armies of the Ch'oe clan.

The Buddhist opposition to the military rulers was essentially a power struggle. Most of the military leaders were, like Ch'oe Ch'unghŏn, ardent followers of Zen. However, with the elimination of the real power of the monarch and the bureaucratic elite, the monasteries had lost a major source of patronage and protection. This was aggravated by the ancestry of the Buddhist leadership, which was drawn to a great extent from primary and cadet branches of the royal and elite clans. Ch'oe Ch'unghŏn had proclaimed his intention of breaking the lineage link between the Buddhist elite and the royal clan. He also did his best to prohibit commercial activities by monasteries.

The efforts of Ŭich'ŏn had resulted in a decline of the Zen school, but during this period the monk Chinul (1157–1210) led a Zen revival by unifying various Zen schools into the Zen *Chogye* school. This meant that in addition to the five Kyo schools from the Silla period there were the Zen schools unified into the *Chogye* school and the *Ch'ŏndae* (c. *T'ien-t'ai*) school founded by Ŭich'ŏn. The growth of Zen schools during the military period led to a decrease in secular activities as the Kyo schools declined and the meditative Zen schools did not involve themselves in secular affairs to such an extent. This resulted in a lessening of Buddhist influence on the elite, which made the later acceptance of the philosophy of Chu Hsi much easier.

THE CH'I-TAN INVASION

As the Ch'oe clan gained control in Koryŏ, external changes were taking place in western Asia which would profoundly affect the entire Far East.

In 1209, the Mongols commenced their drive against the Chin empire, which held sway over North China and Manchuria and to which Koryŏ was tributary. Among the unsettling effects which this produced was a revolt by Ch'i-tan peoples who had been conquered by the Chin. These Ch'i-tan rebels were driven eastward by the Mongols and in 1217, they crossed the Yalu, ninety thousand strong, and plundered the Koryŏ northern districts. Koryŏ forces, principally the strong private forces of the Ch'oe clan but including the weak government armies and some monks troops as well, had managed to hold the Ch'i-tan armies in the north.

As the Koryŏ military recovered and turned to take the offensive against the Ch'i-tan invaders in the winter of 1218, unexpected allies appeared from the northeast. A large force of Mongols and Eastern Jürčen troops entered Koryŏ in pursuit of the Ch'i-tan, who had seized several Koryŏ cities as defensive bases. The Koryŏ military quickly joined them, and the Ch'i-tan were rapidly defeated. With a Mongol force already within her borders, Koryŏ, although distrustful of the Mongols, had little recourse but to enter into tributary relations.

THE MONGOLS IN KORYŎ

The frequency of Mongol delegations to the Koryŏ capital was matched only by the increasing rapacity of their demands. In 1221, a delegation from Temüge-otčigin, the youngest brother of Činggis, was still in the capital when a large embassy arrived from Prince Alčitai with more demands for goods. It became, the Koryŏ records relate, "a matter of slaking their thirst for valuables or of making bloody sacrifice of the living."

In early 1224, an opportunity arrived to throw off the yoke of the insatiable Mongols. The armies of Činggis were deep in campaigns far to the west, and Muqali, the brilliant commander of the Mongol forces in the east, had just died. The Eastern Jürčen in the Tumen River–Hamhŭng plain area were the first to declare their independence. They also suggested an alliance to which Koryŏ did not respond until 1229. In the fall of 1224, a Mongol envoy to Koryŏ was killed just across the border, and from this point Koryŏ-Mongol relations were broken.

THE MONGOL INVASIONS

Succession disputes, preoccupations with campaigns elsewhere and set-backs in North China delayed the inevitable Mongol return. Koryŏ used the respite to make hasty military preparations. But in the autumn of 1231 a large Mongol army crossed the Yalu to begin what was to be an on-again off-again conflict lasting some 30 years.

The Koryŏ main armies marched bravely north but were quickly defeated by the mounted forces of Marshal Sartaq, the Mongol commander. In the three decades of fighting which ensued Koryŏ never again managed to field a large army against the invaders. The great valor of men like Pak Sŏ, the defender of the city of Kuju in the northwest, proved insufficient. As often happened in Korean history, in military engagements against superior forces, battles were won but the wars were lost. The Koryŏ military experience with the Mongols was a repetition of similar experiences with other northern peoples in many respects. The military forces of these northern peoples were highly organized, chiefly mounted troops, which gave them great mobility. They were also experienced campaigners. The inexperienced Koryŏ foot soldier had little chance against these professionals. The Korean experience is summarized by Yun Kwan's report on military setbacks against the Eastern Jürčen a century earlier: "The enemy rode, we walked. We were no match for them."

The month-long Mongol siege of the walled town of Kuju is a classic example of heroic resistance. The siege saw a full array of medieval assault weapons used in the many attempts to take the city. Lines of catapults hurled boulders or molten metal at the city, tunneling efforts to undermine the walls were made, siege towers and scaling ladders were used in assaults, fire carts were rolled against the wooden city gates, and fire-bombs of human fat—made by boiling down captives—which were practically inextinguishable, were used.

It is related that an old Mongol general riding around the city to inspect the ramparts during the siege sighed and remarked: "I have followed the army since I bound my hair [into plaits as a youth] and so I am accustomed to seeing the city of the earth attacked and fought over. Still I have never seen [a city] undergo an attack like this which did not, in the end, submit." But Kuju held, and the attackers finally withdrew when peace negotiations were opened.

In the spring of 1232, the bulk of Mongol forces began to withdraw, leaving the Koryŏ northwest under the control of Mongol resident commissioners supported by Koryŏ rebels.

RETREAT TO KANGHWA ISLAND

When the Mongol forces had withdrawn, the military ruler Ch'oe U ordered the court to move to Kanghwa, a large island in the Han-Imjin River estuary. This was carried out in the summer of 1232, and in such haste that the king was billeted in a local inn on the island. The Mongol resident commissioners in the northwest were killed, and a mass flight of people from the area ensued. Orders were issued for the general populace either to take refuge at those major cities which had adjacent mountain citadels of refuge (*sansŏng*) or to flee to the thousands of offshore islands.

Sartaq's second invasion in 1232 was cut short when the Mongol commander was killed by a chance arrow from the bow of a Buddhist monk. Another series of invasions began in 1233 under Tanqut-bātur and Prince Yekü. A truce of a fashion was arranged by sending a distant member of the royal clan as a hostage disguised as the crown prince. This "truce" lasted during the period 1241 to 1247. The fighting recommenced in 1247 but calmed the following year with the death of Güyük, the Mongol emperor. Prince Yekü remained in Koryŏ until 1253. In 1254, there was another invasion under Jalairtai. The fighting of the 1250's took place during a period of recurring drought which brought tragic consequences. The Koryŏ records relate that "those who died of starvation were multitudinous; the corpses of the old and weak clogged the ravines and it reached the point where some even left their babies tied in the trees." The countryside was in ashes. Under the pressure, the Koryŏ court once more submitted and commenced diplomatic maneuvers to avoid meeting the Mongol demands. During this period the provinces were generally on their own. Since the Mongols commonly split their forces into smaller, wide ranging groups, fighting was widespread but in the nature of localized attacks on individual towns or strongholds rather than confrontation of large armies in the field.

Koryŏ rebels joined the Mongols by the thousands; others were forced into service. The Mongols lived up to their reputation for cruelty in battle when a city did not submit. It was a common practice in such instances to divide the artisans, women, and children of tender years among the soldiers and then to kill all the rest. Koryŏ resistance was carried out largely by the sturdy and enduring Korean peasants, who were organized into local guerrilla forces which specialized in ambush tactics.

THE LATER MILITARY RULERS

In 1258, the Ch'oe clan was overthrown by the military official Kim Chun. It is ironic to note that Ch'oe Ŭi failed to escape because he was too fat for his bodyguard to boost over the back wall while the attackers were breaking down the front gate. The power of Kim Chun, the new military ruler, was balanced to a great extent by the authority of the civil official Yu Kyŏng, who exerted great influence. The aging monarch Kojong, wary and weary of the military, moved into Yu's house for protection. With the overthrow of the Ch'oe clan, a peace agreement was concluded with the Mongols in 1259, and the real crown prince was sent to the Mongol court as a hostage. No response was made to the repeated Mongol demands that the Koryŏ court leave the island and return to the city of Kaesŏng.

While the crown prince was en route to the Mongol capital, he met Prince Qubilai in the field. At this time the princes learned that their fathers had died. As Qubilai rushed his armies north to claim the Mongol throne, the Korean prince hurried back to take the throne of Koryŏ. This was Wŏnjong (r. 1259–1274).

For a decade relations with the Mongols were relatively peaceful. Then the embers of the power struggle reignited as Kim Chun attempted to consolidate control. King Wŏnjong then supported the military commander Im Yŏn in a power play which lasted into 1269 and eliminated Kim Chun and other contenders. Im Yŏn, now without serious opposition, seized power and deposed Wŏnjong, placing the latter's younger brother on the throne. Im was soon pressured into restoring Wŏnjong by the crown prince, who returned from the Mongol court escorted by a large force of Mongol soldiers. Wŏnjong left immediately for the Yüan Mongol court. To ensure the elimination of the military rulers, he submitted to the Yüan on a basis of full cooperation and support. As a further assurance, a marriage agreement was conciuded between the Koryŏ crown prince and a Mongol princess. Wŏnjong returned to Koryŏ accompanied by a large Mongol army to ensure his position. The Im clan on Kanghwa Island had planned to resist but were swept from power by Pae Chungson, leader of the powerful Koryŏ military units (*sambyŏlch'o*). Since Pae and his fellow officers were identified with the military rulers, their replacement of the Im clan probably made little difference to Wŏnjong. He was determined to break the hold of the Koryŏ military. This had led him readily to accept Mongol support. The military on the other hand could not bring itself to surrender to the Mongols, whom they had fought for 30 years and from whom their leadership could expect reprisals. The result was open rebellion, which created chaos on Kanghwa. Emptying the warehouses and taking the families of the court officials as hostages, the rebels seized all the available shipping and sailed southward. The rebellion lasted almost 4 years. At their height the rebels held some thirty islands, including Chin Island—their first major stronghold—and Cheju Island, where they were finally subdued in 1273 by a Koryŏ-Mongol invasion.

With the rebellion ended the period of the Koryŏ military rulers. The position of the military rulers from the Ch'oe clan to the Im clan was analogous in many ways to that of the Japanese Kamakura shogunate, with which they were partially contemporary. Behind the façade of the monarchy, real power was exercised through the position of the Supreme Directorate (*Kyojŏng togam*) which each of the military rulers headed. The institution of a separate administrative structure parallels the *mandokoro* of Japanese military rulers. The fiction of royal supremacy was always retained, and the military rulers always received their "appointment" as head of the Supreme

Directorate from the monarch. Again, the Koryŏ military rulers never attempted to seize the throne themselves, which they could have done with ease at any time. The tough political realities of the day seem to have been the primary reason for their reluctance. By the time a semblance of social stability was regained and power consolidated under the Ch'oe clan, the Mongols had arrived and were pressing demands for the king to visit the Mongol court. Under these circumstances it is understandable that the military rulers would be content to rule from behind the throne. To this might be added the lengthy and undoubtedly tedious ceremonial duties required of the Korean monarch. This situation had an interesting bearing on Koryŏ-Mongol relations. The monarch and the civil bureaucracy who negotiated with the Mongols tended to advocate peace, while the military rulers continued the resistance. Submission to the Mongols could only have meant the reduction of the power of the military rulers, if not their elimination.

THE INVASIONS OF JAPAN

Mongol military colonies established in Koryŏ were usually charged with specific duties among which was shipbuilding, begun in 1259 and originally intended for use against the Southern Sung. However, in 1266, Cho I, a former Korean Buddhist monk who had become an interpreter at Qubilai's court, interested the Yüan emperor in Japan. When Mongol envoys guided by Koreans repeatedly returned empty-handed from Japan, Koryŏ was given the task of constructing ships for the invasion of Japan. The rebellion of the Koryŏ military disastrously delayed the first invasion attempt. In the final period of this rebellion, 1272 to 1273, some 132 ships constructed for the Japan invasion were lost: 85 destroyed by the Koryŏ rebels and 47 sunk in storms.

When the Korean ruler Wŏnjong died in 1274, the period of resistance had ended, and a period of alliance began. The invasion fleet lay scattered in half a dozen harbors in the south, and the main body of the Mongol expeditionary force had already crossed the Yalu. Koryŏ had become a full-fledged participant in the Mongol adventure of conquest and one small fragment in the vast Mongol empire, which stretched eastward to the Danube.

For each of the two invasions of Japan, in 1274 and 1281, Koryŏ furnished some 900 ships and some 15,000 seamen to man them. For the first invasion Koryŏ levied 5,000 soldiers and for the second invasion 10,000 troops. Both invasions ended in complete disaster when the fleets were destroyed in heavy storms, which the Japanese called "divine wind" (*kamikaze*). The first invasion left the port of Happ'o on October 29 1274 and attacked Tsushima. Eight days later the force landed on the islands of Iki.

In mid-November the invasion fleet had gathered offshore of the city of Hakata. An attack was launched, and after a successful day in the field the Mongol commanders reembarked their forces to prevent a surprise night attack. That night a violent storm struck destroying the fleet.

Two fleets were assembled for the second invasion in 1281. In May 1281, one fleet of 3,500 ships carrying an army of some 100,000 men sailed from South China, while a second, smaller fleet of 900 ships carrying some 40,000 men left the Korean port of Happ'o. The two fleets finally rendezvoused at Shiga Island in late June after attacks on the islands of Tsushima and Iki. Assembling off Hirato in August 1281, the fleet was scattered and many vessels sunk by a typhoon. The survivors limped back to Happ'o, and the invasions of Japan were ended.

The Koryŏ loss is estimated at one-half of the men in the first invasion and one-third of the men in the second. Further invasions were cancelled because of the Mongol invasions of Champa and Tongking in the south and the revolt of Prince Nayan in the north.

UNDER MONGOL DOMINATION

With acceptance of Mongol rule, Mongol institutions and customs were adopted wholesale and included everything from the administrative structure and official titles down to clothing and the braided hairdress of the Mongols. Koreans were also brought into contact with many new peoples and customs at this time. Muslims were first reported in Koryŏ in 1270. While an Office of Interpreters had long existed for relations with neighboring people, contacts with the Mongols increased the demand for language specialists. The study of the Uigur script, the smaller Jürčen script and the 'Phags–pa or square script of the Mongols commenced.

Mongol resident commissioners in the capital managed major affairs of state during the period 1270 to 1278. After that the principal Yüan dynasty representatives were the directors of the Bureau for Conquest of the East, to which the Koryŏ monarch was appointed titular head. This bureau, originally established in 1280 for the second attempted invasion of Japan, was retained with the idea of future invasion attempts in mind. It became increasingly involved in internal administrative matters and supervised the Koryŏ government service examinations until it was abolished in 1365. Five major regional military headquarters, Commands of Ten Thousand (*Mandobu*), were established in the country to maintain control. The great tragedies of the two invasions came to a nation already beggared by decades of wars and bankrupt by Mongol demands for goods.

Highly prized by the Mongols were Korean otter furs. Other items on the tribute lists included eating and drinking utensils of precious metals, textiles, and varieties of paper. Hunting birds such as the peregrine falcon, goshawk, and sparrow hawk, long raised by the Koryŏ elite, were also popular.

In 1274, the formal marriage of the Koryŏ crown prince, later King Ch'ungnyŏl (r. 1274–1308), to a Mongol princess took place, linking the Yüan and Koryŏ royal families in marriage. In the century that followed seven Mongol princesses were married into the Koryŏ royal family. The offspring of three of these unions held the throne. Hostages were taken from the royal family and from the families of the high officials until 1283. By that time Mongol influence in Koryŏ was such that it could and did force Korean rulers off the throne.

Through the action of Koryŏ rebels who had submitted to the Mongols, the northeast was lost in 1258 and the northwest in 1269. Cheju Island was turned into a pasturage. Most of this territory had to be retaken forcefully in the latter half of the fourteenth century. A large Korean community also developed in the Liaoyang area during this period. This began with the settlement there in 1232 of the Koryŏ rebel Hong Pogwŏn and some 1,500 Korean families. By 1330 this Korean community had a population of over 5,000 families. Hong's son Tagu, with the Korean army of Liaoyang, helped crush the revolt of Prince Nayan against Qubilai in 1287. A by-product of this revolt was the invasion of Korea by rebels in 1289 to 1290, which was subdued by Yüan-Koryŏ forces. A cadet branch of the Koryŏ royal family was also settled in this area and given appointments as governors of the various Korean communities there. Later Koryŏ monarchs were given honorary control of the area and invested with the title of "king of Simyang." Twice, when the title passed to princes who were not in line for the throne, the Liaoyang Korean community served as a base to support their aspiration to the throne of Koryŏ.

BELLES-LETTRES

During the period that Mongol resident commissioners handled affairs of state, the court had more leisure for music, dance, and a variety of entertainments, thus ushering in what was apparently a rather bawdy period at court. A nationwide search was conducted for talented dancing girls and musicians. Even slave girls and female sorceresses with musical talent were sent to court to form dancing troupes.

The most striking of all literature of Koryŏ was the popular, earthy songs of folk origin introduced at court during this period. The lyrics of these songs, usually called *changga* (long songs), were collected in the fifteenth and sixteenth centuries in two texts on music, the *Akhak kwebŏm* and the *Akchang kasa*. The songs are largely limited to romantic themes and have a refrain which commonly contains onomatopoetic references to the sounds of musical instruments. The most popular at the Koryŏ court was, a rousing table-thumper, *Ssanghwajŏm* [The *Mandu* (a meat pastry) Shop], the first two verses of which, sans refrain, are set forth below:

> *When I went to the Ssanghwa shop to buy* mandu
> *The old Muslim caught my hand.*
> *Should these words go beyond this shop,*
> *I will say you have exaggerated,*
> *Little minstrel.*
> *To his chamber to sleep I too will go.*
> *There is no place so disheveled as that slept in spot.*

> *When I went to the Monastery of the Tripitaka to light a lantern*
> *The monk caught my hand.*
> *Should these words go beyond here,*
> *I will say you have exaggerated,*
> *Little bonze.*
> *To his bed to sleep I too will go.*
> *There is no place so disheveled as that slept in spot.*

In this earthy and spirited work a scene is set, and then the woman involved speaks to her lovers in turn, telling them to be discreet and calls them by a pet name, e.g., little minstrel, little bucket, etc.

A further characteristic of the *changga* is the use of grammatical parallelism, a feature found in the contemporaneous *kyŏnggi* style verse and in the *kasa*, where it is developed very effectively.

The anonymous authors of the *changga* occasionally achieved some rich imagery, as in the following two verses from *Ch'ŏngsan pyŏlgok* (Song of the Verdant Mountains), which uses the images of birds. Birds are commonly used to convey solitude, suggested by their being messengers between parted lovers, and to evoke the ideas of fleeting time and the brevity of life, suggested by the flight of the birds southward, heralding the coming of winter. The onomatopoetic refrain evocative of the high, mournful pitch of a flute has been retained in the following translation.

> *Cry, cry you birds*
>   *asleep or awake.*
> *More grieved than you,*
>   *I too go on crying,*
>   *asleep or awake.*
> *Yalli yalli yallasyŏng*
> *Yallari yalla.*

> *I watch the birds going,*
> *the birds going,*
> *I watch the birds passing*
> *(Shadows reflected) beneath the water.*
> *With moss-spotted plough*
> *I watch the birds passing*
> *(Shadows reflected) beneath the water.*
> *Yalli yalli yallasyŏng*
> *Yallari yalla.*

However much we may appreciate the words, it is well to remember that the *changga* were songs and that in the form we now have them, they were meant to be sung as part of a performance at court. The *Chŏngŭpsa*, for example, was incorporated into a drum dance performed at court during the Koryŏ and early Yi periods. In the Koryŏ court version, two dancing girls were involved, and the dance is described in the Monograph on Music of the *Koryŏsa* in the following terms:

> . . . the sound was amply strong; the dance changed and turned, [dancers] fluttering to and fro like twin butterflies circling flowers; they were as bold as two dragons fighting for pearls.* It was the most unusual work in the repertoire.

About the same time a verse form commonly referred to as *Kyŏnggi* developed. It appears to combine older Korean and Chinese verse forms. During the late Koryŏ period these verses were either verse games or simple poetic counterparts of the prose personification tales, in that they made maximum use of the visual appeal of Chinese characters in an amusing display of academic learning. This choice of style restricted their circulation to literati.

The influence of the prose tales of marvels of the earlier period continued. The literature of the Silla period in this tradition was popular in the Koryŏ period and, in 1279 the Zen monk Iryŏn anthologized it in the *Samguk yusa*.

As a result of the extensive contacts with Sung China, prose tales usually referred to as *p'aegwan munhak* (*C. pai-kuan wen-hsueh*) developed, and from the twelfth century collections of these tales appeared. The *p'aegwan munhak* stories are chiefly entertaining chats or tales on literary subjects, customs, and traditions. The setting of the tales is, importantly, Korea not China. The development of the *p'aegwan munhak* was probably stimulated by the flight of the literati into the provinces during the purges of the early period of the military rulers. There they formed literary associations, such

*A common artistic motif of the period.

as the Seven Sages of the Left Bank, whose members included Yi Inno, O Sejae, and Im Ch'un. Many of the anthologies owe their existence to the literary encouragement and patronage of the military ruler Ch'oe U, who ordered the collection of works of contemporary scholars of note. Representative of *p'aegwan munhak* collections are the *Paegun sosŏl* of Yi Kyubo (1168–1241), the *P'ahanjip* of Yi Inno (1152–1220), the *P'ohanjip* of Ch'oe Cha (1186–1260), and the *Yŏgong paesŏl* of Yi Chehyŏn (1287–1367).

During this period personification stories cast in biographical form came into vogue. These amusing displays of scholarly wit use some common object, such as money, turtles, tadpoles, or paper. In the Biography of Master Yeast by Im Ch'un, for example, wine is personified, and every possible allusion to wine is made in the names of the persons or places involved. It is believed that some of the personification tales are moralistic exhortations referring to the conduct of the ruler. Since such accusations could not be openly written, the locale of the stories was set in China.

The interests of the Korean elite are admirably revealed in a subgenre of literature distinguished as "talks" (*hwa*), which are brief, chatty pieces centered on such pursuits as the composition of verse, calligraphy, and painting and discussions of history, of prose, and of books in general. The summary example below, from the *P'ahanjip* of Yi Inno, follows the triple construction in dealing with painting, calligraphy, and the composition of verse.

> The scenery of the streams and mountains of Chinyang, the ancient imperial capital, is the finest in the region south of the mountain pass. A certain party composed a picture of it and presented it to Minister Yi Chijŏ who put it up on his wall to look at it. Once, when Chŏng Yŏryong of the Bureau of Military Affairs went to visit, the minister pointed at the picture and said: "This is a picture of your home, sir; a verse would be appropriate."
>
> Chŏng took his writing brush and forthwith wrote:
>
> > *How many green mountains pillow the azure lake!*
> > *Sir, you say this is a picture of Chinyang*
> > *How many thatched houses are by the water's edge?*
> > *Is a picture of my hut among them or not?*
>
> Everyone present acknowledged his cleverness and agility.

ARCHITECTURE AND THE FINE ARTS

The three oldest surviving wooden structures in Korea are Koryŏ-period Buddhist halls. There are two at Pusok-sa dating from 1376 and one at

Sudŏk-sa built in 1308. The latter is said to show influences from architectural styles of South China. Excavations show that many monasteries were extremely large, and records give us an idea of the splendor of such structures as the gold and silver pagoda at Hungwang-sa. One of the architectural wonders of the temporary capital on Kanghwa Island was the winged pavilion built in the shape of a cross by the military ruler Ch'oe U. It stood to the east of his polo field, where he had another pavilion built said to have been capable of seating 1,000 persons to watch the matches.

Carving was highly developed, and monastery artisans used ivory and whalebone to carve delicate bas-relief figures of Buddhas and Bodhisattvas on title plaques attached to sutra cases. Figures carved in great detail on stone were another product of the Koryŏ Buddhist artisans. An excellent example survives from the late Koryŏ period in the graceful marble pagoda of Kyŏngch'ŏn monastery, which dates to 1348.

One of the most interesting aspects of Koryŏ art is the extensive use of inlay techniques in some of the more beautiful works surviving from this period. These include surviving examples of lacquerware chests inlaid with mother-of-pearl, silver inlay on bronze vessels, and records of such items as a scabbard inlaid with tortoise shell which have not survived. Attesting to the high skill of the Koryŏ gold- and silversmiths are many fine surviving examples of *kundika* (water pourers), while the records tell of enormous numbers of vessels of precious metals taken away by the Mongols.

The names of several Buddhist artists and a few court painters who painted landscapes and portraits are known, but from this period which spanned half a millennium, only a few works survive. Several monarchs were noted painters, including Hŏnjong, Injong, and Kongmin. A hunting scene attributed to the last survives. The earliest extant work is a painting of Tāthagata or *Yorae* Buddha done in gold on a lacquer screen by the monk Yongno in 1307. Murals survive at Sudŏk-sa and Pusok-sa monasteries depicting Buddhist scenes.

CERAMICS

Painting as a decorative technique for ceramics began with gold-painted pieces and continued with dabs of white or black clay and then underglaze and overglaze techniques. The underglaze technique used iron oxide to produce a brown color and copper oxide to produce a bright red. It is believed that the Korean use of copper oxide predates its use in China by about a century. The painted-underglaze technique became widely used in the late thirteenth century as the principal method of decoration. A black Koryŏ ware was produced, notably at the Kangjin kiln in South Chŏlla Province, by the thirteenth century. This ware has a black glaze with floral or other designs painted on in white clay. A white Koryŏ ware resembling certain Chinese porcelains (e.g., *ying ch'ing* ware) was also being produced at kilns in the Puan area of North Chŏlla Province by the late thirteenth century. The production of celadon continued, but the great period of Koryŏ celadon had passed.

THE END OF MONGOL CONTROL

One of the Mongol requirements which the Koryŏ authorities had to face was the supply of women for the imperial harem. The demand was so great that two special offices had to be established to fill the levies. Each woman chosen was given a cosmetics allowance of 12 bolts of cloth.

By far the most important of all the girls sent to the Yüan imperial harem was Yüan Empress Ki, the daughter of Ki Chao. She entered the harem of Emperor Shun (r. 1333–1368), the last emperor of the Yüan, and in 1341 became his second empress. Her family in Koryŏ became a real power in the land, particularly her brother Ki Ch'ŏl. He led a strong pro-Mongol faction which included men who had daughters in the imperial harem.

At this time the Yüan dynasty was in decline in China, and there was a widespread rise of rebel groups. One of these groups, which would found the Ming dynasty, had seized South China and in 1356 had taken Nanking. In the same year King Kongmin raised his own revolt against the Yüan and eliminated Ki Ch'ŏl and his clique. Empress Ki quickly persuaded the Yüan emperor to replace the Koryŏ monarch. The Mongol force sent to put down the Koryŏ revolt was practically annihilated. This marked the beginning of the end of Mongol power in Koryŏ.

A by-product of the disintegration of the Yüan empire was the invasion of Koryŏ in 1359 and 1361 by a large Chinese rebel army from the Hopei-Chihli area of North China. Known as the Red Banner bandits, they swept across Manchuria and brought temporary devastation to the Korean northwest. They sacked and burned the capital, forcing the Koryŏ court to flee to Kanghwa Island, while scattered rebel troops pillaged the countryside. The capital was finally retaken in early 1362, and the rebel army pushed back across the Yalu. Elements of other armies fighting in Manchuria continued to spill into Koryŏ from time to time.

By 1368, the Ming had pushed the Mongols out of China. The Mongols fled back to their old homelands, where they founded the Northern Yüan, which survived into the early seventeenth century, finally becoming subordinate to the Manchu Ch'ing dynasty.

While King Kongmin pursued a policy which was anti-Mongol and thus pro-Ming, the major portion of his energies was consumed in regaining through military campaigns territory lost in the north, in attempting to combat the raids of the Japanese freebooters (*Wakō*), which were growing in intensity at this time, and in internal reforms.

When the son of Ki Ch'ŏl assembled Yüan refugees in Manchuria in 1368 with the intention of avenging his father's death, King Kongmin dusted off the tradition that Koryŏ was the successor to the old state of Koguryŏ and thus the rightful sovereign of Manchuria and sent two of his best generals, Chi Yongsu and Yi Sŏnggye (1335–1408), into Manchuria. Yi Sŏnggye was the fifth-generation scion of a military family which had for three generations held the post of Chief of One Thousand in the Korean northeast. When his father died, Yi Sŏnggye inherited his rank and position. He had already distinguished himself in an early campaign in the northeast in 1361 when he was only twenty-five. The Manchurian campaign was the first step in a career which would, 24 years later, put him on the throne of Korea.

While Yi Sŏnggye swept north through the Hamhŭng plains, General Chi drove west toward Liaotung and took the city of Liaoyang. The Koreans were unprepared to hold their gains and recalled their armies, although they repeatedly brought up their claim to all lands east of the Liao River. Ming forces soon moved into the area, permanently settling the question.

THE EMERGENCE OF A NEW ELITE

Following the overthrow of the military rulers, powerful elite families aligned with the Mongols emerged. These families fell heir to the great estates built up by the military rulers and to the new conditions which allowed vast accumulations of land. The elite still resided in the capital as absentee landlords. But their acquisition of state lands led to a financial crisis in the central government, and stipends for officials were abolished. While this made little difference to the landowning elite who held the higher offices in the civil bureaucracy, it put the lower echelons in a difficult position, since they received neither land grants nor stipends. They could as a consequence be expected to back internal reform measures and to oppose the old elite families, many of whom were pro-Mongol.

There were several factors which distinguished this newly rising elite group. Prior to the downfall of the military rulers, appointment to a provincial post was considered a degrading form of exile from the center of wealth, power, and activity: the capital. Now, however, members of the new elite actively competed for regional posts where they could use the power of their office to economic advantage. Moreover, many of these newcomers were from provincial families and had entered government service through the examination system. This gave them a closer identification with the land and its management. They were also distinguished by their adherence to a new philosophy, notably the ideas of the Sung philosopher Chu Hsi. These ideas had been incorporated into the curriculum of the National Academy and then given major emphasis on the government service examinations. The works of the Chinese philosopher Chu Hsi (1130–1200) are said to have been introduced into Koryŏ by An Hyang (1243–1306), who played an important role in revitalizing the curriculum of the National Academy in the late thirteenth century. The first important stimulus for the adoption of this new philosophy was provided by King Ch'ungsŏn (r. 1309–1313). This monarch was of scholarly bent and spent a considerable amount of time in the Yüan capital while he was crown prince. The study center, Hall of Ten Thousand Volumes, he established in the Yüan capital became a meeting place for Chinese and Korean scholars. In 1314 he had 10,000 volumes of books purchased, and he received several thousand more volumes from the imperial collection of the Northern Sung donated by the Yüan emperor. The Korean scholars involved, notably Paek Ijong and his disciple Yi Chehyŏn (1287–1367), became zealous adherents of the philosophy of Chu Hsi. They and others after them made it the major focus of study at the Koryŏ National Academy and the principal subject on the government service examinations.

The adoption of this philosophy cut the ground out from under Buddhism. In this period attacks on Buddhism began with the condemnation of the misconduct of monks and practices of the monasteries. Later, emphasis was shifted to a blanket condemnation of Buddhism per se.

The new elite withdrew its patronage from Buddhism and began to institute Confucian ceremonial practices, both public and private, from marriages to funerals, replacing Buddhist practices.

GENERALS AND PUPPET KINGS

In 1365, a personal tragedy, the death in childbirth of his Mongol wife, overcame King Kongmin. A noted artist, the king painted a portrait of his queen and had a large hall built to enshrine it. It is said that he sat there facing the portrait night and day engulfed in sorrow. Alone and without heir, he turned over a large measure of control to Sin Ton, a Buddhist monk of humble origins. Sin Ton continued the reform movement King Kongmin had instituted aimed at breaking the powerful pro-Mongol elite families. Sin Ton was, however, exiled and later killed when he became too arbitrary in his actions. King Kongmin was himself assassinated by a palace eunuch in 1374.

The government was seized by Yi Inmin, the leader of a strong elite clan, who then put the 10-year-old son of Panya, a palace slave girl, and a boy claimed by King Kongmin as his own son, on the throne. This boy was canonized King U (r. 1374–1388). Yi Inmin retained de facto power. Ming China had recognized King Kongmin in 1369 and had given him a gold seal and the Ming calendar, while the Korean court turned over the Yüan seal they had been given by the Mongols. Then Ming Emperor T'ai-tsu refused to recognize King U. The pro-Ming policy was reversed overnight.

Despite opposition by members of the new literati, such as Chŏng Mongju (1337–1392), envoys were sent to the Northern Yüan court who demanded that Koryŏ attack the Ming armies in the Liaotung area. The Yüan demands led to a quick cooling off of relations with the Mongols and a return to attempts to establish more amicable relations with Ming China. After leading two embassies which were turned back, Chŏng Mongju finally managed to gain an audience in 1384. Annual tribute required of Koryŏ included 5,000 horses, 500 Korean pounds (*kŭn*) of gold, 500 Korean ounces (*yang*) of silver, and 50,000 bolts of cloth. The opening of relations with the Ming, however, did not eliminate the pro-Yüan bias of many of the old-guard elite families. The new elite who composed the second level of authority generally favored the Ming. The military was also coming into its own. The years of fighting during the late fourteenth century had increased the power and prestige of a number of military officers. The preconditions for a major change were slowly forming.

THE WAKŌ

The *Wakō* (freebooters) operated from bases in southern Japan and from islands such as Tsushima and Iki in the Korea Straits. In normal times peasants there eked out an existence from the rocky soil, which they supplemented by fishing. In the early Kamakura period they turned more and more to maritime activities which were at times commercial but increasingly piratical in nature. *Wakō* raids on Koryŏ began in 1223 but were not severe.

Piracy was certainly no monopoly of the Japanese but had been endemic in Korean waters since time immemorial. Jürčen pirates had dominated the Sea of Japan in the first half of the eleventh century, raiding both Korea and Japan. Ullŭng Island was pillaged so often by them that it was widely believed to be uninhabitable. At one time Koryŏ had a fleet of seventy-five warships on station in Wŏnsan Bay as a defense against the Jürčen pirates. Sung pirates were no strangers to Korean waters either, while the southern Korean islands were controlled by Korean pirates in the second quarter of the twelfth century, some 800 of them recorded as having surrendered at one time.

The *Wakō* crews were often mixed as Koreans and Chinese joined them, but their leadership and their spirit of bold adventure were essentially Japanese contributions. During the fourteenth century they scourged the China coast and became a major disaster for the narrow peninsula of Korea.

Coastal areas of China were evacuated in depth, while daring *Wakō* adventurers sailed far up the Yangtse River. Coastal evacuation was attempted in Koryŏ as well, but it simply brought the raiders inland. They plundered and sacked, not only every major town, but even remote mountain villages. The maritime grain transport system was wrecked as the *Wakō* seized hundreds of grain ships in a single haul. The Koryŏ authorities tried several measures. A mission led by Chŏng Mongju was sent to Kyūshū and succeeded in obtaining the release of several hundred Korean captives. Ships armed with cannon built by Ch'oe Muson reportedly destroyed some 500 *Wakō* ships in an engagement in the Yellow Sea off the mouth of the Kŭm River. Plans were even discussed which called for the entire population to be moved inside of walled cities and given military training.

The *Wakō* incursions in Korea do not seem to have been a reaction to the attempted Mongol invasions of Japan, since they averaged less than one every 10 years during the period 1223 to 1328. This average rose to more than three attacks a year during the period 1350 to 1374. The intense period of *Wakō* activity in Korea was reached during the years 1375 to 1388 when 378 raids are recorded, or an average of 27 a year. A retaliatory attack on the *Wakō* lair at Tsushima, proposed 2 years earlier, was carried out in 1389. A Korean force of 100 warships attacked the base at Tsushima and reportedly sent 300 *Wakō* ships to the bottom. The raids did not cease, but the effectiveness of the Korean attack on Tsushima is reflected in the decrease of the incursions, which dropped to an average of four a year during the ensuing decade.

GUNPOWDER AND FIREARMS

The manufacture of gunpowder and firearms in Koryŏ is usually attributed to the perseverance of a single individual, Ch'oe Muson. Ch'oe is related to have desired to perfect a weapon to combat the raids of the *Wakō*. He finally learned the secret of gunpowder manufacture from a member of a mission from China, it is related. He then persuaded the state to establish a Bureau of Armament in 1377, and he was placed in charge. Ch'oe manufactured a large variety of firearms, especially cannon. He also experimented with naval armament and constructed ships equipped with cannon to fight the *Wakō*. But this development was like the short-lived *haru sari* (mayfly), and there appears to have been little continued technical development beyond Ch'oe's efforts.

THE RISE OF YI SŎNGGYE

Among the Koryŏ military leaders who rose to fame through victories against the Jürčen and the *Wakō* was Yi Sŏnggye, whose father had gained

The Yi Dynasty: Provincial Boundaries from 1450 A.D.

RESTRICTED AREA

Mt. Paektu

Tumen

Kyŏngwŏn

Hoenyŏng

Kyŏnghŭng

Hamgil

Kanggye

Yalu

P'yŏngan

Ŭiju

Ch'ongch'on

Anju

◉ Hamhŭng

Yŏnghŭng

Taedong

◉ P'yŏngyang

Hwanghae

Key symbols:
▣ Seoul
◉ Provincial administrative centers
● Other towns

◉ Haeju

Kangwon

Kangnŭng

SEOUL
▣

◉ **Wŏnju**

Han

Ch'ungju

Kyonggi

Ch'ungch'ong

Oryong

Sangju

Andong

Kongju ◉

Ch'up'ung

Naktong

Kyongsang

Chŏnju ◉

Taegu ◉

Kyŏngju

Miryang

Yŏmp'o

Cholla

Chep'o

Pusanp'o

Naju

Kŏje Is.

Tsushima Is.

Yi Sunsin Hq

Last naval action 1598

Cheju

merit in campaigns to recover the northeast. In opposing the pro-Mongol policy of the old elite, Yi Sŏnggye was supported by officials of the rising new elite, such as Chŏng Tojŏn (d. 1398). At this time a military coup led by General Ch'oe Yŏng and backed by Generals Cho Minsu and Yi Sŏnggye seized the government. As these changes were being effected, there was a shift in relations with the Ming. Koryŏ envoys to the Ming court were turned back in Liaotung on the pretext that Koryŏ tribute horses were old and weak, but the reasons appear to have been Ming suspicions of the new de facto rulers and territorial ambitions in eastern Manchuria. The Koryŏ capital buzzed with rumors of outrageous Ming demands for young girls, eunuchs, artisans, and livestock. The ignition point was the Ming establishment of a garrison in the Hamhŭng plains north of the Iron Pass in 1388. This enraged the chief military leader General Ch'oe Yŏng. Ch'oe ordered a campaign against the Ming forces in the Liaotung area which he intended to supervise from his headquarters in P'yŏngyang. When the Koryŏ armies reached Wihwa Island in the Yalu, Yi Sŏnggye, who had opposed the campaign strictly on military grounds, revolted. He turned the army back toward the capital and, with General Cho Minsu, seized power. Ch'oe Yŏng was killed and King U was deposed. King Ch'ang, the 9-year-old son of King U, was placed on the throne, with primary power in the hands of Generals Cho and Yi and the literatus Yi Saek, who supported Cho. In 1389 Yi Sŏnggye and his followers carried out a brief purge. King Ch'ang and King U were demoted to the status of commoners and then killed. General Cho was also made a commoner. Several literati, including Yi Saek and Kwŏn Kŭn, were jailed and later banished. Ostensibly these contenders were eliminated in quarrels stemming from the land reform program. The same quarrels provided Yi Sŏnggye and his supporters the excuse to depose King Ch'ang and to "restore" the throne; the Ming refusal to recognize King Ch'ang was undoubtedly a major factor leading to his replacement.

Yi and his backers placed a distant royal relative, later King Kongyang (r. 1389–1392) on the throne and used him to advance the land reform program and to attempt to reestablish friendly relations with Ming China. Just as King U had been under the control of Yi Inmin, and King Ch'ang had been a tool of the generals, King Kongyang became a puppet of Yi Sŏnggye. The new elite who supported Yi Sŏnggye immediately implemented reforms to strip the old elite of their holdings and to reestablish a fiscal basis for government, particularly military, operations. A cadestral survey was carried out in the period 1388 to 1390, and all the old land registers, public and private, were piled up in the marketplace and burned. Proposals were also made to confiscate the lands of the monasteries, but these were impossible to carry out at the time. The withdrawal of the patronage of the new elite was, however, a serious blow to the monasteries.

The few Koryŏ loyalists among the new elite who opposed Yi Sŏnggye were silenced. Some like Yi Saek were jailed and banished; others like the statesman Chŏng Mongju and the literatus Yi Sungin were murdered. In 1392, Yi Sŏnggye took the throne himself. A thorough purge placed the new monarch and his supporters in firm control. The announcement of the end of the Koryŏ period to King Kongyang, who was then sent into exile and later murdered, seems to have been made in almost matter-of-fact fashion.

The Wang dynasty fell and with it went Korea's great period of Buddhism. In a few years the Koryŏ capital of Kaesŏng would be a second-rate commercial town, its palaces and offices no longer maintained. The late Koryŏ scholar Wŏn Ch'ŏnsŏk writes of a return visit to Manwŏldae (Full Moon Terrace), site of the royal palace in Kaesŏng:

> *It is natural that nations rise and fall*
> *And now on Full Moon Terrace too, the grasses of Autumn.*
> *Half a millennium of kingly reign*
> *dissolves in the sound of the herder's flute.*
> *Pausing here at sunset*
> *I cannot hold back my tears.*

8
Early
Chosŏn

On the morning of August 5, 1392, Yi Sŏnggye, canonized T'aejo, mounted the phoenix throne in Kaesŏng as the first ruler of Chosŏn. A major source of support for T'aejo had been the new elite group. One of his initial acts was to reward those who had supported him in the struggles for the throne. Thirty-nine of his most loyal and powerful backers were given the title of "merit subject." A number of others were given the title of "minor merit subject." In the many struggles centering around the throne, the supporters of the victor were in each of the twenty-eight recorded incidents awarded the title of merit subject, first to fourth class. The merit subjects were the pinnacle of the elite pyramid of power throughout the period and the prime movers of the dynasty.

The reorganization and readjustment of domestic institutions and the important problems of foreign relations absorbed their energies in the early years. Culturally and intellectually the first century of the Yi dynasty was a brilliant period, which reached a zenith during the reign of the fourth monarch, Sejong (r. 1418–1450). An immense centralized bureaucratic apparatus was slowly constructed which permeated the countryside to a degree never realized during the Koryŏ period and a rigid and tightly controlled social structure developed. The periodic struggles for power during this century of development led to the rise of intense factional struggles among the bureaucratic elite during the century which followed.

After some hesitancy, Hanyang (Seoul) was chosen as the capital of the new dynasty, and construction work was begun in 1394. The move probably had practical political reasons as well as symbolic ones, for the old elite and the Buddhist monasteries might have been expected to retain a great deal of influence in Kaesŏng. Although the new capital was begun, not until the reign of T'aejong (r. 1400–1418) would Yi monarchs take up permanent residence there.

THE REVOLT OF THE PRINCES

When he took the throne in 1392, Yi Sŏnggye was fifty-nine. By 1398, he was sixty-five, and the matter of selecting his successor had become urgent.

Chronological Overview

Date	China	Manchuria	Korea	Japan
1392	Ming		Chosŏn	Ashikaga Bakufu
1592			Japanese Invasions	
1598				
1600				
1627		Later Chin	Manchu Invasions	Tokugawa Shogunate
1637				
1644				
	Ch'ing			

The founder of the Yi dynasty had two principal wives. His first wife, of the Han clan, presented him six sons before her death. His second wife, of the Kang clan, bore him two sons, and these were presented to him for his choice. T'aejo selected Prince Yi Pangbŏn (d. 1398), the eldest son by Queen Kang, as crown prince, but this was opposed by many ministers who favored Prince Yi Pangsŏk, the second son of the Kang-clan line. The chief supporters of Prince Pangsŏk were Merit Subjects Chŏng Tojŏn, earl of Ponghwa, who had been tutor to the prince, and Nam Ŭn (d. 1398), lord of Sŏnsŏng. When rumors circulated that the princes of the Han-clan line were to be deposed, the boldest of them, Prince Yi Pangwŏn (1367–1423) acted. Assembling his private forces and supported by several of the higher ministers, he broke into the residences of Chŏng Tojŏn and Nam Ŭn and killed them. The two princes of the Kang line were cut down on the road.

This occasioned the award of the title merit subject to sixteen ministers and two princes for their support in the revolt. Prince Pangwŏn, who seems to have been the de facto power, did not take the throne himself, but deferred to the appointment of one of his brothers, Prince Yi Panggwa (1357–1419), as crown prince. T'aejo, sick and aging, abdicated in the autumn of 1399. He spent the remainder of his days travelling about the countryside with a small retinue, often residing for extended periods in the northeast. He later returned to Kaesŏng, where he died at the age of seventy-four in 1417.

Prince Panggwa, canonized Chŏngjong (r. 1399–1400), held the throne for only four months. In early 1400 a second struggle for the throne led by Prince Panghan erupted. Panghan, who had the support of only two of the powerful merit subjects, was quickly captured and exiled by Prince Pangwŏn. Pangwŏn then took the throne himself. This was T'aejong (r. 1400–1418), who immediately awarded the title of merit subject to thirty-eight of his backers. He provided a residence for his deposed brother Chŏngjong at Kaesŏng, where the latter lived the 19 remaining years of his life.

THE NEW CAPITAL

Construction of the new capital at Hanyang was placed under the supervision of Pak Chach'un, President of the Ministry of Public Works. A nationwide levy in 1404 provided a labor force of 118,000 which completed construction of essential palaces and government offices. In 1405, the city was still under construction but sufficiently completed for T'aejong to transfer the capital from Kaesŏng. T'aejong himself took up residence in the Ch'angdŏk palace. In 1412 a second levy on all the provinces brought 100,000 workers into the capital to finish major construction efforts. Seoul was primarily a city of government and officials, dominated by walled palaces and the walled mansions of the scholar-officials. Roads ran in from the principal gates in the city wall to intersect a short distance from the main palace gate. Government inns were maintained for foreign envoys from China, Japan, and Manchuria near the principal gates, which were also busy market areas. Shrines to the gods of the earth and grain (*sajik*) and the royal ancestors were built as well as numerous government buildings. It was a city of single-story buildings with the few exceptions being two-story palace buildings or multi-storied pagodas in the palace gardens and the double-storied towers built over the principal palace and city gates. In the northeast section of the city was the Sŏnggyun'gwan National Academy, with the national shrine to Confucius and to the Chinese and Korean Confucian sages. Half of the residences in the city were tiled-roof homes, reportedly due to special efforts urged by the monk Haesŏn. The remainder were the thatched huts of the masses who supported officialdom in this new city which had sprung up amid the hills and mountains on the small plain north of the meandering Han River. Stone bridges arched over a stream run through the center of the city to provide water, and a permanent market with shops erected side by side lined both sides of one major road. A defensive wall climbed the hills and snaked down through the valleys around the city. Two citadels of refuge, *Pukhan sansŏng* to the north and *Namhan sansŏng* across the river and to the south, were constructed in two of the more inaccessible mountain ranges ringing the city.

THE REIGN OF T'AEJONG

In the 18 years of his reign King T'aejong proved a strong-willed, active monarch. Under his forceful guidance was begun what would amount to a Korean renaissance. During the eventful reign of this monarch five high schools were established in the capital in 1411 with grants of land for their support (one was later abolished); paper money was issued (1401); a number of fonts of metallic type were cast and the reprinting of Chinese texts begun (from 1401) to meet the demands of the increasing number of Korean scholars and students and for export to Japan; the maritime grain transport system was revitalized with the construction of some 250 transport vessels (1402); several land surveys were carried out; *materia medica* were compiled; the regional tribute system was reorganized (1416); the guidelines for the regional administrative system were effected, and the authority of the six ministries of the central government was increased; detailed law codes were promulgated; and relations were established with China and Japan.

T'aejong was a monarch who had been thoroughly steeped in the teachings and traditions of Chu Hsi orthodoxy. His Confucian orientation made him sympathetic to the anti-Buddhist intellectual climate of the period. At the same time he was endeavoring to break the power of the influential families, many of whom had their own military retainers, and to bring the unregistered lands of these powerful clans back on the tax registers. T'aejong's actions might be seen as efforts to strengthen the position of the ruler and to provide a financial basis for the state sufficient to meet the expenses of government and the large military outlays required for national defense. As one part of these efforts T'aejong implemented a large-scale reduction of the influence and resources of the monasteries. Strict regulations limited the number of monks at each monastery and the number of slaves and amounts of land the monasteries were allowed to retain. Yet even after these measures were carried out, some 250 monasteries remained.

The intrigues of royal relatives around the throne had been a recurring problem in traditional Korea and one of which T'aejong was well aware. T'aejong's solution was to exclude royal relatives from participating in government. To ensure their financial needs, an office was established to handle the affairs of royal Yi clansmen of the ninth degree of relationship and to the sixth degree of relationship for royal in-laws. After that, presumably, offspring of collateral branches of these families were on their own. Despite regulations to the contrary, many of them seem to have entered government service.

Among the new social institutions which developed at this time were discriminatory restrictions on the *sŏŏl* (illegitimate *yangban* offspring) and upon wives other than the first wife. Women in general were forbidden to remarry. In 1413 T'aejong implemented the *hop'ae* identity tag system. The *hop'ae* tags distinguished five general groups:

Ivory tags for the highest military and civil officials.

Deer horn tags for lesser officials.

Yellow tags of poplar wood for *yangban* with the degree of *chinsa* or *saengwŏn*.

Small square wooden tags for all others down to commoners.

Large square wooden tags for all outcastes and slaves.

For commoners the tags were inscribed with the name, birthplace, and birth-date, and slaves' tags additionally included the complexion and height of the bearer. These tags facilitated the compilation of census and tax records and also served to define and rigidify the class structure of Yi dynasty society.

Every male aged fifteen to seventy was responsible for making his own identity tag, which he then presented to a government office where it was validated by being branded with an official seal. The tags facilitated the implementation of the regulations forbidding movement outside a province, and stations were set up at provincial borders to check on all travellers. Rewards were offered for reporting persons who forged, altered, or dis-regarded their identity tags. The restrictions on movement were enforced only periodically during the early Yi period, in 1413 to 1416 and 1460 to 1469, i.e., at the time of their initial implementation in the reign of T'aejong and again during the reign of Sejo when bad crop years and epidemics led to mass flight of peasants from P'yŏngan, Hwanghae, and Kangwŏn Provinces. From 1675 the *hop'ae* identity tag system appears to have been enforced more successfully. Undoubtedly this was due in part to the assumption of imple-mentation and enforcement by the Office of Border Defense (*Pibyŏnsa*), which was also responsible for enforcing the five-household mutual guarantee system (*ogajakt'ong*).

T'aejong, himself a military-minded individual, kept firm control of the army even following the ascent of his son to the throne. His release from ceremonial obligations gave him more freedom to participate in political decisions, while his control of the military enabled him to eliminate the private armies of the members of the royal household and powerful ministers. In so doing he not only ensured the successful transfer of power to his son during his own lifetime but also the continuation of the reign after his death.

THE REIGN OF SEJONG

In 1418, T'aejong followed the precedent of his father and abdicated in favor of his son To. This young man, canonized Sejong (r. 1418–1450), was then twenty-two. He was destined to rule 32 years and have the most brilliant and fructuous reign in Korean history.

Central to the intellectual and cultural efflorescence of Sejong's reign were the scholars of the Hall of Assembled Scholars (*Chiphyŏnjŏn*) established by the king. In this center gathered some of the finest intellects of the day. One intention behind the formation of this institution seems to have been to create an elite center for the accumulation and dissemination of knowledge which would, presumably, be useful in government and to the populace. Scholars of the Hall of Assembled Scholars carried out research, drawing heavily from centuries of Chinese experience, and published books in a large number of fields.

Throughout the centuries of traditional Korea the great bulk of the populace, perhaps as many as 80 percent, were engaged in food production. The majority devoted their lives to the cultivation of food grains, particularly wet-field rice. The Confucian expression "agriculture is the basis of government" was a practical fact of life in Korea. Therefore, it is not surprising to find that Sejong and his scholars paid particular attention to agriculture and to the related fields of mathematics, measurement, and meteorology.

Several cadastral surveys were carried out, and irrigation was improved by the utilization of Chinese types of water wheel. In 1430, at the recommendation of the Ministry of Finance, a more efficient Japanese water wheel was introduced. These efforts were particularly effective in P'yŏngan Province, where irrigation works had been scarce.

One of the most talented "scientists" of the early Yi period was Yi Ch'ŏn (1376–1451), who contributed improvements in the fields of firearms, musical instruments, metallic type, and astronomical instruments. During the period 1432 to 1438 Yi and Chang Yŏngsil brought out an improved armillary sphere—a celestial globe with stars represented on its surface which was over 10½ Korean feet in circumference—directional and time indicators, and several types of improved clepsydras. In 1442 copper rain gauges were made and distributed to the eight provinces, producing accurate rainfall records some two centuries before they would be compiled in Europe. Weights and measures were standardized; the linear measure adopted was engraved on stone to ensure accuracy.

A number of books on agriculture were compiled, such as Chŏng Cho's (d. 1434) *Nongsajipsŏl* of 1429. These books are said to have prompted better utilization of fertilizers, enabling the practice of leaving a field idle for a season to be discontinued, thus bringing more land under constant cultivation. A notable effort was made in the construction of thousands of reservoirs and catch basins as a drought-relief measure.

The detailed land surveys undoubtedly stimulated the compilation of gazetteers, works which combined elements of physical, economic, and cultural geography and local history for each town and its environs. In 1432 Maeng Sasŏng (1359–1438) brought out his New Gazetteer of the Eight Provinces (*Sinch'an p'aldo chiriji*), which provided a useful reference guide for officials of the central government. In the field of cartography maps of each province were prepared in 1463 by Chŏng Ch'ŏk (1390–1475) and others in the *Tongguk chido* (Maps of Korea).

The area of political history is represented by the *Ch'ip'yŏng yoram* of 1445, which covered both Chinese and Korean historical events. Five years later a military history of Korea, *Tongguk pyŏnggam*, was published.

The Korean tradition in the field of medicine continued with the re-printing of Chinese and Korean medical texts and the compiling of new Korean *materia medica*. The physician No Chungnye, who had studied in China, was active in the compilation of several *materia medica* including the *Hyangyak ch'aejip wŏllyŏng* of 1431 and the *Hyangyak chipsŏngbang* of 1433. The compilation of an encyclopedia of Chinese medicine in 1445 led to the production of a single comprehensive work, the twenty-five volume *Tongŭi pogam* (Treasured Mirror of Korean Medicine), compiled in the period 1597 to 1611 by the royal physician Hŏ Chun. This work was later reprinted and widely used in China.

Work in Korean history had been active during this period, attempting to finalize a version of the history of the previous dynasty. The *Koryŏsa* (History of Koryŏ), which had been underway since the early years of the dynasty, was finally presented at court the year following Sejong's death. It was followed by a chronological history of Koryŏ, the *Koryŏsa chŏryo*.

The moral and ethical principles espoused by the Confucian-oriented elite of the early Yi dynasty were summarized in illustrated collections of exemplary biographies drawn from Chinese and Korean history which depicted the ideal behavior of loyal subjects, dutiful sons, virtuous wives, and appropriate relationships between superiors and inferiors. The first of these works was the *Samgang haengsil* (1432), compiled in the Hall of Assembled Scholars under the direction of Sŏl Sun. In 1434 it was printed in a metallic-type edition and widely distributed throughout the provinces. There were many subsequent works of this type during the Yi dynasty, and the brief biographical sketches of dutiful sons and daughters who sacrificed themselves for their parents, of wives who gave their lives for their husbands, and of loyal subjects had a widespread appeal. In their own fashion these tales were more influential than any other single source in spreading the values of the Confucian-oriented Yi dynasty elite through the lower levels of society.

The printing and reprinting of this vast outpouring of books, many of which found their way into the Japan trade, stimulated the casting of new fonts of movable type and improvements and refinements in printing techniques.

The same motivations which prompted efforts to improve agriculture underlay certain attempts in social engineering involving the various outcaste groups. These outcastes were declared "new commoners" (*sin paekchŏng*). The result of this effort was not a rise in the status of these unfortunates but a degrading of the term *paekchŏng*, which had formerly meant simply a commoner, to refer to the pariah class. Instructions were issued to prohibit them from moving their place of residence. This restriction was extended to the populace at large, who were limited to their home province. The new commoners were also prohibited from entering the regional schools

THE DEATH OF CHŎNG MONGJU 夢周殞命 麗高

Woodblock prints from the eighteenth-century collection of exemplary biographies, *Oryun haɛngsildo*. The publication of these biographical sketches of loyal subjects, dutiful sons, virtuous women, and the like began during the reign of King Sejong. They were meant as instructional materials and were widely distributed with texts in Korean or Chinese.

金氏撲虎　本朝

(*hyanggyo*). When new lands were acquired in the north as a result of campaigns against the Jürčen people during the sixteenth century, large numbers of these new commoners were moved from the heavily populated southern provinces to settle these areas. The new territories also made possible an expansion of the bureaucracy and created new positions for the proliferating elite class.

Increased agricultural yields, the opening of vast new lands to settlement in the north, large-scale commercial activity, and decades of peace contributed to a period of prosperity. These same factors increased the food supply and began a population explosion.

THE KOREAN ALPHABET

Research and study in the field of Chinese phonology had been carried on for some time in Korea. Again, Koreans had long paid attention to the study of foreign languages and scripts, particularly Chinese, and languages studied at this time included Japanese (from 1413), Jürčen, Mongolian, and Ryukyuan. King Sejong himself took an intense personal interest in phonological studies and initiated a project to develop a script suitable for writing the Korean language. It seems probable that King Sejong's initial intention in beginning work on a Korean alphabet was influenced by considerations of improving instruction in the pronunciation of spoken Chinese, but he could hardly have been unaware of the far-reaching importance the alphabet would have, as his later remarks indicate.

At this time the clumsy *idu* system of using Chinese characters phonetically for Korean grammatical endings and inflections had given rise to a highly abbreviated form of *idu* called *kugyŏl*. At its best *kugyŏl* approximated a crude syllabary and was thus unsuitable either for indicating the pronunciation of Chinese or for writing Korean sounds.

Work on the alphabet proceeded slowly and Korean scholars on trips to Liaotung and Peking consulted many Chinese phonologists. Finally, in

Korean Writing Systems

Sound	Idu	Kugyŏl	Han'gŭl	Meaning
ŭn	隱	ㄹ	은	topical particle
i	是	㇏	이	subject particle
hako	爲 古	㕦	하고	does (is) and ....

1446 the alphabet was promulgated in the work *Hunmin chŏngŭm* (Correct Sounds for Instructing the People). First called *chŏngŭm* (correct sounds), the alphabet soon gained the depreciatory name of *ŏnmun* (vulgar script). The current designation *han'gŭl* [script of the (Korean) Han people] was devised by the modern grammarian Chu Sigyŏng (1876–1914). At the time of its promulgation the alphabet had twenty-eight letters, seventeen consonants, and eleven vowels. Three consonants and one vowel were dropped through the centuries. In the preface to the *Hunmin chŏngŭm* King Sejong sets forth the reasons behind the undertaking.

> The sounds of our language differ from those of China and they do not accord with written [Chinese]. Therefore, there are many of the common people who have something they wish to express but are ultimately unable to bring out their feelings. In sympathy with this, I have newly made twenty-eight letters, simply desiring that men become familiar with them and easily put them conveniently into daily use.

The new alphabet was tested, it is believed, by using it to write the *Yongbi ŏch'ŏn'ga* (Song of the Dragons Ascending to Heaven), a lengthy 125-stanza dynastic hymn eulogizing the ancestors of the house of Yi. The alphabet encountered the fierce opposition of many scholars at court, who seem to have believed it would lead to estrangement with China and be used to vulgarize the ancient classics, or even worse, cause the lower class functionaries to ignore them. Denigration of the alphabet as unworthy of the regard of a learned man remained among the Korean scholar-officials throughout the Yi dynasty and lingers on today. The result was that several centuries were to elapse before the full potential of the alphabet would be realized.

TRANSLATIONS

Following the promulgation of *han'gŭl* a considerable effort was directed toward translating Chinese texts into Korean. The works selected for translation illustrated the philosophy of the Korean intellectuals. The seven Chinese classics, for example, were translated twice in the sixteenth century. Chinese belles-lettres were represented by translations such as the twenty-five volumes of poetry drawn from the works of the T'ang poet Tu Fu (712–770). One of the great translators of the period was the grammarian Ch'oe Sejin (ca. 1473–1542), who translated such works as *Women's Instructions* (*Yŏhun*) and the *Classic of Filial Piety*. Ch'oe's most noted work was an *ŏnhae* ("explained in Korean") text, the *Hunmong chahoe* of 1527, a Chinese primer for school children which established the basic orthographic system used. Translations of Buddhist texts were undertaken in the final years of the reign of Sejong and in the reign of his son Sejo under the direction of the Zen monk Sinmi.

BELLES-LETTRES

During the period which encompassed the final years of the Koryŏ and the initial years of the Yi dynasty, i.e., in the fourteenth and fifteenth centuries, two new poetic forms emerged. These were the *kasa* and the *sijo*. Both belong to the category of lyric poetry, which is to say they were written to be sung. They probably had antecedents composed in Chinese, but it was not until after the development of *han'gŭl* that they took the distinctive form in which we now know them. The writers of *kasa* and *sijo* reflected the new philosophy of the period. One result was a new attention given to the beauties of nature. A favorite theme of these writers was the charm and pleasures of a rustic life. A common structural device was to incorporate such themes into a seasonal framework. The development of the private academies (*sŏwŏn*) in the countryside and the large numbers of scholar-officials sent into exile as a result of the factional struggles contributed to the use of nature in poetry.

The *kasa* is a long descriptive and often episodic narrative in poetic form characterized by the extended use of grammatical parallelism. It might well be described as a Sino-Korean hybrid with Chinese phrases and allusions occupying a dominant position. The *kasa* became a favorite of the Korean Confucian scholar who, often in exile during the stormy years when political factionalism raged at court, used it to display his knowledge of Chinese classics and belles-lettres. The *kasa* reached its zenith in the late sixteenth century in the works of *Songgang** Chŏng Ch'ŏl (1536–1593) and Pak Inno (1561–1643), although the form continued into the late eighteenth century. [Extracts from Pak's *T'aep'yŏnggok* (Song of Peace) of 1598 are contained in the section The Japanese Invasions.] Chŏng Ch'ŏl is probably the most highly regarded author of *kasa* verse. Forced into exile in 1585 because of factional struggles at court, Chŏng wrote *Samiin'gok* (Thinking of My Lord), a lengthy *kasa* poem which follows the tradition of the ancient Chinese *Ch'u tzu* (Songs of Ch'u) in depicting the monarch as a lover and the exiled minister as the forgotten woman. In Chŏng's *kasa* poetry are liberal allusions to Chinese classics and Chinese and Korean poetry. This gives them a somewhat contrived and artificial flavor to the modern mind, but these same features were highly appreciated in his own day. Chŏng seems more at ease in his descriptive passages illustrated below with the final section "Summer Scenes" and the section "Winter Scenes" from his *kasa*

*Songgang was Chŏng Ch'ŏl's literary name. Eminent Korean scholars are commonly referred to simply by their literary name.

Song of Star Mountain (*Sŏngsan pyŏlgok*). The reference to a dragon rising from the water, while ostensibly meaning only the dragon sandbar of the poem, is an allusion to the Korean dynastic ode *Yongbi ŏch'ŏn'ga* and the first hexagram of the Chinese *I Ching* (Book of Changes) to which the former alludes.

Summer Scenes

Below the pair of gnarled pines at the fishing hole,
I let the boat drift as it will.
Before I know it I've passed the isle
where red smartweed and white duckweed bloom
and the prow of the boat nudges
the Dragon sandbar below Hwanbyŏk Hall.
Enraptured by the evening sunset
the boys tending cattle
on the grassy banks of the clear river
trill on their flutes
while the dragon dozing beneath the water
seems to wake and rise.
The crane has left its nest and,
coming through the mist,
seems to soar through half the sky.

Winter Scenes

Scattering the leaves piled in the mountains
the North Wind marshals banks of clouds
and comes driving the snow.
The Lord of Heaven luxuriously
makes flowers of jade
and beautifully decorates
the countless trees of a myriad forests.
The rapids before us are frozen solid
and the lone plank bridge is all askew.
That old monk with his stick on his shoulder,
toward what monastery might he be going?

With the *sijo* Korean verse was able to shake off centuries of accumulated Chinese tradition in poetry. The brief, three-line *sijo* proved remarkably suitable to the Korean poetic imagination. It quickly became the most popular of Korean verse forms, and *sijo* were written by generals and statesmen, by *kisaeng* and kings. Rural pleasures, loyalty to the monarch, and reflective or philosophical themes were common, but *sijo* were written on almost every subject imaginable. Yun Sŏndo (1587–1617) is considered by many to be the greatest of *sijo* authors, but the range of choice is truly so vast that it is difficult even to choose a verse or so to illustrate the form.

In the following *sijo* Sŏng Sammun (1418–1456), one of the six ministers executed for involvement in the attempted restoration of Tanjong, speaks of his loyalty toward the deposed monarch, using the common symbols of the evergreen pine tree to denote constancy and the white snow for adversity.

> *What shall I become*
> *when I die?*
> *A towering pine*
> *on the highest peak of Mount Pongnae.*
> *And when snow blankets Heaven and Earth*
> *Lone and green I'll stand.*

Of a less serious nature is this *sijo* by U T'ak (1263–1343):

> *A staff in one hand,*
> *brambles in the other;*
> *I'd block the path of age*
> *with brambles*
> *And drive off white hairs*
> *with the staff.*
> *But the white hairs knew this beforehand*
> *and came by another road.*

The joining of several *sijo* together to form linked verse was particularly popular for exploring the possibilities of subjects such as boating, angling, or rustic pleasures in the four seasons. Of all traditional Korean poetic forms, the *sijo* alone seems to have been capable of expressing the Korean spirit.

The development of Korean prose forms in the early Yi period was a continuation of older traditions and was dominated by Chinese influence. Adaptations of Chinese works were made in which the setting was changed to Korea, names of persons and places changed, and episodes added or deleted. The earliest of these adaptations was Kim Sisŭp's *Kŭmo sinhwa* (New Tales from Mount Kŭmo), which drew from the *Chien-teng hsin-hua* of Ch'u Yu (1341–1433), a work widely imitated in Ming China, Korea, and Japan. The *Kŭmo sinhwa*, a collection of short tales with tragic endings, continues the heavy emphasis upon the supernatural found in the earlier *ch'uan-ch'i* tales, but adds new elements in that more attention is given to characterization and to plot.

The older tradition continued in works like the *Hwasa* (History of the

Flowers). This moralizing personification tale which appeared in the late sixteenth century has been attributed to Im Che (1549–1587). Arranged in what is implied chronological order after the manner of dynastic histories, the author reserved a place for his own comments in the form of "Comments of the Historian." The story is an unabashed attack on factionalism and Buddhism and contains in its own fashion a summary of the ills of the Yi dynasty body politic. Its ultimate answer to malpractices in government is that the ruler should have "good" ministers, "good" in the Confucian terms of individual moral character. In the "Concluding Remarks" the author observes:

> Flowers may spring forth on rocky elevations or amid fetid fields, yet they do not fight for high or low position, to be noble or commoner, but blossom alike.

COURT SPECTACULARS

Although little is known of popular performances during the early Yi dynasty, there is considerable information available on the elaborate performances sponsored by the court. One of these was held on New Year's eve in the halls and gardens of the Ch'anggyŏng palace with performances by *kisaeng* dancing girls and with singing boy performers at the nearby Ch'angdŏk palace. The performances, which lasted all night long, were held to exorcise evil. One of the more spectacular was the fire-viewing ceremony put on by the government armory. As the monarch watched from Pine Tree Hill in the rear garden of the palace attended by civil and military officials of the first and second ranks, numerous pyrotechnic displays were presented. In one of these a cannon was turned into a gigantic firecracker by stuffing it with gunpowder and ramming the barrel shut with thick paper. When the cannon exploded, thousands of fire-arrows were shot through the night sky from a nearby mountain, giving every appearance, it is related, of a meteor tracing through the sky.

PAINTING

Painting during the early Yi period was patronized principally by the court and the *yangban* elite. Professional painters associated with the Office of Court Painters (*Tohwasŏ*) produced formal and idealized court portraits, academic landscape paintings for screens and fans, and the like upon order. Under court influence Chinese styles and motifs dominated Korean painting. The professional artist was also the court photographer of his day and depicted not only grand occasions at court but also significant events of the period such as the conquest of rebel strongholds and other government victories.

Gentlemen painters of the scholar-official class had an early introduction to art, as calligraphy was a normal part of the curriculum of every *yangban* youth. Yet the amateur ideal persisted since professionalism implied *chungin* status. Rapidly executed ink drawings on silk were predictably popular among the leisure class. One of the great gentleman painters of the sixteenth century was An Kyŏn (1501–1560), famed for his landscapes in the academic style.

An excellent representative of the gentleman of leisure of this period is Kang Hŭian (1419–1464) of Chinju, a small town in the Korean southeast. Kang followed his father in an official career and like most of the *yangban* of his day had wide interests. He accompanied a Korean embassy to China, where he was able to see the works of Chinese painters at first hand. He was particularly adept at the three-fold construction involving painting, verse composition, and calligraphy. Kang also had an avid interest in flower raising, which had become popular at court in the early fourteenth century when a Mongol princess introduced numerous flowering plants from the continent. This interest is reflected in his widely circulated manual on flower raising *Ch'ŏngch'ŏn hwasorok*, which introduced, among other things, the cultivation of the Japanese azalea to Korean gentlemen of leisure.

PERSECUTIONS OF THE BUDDHISTS

By the beginning of the Yi dynasty Buddhism had lost state patronage. The Chu Hsi oriented bureaucratic elite not only withdrew their patronage from Buddhism but launched a strong attack against it. This was spearheaded by Chŏng Tojŏn, a particularly vehement opponent of Buddhism. The view that Buddhism was destroying society and was an evil to which monarchs in particular should be alert found widespread expression in Korean literature as well.

An extensive proscription of Buddhism was implemented in the fifteenth century. Monasteries lost their tax exempt status, and a limit was placed on the number of novices permitted to become monks. Although the opposition of the literati to Buddhism involved differences in moral and philosophical principles and positions, it is nonetheless interesting to note that the proscriptions coincided with a period when surplus land for official positions was in short supply and when Buddhist texts, images, and monastery bells were in great demand in trading activities with Japan. In 1406, a wide-scale confiscation of monastery lands and slaves was begun. Strict regulations limited the number of monks at each of the 242 remaining monasteries as well as the number of slaves and the amount of land allowed. This proscription was continued by King Sejong with a prohibition on monastery construction (1423), confiscation of all save some thirty-six monasteries (1424) which together were allowed to hold 80,000 Korean acres (*kyŏl*) o land. The result of these actions would almost double the amount of land on the government tax registers. Sejong further merged the seven Buddhist schools into the two schools of Kyo and Zen.

Ironically, in the final years of his reign this same ruler, grief-stricken at the death of his queen, turned to Buddhism for solace and installed a Buddhist shrine inside the palace over the protests of his ministers. King Sejo, Sejong's second son, continued to patronize Buddhism under the influence of the great Zen translator Sinmi, who had been his confidant since his youth. A more confirmed patron of the faith than his father, Sejo believed that he had witnessed an appearance of Avalokiteśvara on a visit to the monastery of Sangwŏn-sa in 1461. Sejo's most notable acts of faith were the construction of Wŏn'gak-sa monastery in Seoul and the establishment of an office to translate and print Buddhist texts.

Succeeding monarchs were not always so kind. In 1507 the monk examinations were abolished and with them all official sanction for Buddhism. The occasional patronage of the royal family proved insufficient to restore Buddhism to anything remotely resembling its past glories. The widespread destruction of monasteries, particularly in the southeast, during the Japanese invasions, was a crushing blow. It is a tribute to the strength of local patronage and to Buddhist abilities in commerce that the monasteries were rebuilt in the final centuries of the Yi dynasty. The monasteries were at this time at a low ebb politically and economically while dependent upon attracting novices from the lower social groups. Wood-block reprinting of Buddhist works was continued by monasteries, among which texts of the mystic Chinon (j. Shingon) school—introduced into Korea in 664—were popular but the grand period had passed.

RELATIONS WITH MING CHINA

Among the immediate concerns of the founders of the Yi dynasty was to obtain recognition of their legitimacy from Ming China and to secure support for their authority. When the Ming court demanded a change in the name of the state, still called Koryŏ, the Koreans requested they select between the names Chosŏn and Taenyŏng, the latter being an alternate name for the birthplace of Yi T'aejo. Chosŏn was selected, and in early 1393 it became the official designation of the state. Although relations with Ming China were established on a more or less cordial basis, Ming recognition of the legitimacy of the Yi rulers was not immediately forthcoming.

One of the problems of Ming-Chosŏn relations concerned the Jürče peoples of southern and eastern Manchuria and involved territorial claims to the area, particularly the Yalu and Tumen River regions they occupied. The boundary question remained unsettled until the Jürčen people themselves came to power in China. Prior to the establishment of the Ch'ing dynasty Jürčen attacks on Korean settlements and Korean campaigns to conquer the Yalu-Tumen River areas were periodic occurrences. The Ming authorities were also suspicious of a possible alliance between the Koreans and the Jürčen, particularly when the Korean authorities began bestowing titles on Jürčen chieftains. The new Korean emphasis on national history during this period made Koreans strongly aware that southern Manchuria as far west as the Liao River was the ancient territory of Koguryŏ. Large Korean communities existed in such major cities as Liao-yang, while Koreans probably made up the majority of the population in the area of Manchuria just beyond the Yalu.

Another problem involved the founder of the new Korean dynasty. The Ming records reported that Yi Inim and his son—whom they identified as Yi Tan, i.e., Yi Sŏnggye—had murdered the last four monarchs of Koryŏ. The Korean court sent an embassy to Nanking in 1403 to petition for deletion of the offending passage. Then in 1518 members of a Korean embassy returned to report that the shocking accusation had been published in the compendium of Ming statutes, the *Ta-Ming hui-tien*. This controversy was never completely resolved to the satisfaction of the Korean authorities despite numerous Korean embassies to the Chinese court. In the late seventeenth century the Chinese version of the deposing of the Korean ruler Kwanghaegun was found objectionable; other incidents of a similar nature involving the manner in which certain Yi monarchs had gained the throne arose in the late eighteenth and mid-nineteenth centuries as well.

A final matter was the reluctance of the Korean authorities to supply cavalry mounts to the Ming in the amounts demanded. The Ming court reacted by holding several Korean envoys hostage and had several embassies turned back. In early 1398 a proposal was even discussed which called for an invasion of Korea, a proposition the Ming Emperor rejected.

Relations improved greatly when Prince Yi Pangwŏn was sent to the Ming court as a hostage. The dynastic legitimacy of the house of Yi was finally recognized by the emperors of China when this prince, canonized T'aejong, took the throne of Chosŏn. From that point relations were stabilized with Ming China and became the cornerstone of the Korean foreign policy.

Korea's "China policy" was carried out under the phrase *sadae* (subservience to the mighty), a term drawn from the ancient Chinese text *Tso chuan*. Another phrase popular at this time was the expression *mohwa* (adoration of China), whose *locus classicus* is the Chinese work *Li Chi*. This might be compared to the advice given to his Roman countrymen by Horace in his *Ars Poetica* (ca. 20 B.C.) to study the Greek models night and day.

Four Korean embassies a year wound their way across Manchuria and down to Peking, the northern Ming capital, where they were lodged in the Hui-tung Inn. An essential part of the relations with China was the tribute trade. Horses were a principal ingredient in the early years. In the 31 years from 1392 to 1422, some 45,000 horses are recorded as having been sent to Ming; some 26,000 oxen were also sent in two periods, viz., 1403 and 1430 to 1431. The steady Ming demand for horses seems to have provided a stimulus for horse raising and breeding. There were some fifteen state-operated horse ranches in the early Yi period, with an estimated breeding stock of 24,000 head. A number of works on veterinary science, such as the *Maŭisŏ* (Equinary Medicine), were also published.

KOREAN-JŪRČEN RELATIONS

Ming control over Manchuria was exercised through a number of military garrisons and through effective use of the tribute system to maintain a separation of the various branches of the Jŭrčen peoples. Horse markets were established at Kai-yüan, Huang-ning, and Wu-sun, areas of Manchuria firmly controlled by the Ming military. These markets supplied the Ming authorities with cavalry mounts useful in their campaigns against the Mongols and furnished the Jŭrčen people with agricultural implements, textiles, and a variety of luxury items. Ming authority in eastern Manchuria was relatively weak, and the Jŭrčen people there were practically autonomous.

The Korean policy combined the tribute trade system and a conquer-and-absorb program. Markets were established at the border cities of Kyŏngwŏn and Kyŏngsŏng in 1405. These cities, successors to the Koryŏ period monopoly market at Chŏngp'yŏng, also served as entrepôts for Jŭrčen delegations to the Korean capital. Jŭrčen inns were maintained outside the walls of each principal city on the prescribed routes to Seoul. In the capital the Jŭrčen were lodged at the Inn of Northern Peace, inside the East Gate of the city, a location which provided the maximum physical separation from the Inn of Great Peace, just inside the South Gate of the city, where the Chinese embassies were lodged.

The Korean campaigns northward were begun in the reign of T'aejo with the construction of two walled towns to serve as frontier garrisons and the stationing of ten warships in the upper reaches of the Tumen River, ice-free less than half of the year. Further campaigns during the reign of T'aejong extended the Korean outposts far north of the Tumen River and deep into southern Manchuria, but the fierce resistance of the Jŭrčen peoples soon forced their withdrawal. In the mid-fifteenth century, during the reign of Sejong, internal warfare among the Jürčen peoples provided a long-awaited opportunity, and Korea seized control of all lands south of the Yalu and Tumen Rivers. A number of military stations and walled towns were constructed in the new territories, and settlers were moved into these sparsely settled areas from the heavily populated southern provinces. This colonization occurred over a period of 17 years in the period 1431 to 1447 and essentially set the northern boundaries which mark modern Korea.

There were sporadic encounters along the northern borders, and a particularly large-scale Jürčen attack occurred in the sixteenth century, a few years before the Japanese invasions. The border problem continued to be a sore spot in later Korea-Ch'ing relations.

RELATIONS WITH ASHIKAGA JAPAN

Relations with Japan revolved around the issues of piracy and international commerce, which were not unrelated. In 1418 the head of the Sō clan, hereditary lords of Tsushima, died, and his heir was a young child. Control of affairs passed into the hands of the *Wakō* freebooters. Their subsequent incursions on the Korean coast led to a Korean punitive expedition against them in 1419, which involved some 250 ships and an estimated 17,000 men. About this time Shogun Yoshimitsu of the Ashikaga Bakufu (1392–1568), who apparently was anxious to open trade with both Ming China and Korea, sent word that he would suppress the pirates for a copy of the Korean Tripitaka. A copy in 6,467 volumes was finally sent to his successor the Shogun Yoshimochi in 1423. A quarter of a century later some fifty copies were printed for export to Japan. Campaigns against the pirates of the islands of Iki and Tsushima had been undertaken as early as 1402 by the Ashikaga, but the *Wakō* were not fully overcome until Hideyoshi's

Japanese Trading Settlements in Korea

(After Nakamura Hidetaka, *Nissen kankeishi no kenkyū*, vol. 1, p. 641.)

DATE	Chep'o		Pusanp'o		Yŏmp'o		Total	
	H	I	H	I	H	I	H	I
1466	300	1,200	110	330	36	120	446	1,650
1474	308	1,722	67	323	36	131	411	2,176
	11 temples		2 temples		1 temple		14 Buddhist temples	
1475	308	1,731	88	350	34	128	430	2,209
	11 temples		3 temples		1 temple		15 Buddhist temples	
1493	204	781 (?)	74	288	51	152	329	1,221
	10 temples							
1499	347	2,500	127	453	51	152	525	3,105
	10 temples		4 temples				14 temples	

H Households.
I Individuals.

JAPANESE SETTLEMENT AT CHEP'O

Circle on right is the Japanese settlement at Chep'o. Circle on left is a military garrison. The large square at the top-center is the walled town of Ungch'on, the local administrative center. The rectangles indicate Buddhist monasteries, and the three circles at the bottom are small nearby ports.

SOURCE: From the *Haedong Chegukki* of 1443.

campaigns of 1587 which brought the *daimyō* (feudal lords) of western Japan under firm control.

Increased commercial activities, particularly Korean copper imports and silk exports, led to the establishment of Japanese trading settlements in the three southeastern ports of Naeip'o (or Chep'o), Yŏmp'o, and Pusanp'o. A breakdown of the figures for the year 1475 allows us to see the composition of these settlements more clearly.

	Chep'o	Pusanp'o	Yŏmp'o	Total
Adult male	607	125	42	774
Adult female	605	132	34	771
Elderly male	33	6	8	47
Elderly female	19	8	8	35
Young male	234	40	14	288
Young female	187	34	12	233
Adult Buddhist monks	41	5	1	47
Young Buddhist monks	5	—	—	5

In 1443 a treaty was accorded with the lord of Tsushima governing this trade. Two hundred Korean bushels of rice and of beans were provided as an annual allowance for the lord of Tsushima. Fifty vessels plus four special vessels were permitted to call at the trading ports each year. All were required to obtain a letter of authorization from the lord of Tsushima affixed with his seal. Japanese embassies to Seoul followed one of three prescribed routes to and from the Korean capital. While in the capital they were lodged at the Inn of Eastern Peace, and a separate protocol was maintained according to whether the envoys were from the Ashikaga Bakufu, representatives of such *daimyō* as the Hosokawa, Yamane, or Ōuchi clans, or representatives of the Sō clan. The volume of trade carried by these embassies was large enough to require merchant ships. These ships sailed up the Naktong River and unloaded their cargo, which was packed overland through the Oryŏng Pass in the Sobaek Range and then reloaded on barges near the town of Ch'ungju for transport down through the gorges of the Han River to Seoul.

Korean embassies to the Ashikaga Bakufu were apparently few, the last one being in 1460. Thereafter, Korean missions went only to Tsushima.

The Japanese trading posts in Korea prospered as peninsular outposts of a new era of maritime trade activities which extended from Siam to Seoul. The merchants of Hakata were particularly active in the Korean trade, since that city was a major northern terminus for products from south Asia. A key role in this new era of international commerce was played by the Ryūkyū Islands, which offered a convenient anchorage for the ships of many states plying the long sea routes north and south. After the unification of the islands in 1430 the Ryūkyū merchants themselves became active as middlemen and brokers. Because of the *Wakō* raids, the Ming authorities had closed their ports to unauthorized private trade, and the Japanese were particularly unwelcome. These restrictions may have stimulated the rise of Chinese pirates who, in the late sixteenth century, plagued the coasts of China and Korea and made maritime commerce a high risk venture. These factors increased the commercial importance of the Ryūkyū Islands.

The first embassy from the Ryūkyū Islands arrived in Korea in 1389. Relations were maintained until 1477, during which time some thirteen embassies from the islands visited Korea. The first embassy from Siam arrived in 1391, and in 1393 a Korean embassy was sent to Siam. Several envoys from Java, the first in 1397, also came to Korea. How many Koreans were involved in these far-flung activities is unknown. The naval officer Yang Sŏng, who was shipwrecked in the Ryūkyū Islands, returned to Korea after 8 years to report the existence on the islands of Korean and Chinese communities of over two hundred persons. The Portuguese who had taken Malacca in 1511 and who were engaged in trade in the south mention encountering ships manned by natives of Gores, i.e., Koryŏ. These activities led to the compilation in 1443 of the *Haedong chegukki* by Sin Sukju (1417–1475), the first Korean text on the nations of the Pacific.

In 1510 the Japanese residents in the three ports rioted, which closed the settlements temporarily. They were reopened with a new treaty in 1512 which halved the number of vessels permitted to call annually; an increase of five vessels was later granted.

The total amount of trade carried out in the three southern ports was enormous both in amount and in variety. One of the principal items sought both by the Ashikaga Shoguns and by the Sō clan of Tsushima were Buddhist texts, and thousands of volumes were exported, many taken from temples in the south. The cultural and technological exchange that resulted between the two nations was considerable.

ADMINISTRATIVE STRUCTURE

When Yi Sŏnggye and his followers first came to power, they used the Koryŏ period Central Council (*Todang*, later *Top'yŏngŭisasa*) as a central decision-making apparatus. In 1400 King T'aejong combined the functions of the Central Council and the Chancellery (*Munhabu*) and changed the name to Joint Council (*Ŭijŏngbu*). The Joint Council was the highest government organ, and after 1414 its function was to deliberate matters of national concern. Authority for the daily governmental operations was placed with the six ministries, i.e., Personnel, Finance, Rites, War, Justice, and Public Works. This shift in authority meant a change from the elite council politics of the preceding period to a more bureaucratic structure. One of the results was the compilation and continued supplementation of law codes which detailed regulations, statutes, and procedures for the various ministries, culminating, after several earlier codes, in the *Kyŏngguk taejŏn* of 1469. This volume with its many supplements remained the basic law code of the Yi dynasty.

The Royal Secretariat (*Sŭngjŏngwŏn*), following the merger of the Chancellery with the Joint Council, became the central processing office for all documents in and out from both central and regional administrative offices. It handled correspondence of the king as well. Official posts in the Royal Secretariat were filled by ministers of the Office of Royal Lectures (*Kyŏngyŏnwŏn*), the Office of Historiography (*Ch'unch'ugwan*), and the Office for Drafting Memorials (*Yemun'gwan*). The Royal Secretariat came to have a deliberative and advisory function, while its chief officers sat on the Joint Council.

Three offices whose influence was much greater than their names might appear to warrant were the censorial and advisory organs. Their chief officials were also members of the Joint Council.

The Censorate (*Saganwŏn*) had the function of admonishing the monarch on his personal conduct. Since the correct behavior of the monarch was linked in Confucian theory with the well-being of the state, including natural phenomena, the officials of the Censorate might comment on practically anything. The foundations for criticism were drawn from the ideal concept of monarchal behavior as exemplified in the Chinese classics. The censoring officials were in effect the guardians of orthodoxy.

The Inspectorate (*Sahŏnbu*) investigated the personal history and background of all candidates for public office. The inspector general (*taesahŏn*) had a higher rank than the president of a ministry, which gave the office authority and autonomy. The Inspectorate could approve or disapprove of an appointment to government office. It also debated current policy matters, censured officials, and acted as something in the nature of a court of appeals for contested decisions handed down by the Ministry of Justice.

The Office of Special Counselors (*Hongmun'gwan*), the successor to the Hall of Assembled Scholars (*Chiphyŏnjŏn*), was the authority on the Chinese classics, Chinese and Koryŏ history, and law codes. It functioned to advise the monarch on precedents and was in charge of the writing of all official documents. The Office of Special Counselors included historians who recorded government matters and officials from the Office of Royal Lectures. The office also played an active role in debate and criticism of policies and personnel.

Implementing a decision was a lengthy procedure which involved numerous offices, and every petty detail, including the style of the missive and procedural correctness, was deliberated, criticized, and wrangled over to the extent that the process resembles legislation by negotiation.

REGIONAL ADMINISTRATION

In 1413 the nation was administratively divided into eight provinces or circuits. Towns were designated as centers of administrative regions (*mok*), and the Higher Defense Commands (*Taedohobu*) were the centers of civil and military administration in the provinces. According to the gazetteer *Sejong chiriji*, the regional administration in the early fifteenth century was as shown in the following table:

Yi Dynasty Regional Administration

Provinces	8	Intendant (*Kwanch'alsa*)
Administrative regions	14	Governor (*Moksa*)
Higher Defense Commands	5	Military commander
Defense Commands	34	Military commander
Districts (*kun*) *	101	Prefect (*Kunsu*)
Counties (*hyŏn*)	156	Magistrate (*Hyŏllyŏng*)

*Districts did not necessarily have subordinate counties nor were counties necessarily subordinate only to districts.

The two special cities (*pu*) of Hanyang and Kaesŏng were under the direct control of the central government, while the special cities of Kyŏngju, P'yŏngyang, Chŏnju, and Hamhŭng were in the regional administrative structure. Central government officials were not appointed below the county level. The subcounties (*myŏn*) were under quasi-officials, *hyangban* (rural elite), who were appointed by the regional magistrates to assist them as advisors. The *hyangban* were required to send their sons to the capital as hostages (*kiin*), where they performed menial services. The *hyangban* soon organized, became a power at the local level, and established liaison representatives at the office of the provincial intendant and in the capital to lobby for their interests.

Central government officials were appointed for a period of 3 years, except for the provincial intendant, who received a 1-year appointment. They were by law prohibited from serving in the area of their own ancestral home of record. Each of the regional government offices was divided into a number of offices (*pang*) and were versions in miniature of the central government ministries. Local residents were taken for service in these offices and acted as intermediaries between local officials and the peasantry. There were two categories of these local functionaries. The *hyanggun* (rural constabulary), who acted as guards, performed police functions and supervised local corvée labor parties. The *isŏ* or *ajŏn* "clerks" handled clerical and administrative matters and the collection of taxes and levies. The creation and later institutionalization of this intermediary group between the local government officials and the peasantry played a tragic role in Yi dynasty history. The *ajŏn* clerks were permanent residents of the area, while the central government officials were both unfamiliar with the local area and served on a rotation basis. This meant that the officials tended to rely on the *ajŏn*.

Initial recruitment of the *hyanggun* and *ajŏn* was carried out in the manner of a corvée labor draft, and the luckless individuals selected were required to perform their functions without compensation. These conditions made extortion and corruption a necessity. The result was the transformation of the *ajŏn* and the *hyanggun* into hereditary occupational groups which monopolized local functionary positions and tended to marry within their own group.

While the magistrate was ultimately responsible for his area, in fact he appears to have been left on his own, and his decisions were supported as long as his region remained quiet and he was prompt in forwarding tax quotas and levies of goods. He would make the major decisions, and the *ajŏn* and *hyanggun* would make certain that the peasants carried them out. Many later reformers pointed out the corruption of the *ajŏn*, whom they depicted as a powerful, parasitic force, but there seems to have been little serious consideration given to eliminating them, probably because they had become a necessity. The *ajŏn* and *hyanggun* relieved the *yangban* elite in local posts of any onerous duties and released them to indulge themselves in the study of poetry and the ancient Chinese classics, flower raising, calligraphy, and the composition of verse, and the company of their cronies over a leisurely cup of wine. In short, they were free to enjoy those refined and cultivated pursuits befitting a gentlemanly scholar-official of dignity and position to which the *yangban* elite felt they were entitled by birth. Alert to the romantic and nostalgic cries of the geese winging south over the rugged autumnal splendor of the Korean mountains, the Yi dynasty *yangban* was impervious as his ancestors had been through the centuries to the anguished groans of the peasants.

HYANGYAK (VILLAGE ARTICLES)

The strong orientation of the Yi dynasty scholar-officials to the land made them naturally give consideration to the education of the rural populace in Confucian ethics. This was expressed in many ways and produced an entire literature of its own. These considerations led to the establishment of the *hyangyak* (village articles). The *hyangyak* began as a set of precepts or general moral principles for the guidance of the peasants and turned into an organization at the local level with its own unofficial officials. These organizations were self-governing groups at the local level and had a censoring function. They reported on misconduct and regulated customs to conform to the orthodox Confucian standard. The original motive for establishing the *hyangyak* seems to have been the idealistic one of utilizing them to educate the populace in Confucian practices. The *hyangyak* gave to the *yangban* in the provinces, many of whom had never held official office, an officially recognized ethical-political function which was analogous to some of the duties of an office holder. The local members of the *hyangyak* wrote reports to the central government recommending recognition for those local officials whose behavior conformed to their standards and calling for stern measures to be taken against any who were behaving improperly.

In the *hyangyak* the Koreans were adopting Chu Hsi's revised version of a village institution begun by the brothers Lü in China's Shensi Province centuries before. In the Korean context, however, the institution changed considerably. It is usually said that the first such efforts in Korea were made by the founder of the Yi dynasty, to whom many fine actions were later attributed. The *yuhyangso* of the late Koryŏ period is sometimes considered a forerunner of the *hyangyak*, since it was also unofficial in nature and established to report on rapacious regional officials.

In the early sixteenth century Cho Kwangjo and his clique brought forth the suggestion that the *hyangyak* be established nationwide. Probably the most influential and most widely copied of the various *hyangyak* were the village articles drawn up by the eminent Korean philosopher Yi I for the village of Haeju.

The *hyangyak*, although established for the high principle of instructing villagers in Confucian ethics, had a negative side as well. First, they were controlled by the local elite, i.e., *yangban* and *hyangban*, and immediately took on a bureaucratic air with their own offices and posts. As they had a censorial function as well, they often became more influential than the government officials in the provinces, since they could report the alleged misconduct of any recalcitrant or independent-minded magistrate.

SOCIAL STRUCTURE AND THE EDUCATIONAL SYSTEM

Social classes in the Yi dynasty continued to be clan exogamous, class endogamous, and to be largely occupationally defined. A separate educational structure and government service examination system existed for each of the three groups which made up the ruling and managerial classes, i.e., the civil officials, the military officials, and the *chungin* functionaries. The principal decision makers were the *yangban* members of the civil bureaucracy. Although the term *yangban* meant both civil and military officials, it is generally used to refer to the civil officials alone, since the military officials were considered socially and politically inferior. The *yangban* monopolized bureaucratic positions by a variety of means, including control of the educational system.

The *ŭm* (C. *yin*) system of appointment instituted during the Koryŏ period was retained. The *ŭm* system at this time meant that those qualified by relationship who were at least 20 years old took what amounted to a pro forma examination and then received direct appointment to official posts. The examinations given the *ŭm* candidates amounted to no more than tests of their knowledge of one of the Five Classics and one of the Four Books. The qualification for the *ŭm* privilege extended to the sons, grandsons, sons-in-law, and nephews of merit officials and officials of the second rank and above. The sons and grandsons of those of the third rank qualified, as did the sons of several lesser court ranks, for certain offices.

For the great majority of the *yangban*, however, the road to government appointment was through the education and examination structure. At its best the educational system produced wise and learned men of great dignity and moral principles, who had a respect for learning and seniority; a love of books and antiquity; a fondness for verse, calligraphy, and painting; a deep concern for proper ethical standards in conduct and in attitude; a feeling of close affinity with the rustic life in the countryside; a religious feeling toward their departed ancestors; and a benevolent paternalism toward inferiors. At its worst the system produced doctrinaire and intolerant pedants capable of cruel and malicious acts, all, of course, in the name of the highest principles.

The patents of nobility of the Koryŏ period, viz., duke, marquis, earl, were abolished in 1400 because of the objections of the Ming court and were replaced with the titles of "lord" (*kun*) and "great lord" (*taegun*). In the late sixteenth century the title of *Taewŏn'gun* was created for the non-king father of King Sŏnjo (r. 1567–1608). The title was held by the non-king fathers of two other monarchs, the most famous of whom was the Hŭngsŏn Taewŏn'gun, father of King Kojong, penultimate ruler of Chosŏn.

During the turbulent years of the late Koryŏ and early Yi period and the new opportunities offered during the dynastic change, there was an increase in the number of clans qualifying as *yangban*. The doors to membership in the ruling elite were soon closed, but in terms of participation the political base had been broadened considerably. In this same period government service examinations for military officials were put into effect. The military service provided a safety valve for social tension at the elite level, and the higher ranks were swollen with the *sŏŏl* (see below) and distant relations of high officials and the royal family.

Education and Examination System for Civil Officials

Lower Schools

(Ages 7–8)

Four Seoul Higher Schools
Limit:
100 students annually
(Ages 15–16)

Regional Higher Schools
Limits:
Administrative towns: 90
Military commands: 70
Districts: 50
Counties: 30
(Ages 15–16)

Triennial Lower Examinations

A total of 1,400 candidates admitted for the examinations, 700 for the two-stage examination in poetry, rhyme-prose, memorials, and documentary style leading to the degree of *chinsa*; 700 for the two-stage examination in the Four Books and Five Classics and the degree of *saengwŏn*. The first stage of each examination was held nationwide; the second stage was administered by the Board of Rites in Seoul.

Result: 100 *chinsa* and 100 *saengwŏn* degrees awarded. This qualified the holders for elite status, entry into the Sŏnggyun'gwan Academy, and lower civil positions.

Sŏnggyun'gwan Academy

A limited student body (200) with a residence requirement of 1 year before applying for the higher examinations. Students could also leave for appointment to lower civil offices.

Triennial Higher Examinations

A three-stage examination as follows:

First stage: nationwide examinations given in classics, poetry, documentary style, and the problem essay. Some 340 candidates accepted as eligible for the second stage of the examinations.

Second stage: Examinations conducted by the Board of Rites in the capital. Some 33 candidates selected as successful.

Third stage: Palace examinations in the presence of the king in documentary style, e.g., eulogies, memorials; candidates were ranked by performance. Three were awarded first place, 7 given second place, and the remainder were ranked in third place.

Civil Office

The thirty-three successful candidates were given government appointments with ranks from 6B to 9A, dependent upon their performance in the palace examinations.

Operational and technical matters were handled by the *chungin* functionaries. A hereditary occupational group, the *chungin* filled positions as translators, physicians, court painters, accountants, mathematicians, scribes, judiciary officials, meteorologists, musicians, and specialists in theories of prognostication.

First stage: Examinations in classics, military texts, and military arts for candidates given nationwide by boards of three officials (one civil, two military). Some 15 candidates from each province and 72 candidates from Seoul were selected as successful.

Second stage: Examinations held by the Ministry of War in Seoul for the 192 successful candidates. Some 28 were selected as successful and awarded the degree of *sŏndal*.

Third stage: Grading of the 28 successful candidates (3 first place, 5 second place, 20 third place) through competition in archery, mounted polo, and other military sports.

Intermediate between the *yangban* elite and the *chungin* functionaries were the *sŏŏl*, who were the illegitimate children of *yangban* fathers and lower class females. While these offspring were often given good educations by their fathers, socially their status had been sealed in the reign of King T'aejong, and they faced cruel discrimination by the *yangban* group. They were excluded from the examinations for civil positions and tended to enter military service or to preempt the higher *chungin* functionary positions.

The peasants who made up the bulk of the population were effectively nailed to the land by numerous restrictions, including the *hop'ae* identity tag system and the five-family mutual guarantee system (*ogajakt'ong*). Under the latter, families were organized into units of five households whose members were held jointly responsible for the taxes or service obligations of all members of the unit.

Slavery appears to have increased. If the records may be believed, in 1424 there were 200,000 slaves in the 114 government offices alone. Female slaves in government service were divided into two categories by a simple rule of thumb: if they were plain they became menials called "water fetchers" (*sugŭp*) and if they were attractive they were trained as *kisaeng* (dancing girls) and professional entertainers of government officials. Many of the male slaves were apparently rather independent, maintaining their own homes and paying a tax of one bolt of cloth and twenty sheets of paper money annually for the right to quit at the end of the day and go to their own home. Many private slaves apparently also had this privilege.

ECONOMIC STRUCTURE

Following the burning of the land registers a new land system, the so-called rank-field (*kwajŏn*) system, was put into effect in 1392. The land of the capital province was given to officials in amounts dependent upon their rank. The remainder of the lands went to the royal family, to powerful regional families, to government offices and schools, and to the military, and some were retained as state lands.

The principal difference between the Yi and Koryŏ land systems was the legal recognition of land ownership and the right to buy and sell land. Land could be inherited and was not subject to confiscation except for the most serious crimes. An attempt was made to limit private land ownership to Kyŏnggi Province, but a notice of 1426 informs us that: "The land of the southern provinces is fertile and crops are abundant; over half of the farms and slaves are those of court officials." Lands assigned to support government offices disappeared from the registers and became private holdings. By Sejong's reign there was no longer a surplus of land for distribution to newly appointed officials, who were as a consequence given only quarterly stipends. Prior to this the highest official had received 150 Korean acres of land and a decent stipend. The stipend of a chief official is given in the following table.

Stipend of a Chief Official (Early Chosŏn)

(After *Kosa chwaryo*, ha. 10a.)

Item	Unit	Spring	Summer	Autumn	Winter	Total
Polished rice	Korean bushel	4	3	4	3	14
Unhulled rice	"	12	12	12	12	48
Dry-field rice	"	1	—	1	—	2
Barley	"	—	5	5	—	10
Beans	"	12	—	—	12	24
Silk	Bolt	2	1	1	2	6
Fine cloth	"	4	4	4	3	15
Paper money	Sheet	10	—	—	—	10

The acquisition of new territories in the north ameliorated this situation somewhat, as did the confiscation of large tracts from the Buddhist monasteries. Indeed, the acute land shortage may have been a motivating factor in these actions.

Yangban land holdings were not concentrated but scattered about the country. The literatus Sŏng Sammun, who fell victim to the power struggle in 1456, for example, had estates in eleven different areas of the country. An idea of the situation in the provinces is provided by the following table.

The agricultural system itself took on the characteristics of a landlord-tenant relationship. This development led to the recognition of the right of the peasant to cultivate, i.e., legally he could not be evicted without cause.

Survey of Landownership in Kangwŏn Province, 1435

(After *Sejong sillok* 74.)

Landholdings (in *kyŏl*)	Classification of Family	Number of Households	Percentage
50 plus	Wealthy	10	0.1
20–50	Middle	71	0.6
10–20	Lower	1,641	14.2
6–10	Impoverished	2,043	17.7
5 or less	Beggared	7,773	67.4

More peasants now had the state rather than a private individual as a landlord. The state on its part carried out agricultural policies to ensure successful revenues. As early as 1417 government agricultural offices (*chongnongsa*) were established in the provinces to promote sericulture and agriculture. The growing importance of silk in the trade with Japan led the Ministry of Finance in 1462 to suggest that peasants be required to plant mulberry trees. All commercial trees, such as mulberry, fruit, pine nut, and varnish, were, like everything and everyone, registered with the government. Government relief measures were undertaken in the same light, and peasants in distressed areas repaid government loans of seed grain at interest rates of 20 to 40 percent at the following harvest.

Peasants paid about 50 percent of their harvest to the landowner, and both paid the land tax, which was around 10 percent of the harvest, to the state. The heaviest burden on the peasant was the regional tribute (*kongnap*) levied on households and paid in regional speciality products stipulated in kind and in amount. The regional tribute was assigned to government offices to meet their requirements.

During the reign of King Myŏngjong (r. 1545–1567) the payment of cloth in lieu of military service (*kunp'o*) was instituted. It later became simply another tax. The *ho'pae* identity tag system successfully increased the number of households on the tax registers from 180,000 in the reign of T'aejong when it was instituted to 226,000 by the reign of his son Sejong, or an increase of 28 percent.

The tax burden distinguished the *yangban* and the peasant as vividly as did their tile-roofed houses and thatched huts. The *yangban* paid only the 10 percent land tax. The peasant bore all other burdens. In fact, even the collection of taxes engendered a host of levies on the peasants to pay transportation expenses, damage and loss recovery, paper and supplies for reports, loading and unloading charges, and the hire of private vessels when government ships were unavailable. By the early fifteenth century peasants were desperately trying to free themselves from these burdens by attaching themselves to the estates of *yangban* as outcastes or slaves, since these groups were exempt from the heaviest tax burdens.

PRODUCTION AND TRADE

Products for the royal household, government officials, and government offices were provided by state-operated manufactories. There were some 30 of them in the capital producing 129 different items and engaging almost 3,000 workers. Other manufactories were located in the provinces, particularly in the three southern provinces of Kyŏngsang, Ch'ungch'ŏng, and Chŏlla, with a labor force of some 3,500 workers. Some manufactories such as ceramic works had hundreds of workers, and the division of labor was highly specialized while other manufactories for the production of such items as carved official seals, fans, and combs might have as few as two artisans assigned as the following table indicates.

Major Government Manufactories in the Provinces

(After *Kyŏngguk taejŏn* of 1469.)

Manufactured Items	Workers	Manufactured Items	Workers
Paper	678	Paints, lacquers	311
Metal smelting	464	Varnished items	179
Cushions	385	Enamelers	99
Arrows	370	Armor	50
Bows	277	Brassware	36
Bow-strings	76	Ceramic finishers	24
Wooden articles	340	Ink	20
Leather products	312	Boxes and coffers	12

Small-scale commercial enterprises had existed in the old Koryŏ capital of Kaesŏng, and when King T'aejong moved to Seoul in 1405, it is related that some 800 shops were built which the state leased to merchants. These shops purchased goods needed by the royal household and the central government and disposed of surplus items from government storehouses. By the late Yi period some of these shops had developed into large-scale monopoly enterprises (*yugijŏn*), while Kaesŏng had become a principal commercial city.

The considerable commercial activity generated by international trade had led to a severe shortage of copper, gold, and silver. Precious metals were in high demand by the Japanese feudal lords, who used gold and silver bullion as a monetary reserve. This led to several prohibitions against the export of these metals and to issuance of paper currency which soon became inflated. A new issue of copper coins was tried in 1424 when the *Chosŏn t'ongbo* (Circulating Treasure of Chosŏn) was struck, but it and other issues of coins were quickly drained away by Japanese merchants. The result was a continued reliance on grain and cloth as mediums of exchange. Cotton, which had been introduced in the mid-fourteenth century, gained in importance following the construction of a cotton gin and spinning and reeling equipment—traditionally accredited to Mun Ikchŏm (1329–1398)—and was soon being cultivated extensively. During the late fifteenth century cotton cloth became a principal medium of exchange in commercial transactions including payment of taxes, and cotton became an important "cash crop" for the peasant.

CERAMICS

One of the products of the government manufactories was the distinctive ceramic ware of the period. While there was the expected continuation of Koryŏ wares, particularly the black-glazed and white-glazed Koryŏ pieces, there was a noticeable departure from the forms of the earlier period. The government kilns now catered to the demands of the court and the scholar-official, with the result that the accoutrements of the writing table, e.g., water droppers and brush holders, replaced the forms dictated by a Buddhist-oriented elite of the Koryŏ period. The late Koryŏ white porcelain was widely manufactured for use in the palace. Under the influence of the Ming blue and white porcelain wares the Korean potters began to paint underglazed designs in cobalt blue, obtained at high price from abroad, while continuing the underglazed techniques using iron brown and copper red practiced in the late Koryŏ period.

Perhaps more widely known than these wares is the Korean *punch'ong* ware, a heavy, unpretentious stoneware decorated by a number of techniques, including overglazing and underglazing with a translucent celadon glaze, painting over the white slip, and incising. The *punch'ong* stoneware was in wide use in Korea and formed an important item in trade with Japan.

There is also a noticeable change in shape and design. The molding of vessels in the many varieties of floral and animal shapes gives way to less elaborate forms with simpler lines. The lotus leaf and elaborate, geometrically arranged designs are replaced by designs of wild flowers, bamboo blades, and incised or painted fish.

The wars of the late sixteenth to early seventeenth centuries were particularly devastating to the ceramic industry. *Punch'ong* artisans captured and taken to Japan produced their stoneware under a new name: Mishima ware. Yet the government kilns continued to turn out high-quality work for the palace until the late years of the dynasty.

THE DEVELOPMENT OF THE KOREAN SŎNGNI (NATURE AND REASON) SCHOOL

In the Sung period (960–1279) Confucianism in China underwent a sweeping revitalization at the hands of the Sung philosophers. During this process it evolved into a highly sophisticated and abstract philosophy concerned with the origins of the universe and of all in it. It drew from many sources including Buddhism and Taoism, and when the great philosophers such as Chu Hsi had finished putting their touches to it, it was sufficiently developed to prevail over Buddhism and the existing mystically oriented popular religions.

The early development of the Chu Hsi or *sŏngni* school in Korea during the late Koryŏ and early Yi period took place when external threats from the Jürčen tribes on the northern borders and the *Wakō* incursions combined to heighten the internal instability caused by the change in dynasties. These conditions apparently made Korean intellectuals more receptive to new ideas. At any rate, they did increasingly accept the doctrines of Chu Hsi. Scholars such as Yi Chehyŏn, Kil Chae, and Chŏng Mongju, through their expository writings and their actions in making the doctrines of Chu Hsi the basis of the curriculum in the National Academy, laid the foundations for its acceptance by Korean intellectuals. The intellectual challenge which faced Korean proponents of the *sŏngni* school of refuting the propositions of Buddhism was taken up by Chŏng Tojŏn. Chŏng in his *Pulssi chapp'yŏn* (Comments on Mister Buddha) launched a scathing attack upon the Buddhist views of cause and effect retribution, transmigration, and the Buddhist version of hell. Although the writings of Chŏng Tojŏn and those who followed in his path provided the intellectual climate during which the confiscation of monastery lands was carried out, they also probed deeply into the philosophic questions raised by the Sung philosophers, and in so doing they took the first step toward the development of a distinctively Korean *sŏngni* school.

One of the tenets of the teaching of Chu Hsi was the mutual interaction of the inseparable universal principles *i* (c. *li*), which is often translated "reason," and *ki* (c. *ch'i*) often translated "vital force." If we view these as opposing principles, then *i* might represent such intangibles as logic, intuition, moral principles, or subjectivity, and *ki* might include energy, activity, substance, or objectivity. In the early sixteenth century *Hwadam** Sŏ Kyŏngdŏk (1489–1546) had raised the question of the inseparability of these principles by taking a monist position stressing *ki* in his *Li-ki-sŏl* (A Discussion of *I* and *Ki*). This was followed by the rise of a Korean dualist school which stressed the primacy of either *i* or *ki*.

The greatest exponent of the reason or *i* school (which stressed *i* as the basis for *ki*) was *T'oegye** Yi Hwang (1501–1570). The emphasis of this school was upon cultivation of moral character, learning, and reflection to perfect the self. The influence of this school of thought became strong in the

---

*Hwadam and *T'oegye* are the literary names respectively of Sŏ Kyŏngdŏk and Yi Hwang.

Kyŏngsang area where Yi Hwang was born. *T'oegye's* short tract *Chasongnok* of 1558 was especially influential in Japan, where his works were introduced to Japanese intellectuals by Yamazaki Ansai (1618–1682).

Opposing these views was a school of thought which took the position that *ki* was the controlling agent or prime mover of *i*. *Yulgok** Yi I (1536–1584) was the greatest representative of this vital force or *ki* school, which stressed practical intellectual activity, education, and experience. *Yulgok,* whose mother was the noted painter Sin Saindang (1512–1559), was venerated throughout Chŏlla and Kyŏngsang Provinces. During his youth *Yulgok* had spent several years in meditation and thought at a remote Buddhist monastery in the rugged scenic beauty of the Diamond Mountains. He was a younger contemporary of *T'oegye,* whom he once visited, and a close friend of the scholar-official and poet Chŏng Ch'ŏl. While he wrote many works dealing with Confucian philosophy, *Yulgok* also put forth several plans to reform the government administration. And in 1583, the year before his death and less than a decade before the Japanese invasions, he proposed the training of a large army reserve corps of 100,000 men. Although most of *Yulgok's* proposals were never implemented in his lifetime he left a legacy in his stress on practical studies that would later be carried on by others.

While other philosophical schools of China were known in Korea, the Chu Hsi school became dominant as the state orthodoxy after a considerable amount of time. In time, however, the patronage of a powerful bureaucracy and the incorporation of the works of Chu Hsi into the educational curriculum—the *Chuja karye* (c. Chu Hsi *Chia li*), a work on proper behavior and ceremonies for all occasions, was standard in the lower schools—ensured the primacy of the Chu Hsi school in Korea.

THE USURPATION OF KING SEJO

In 1450 King Sejong died. Not as prolific as Priam, he left only eighteen sons. His eldest son, Hang, had been made crown prince in 1421, and for two decades had assisted his father in state affairs. His health was already failing when he took the throne in 1450. Aware that he would not have a lengthy reign, he immediately invested his 10-year-old son as crown prince. Yi Hang, canonized Munjong (r. 1450–1452), held the throne barely 2 years and died. The throne passed to the crown prince, later given the temple name Tanjong (r. 1452–1455), who was then 12 years old. King Munjong, realizing that the young prince would have a difficult time surviving the ambitions of his uncles, had entrusted the boy's welfare to his closest advisors. These included Hwangbo In (d. 1453)—a scion of a military family who had dis-

---

* *Yulgok* is the literary name of Yi I.

tinguished himself on the northern frontier and whose father had been a general under Yi Sŏnggye—Kim Chongsŏ (1390–1453)—a powerful minister who had gained fame in establishing six military garrisons in the northeast to secure the area for Korea—and the influential Sŏng Sammun (1418–1456), whose father had been a ranking military officer. King Munjong placed his greatest hopes for his young son's future in the scholars of the Hall of Assembled Scholars, with whom he had been closely associated both during his father. King Sejong's reign and his own.

The chief contenders for the throne in the power struggle which erupted following King Munjong's passing were Tanjong's uncles. These were Sejong's second son—the lord of Suyang, who had the backing of the army —and Sejong's third son—the lord of Anp'yŏng (1418–1453), a noted calligrapher favored by many literati. In 1453 the lord of Suyang made his bid for power. Alleging a plot, Kim Chongsŏ, Hwangbo In, and their sons were killed. The lord of Anp'yŏng was banished to Kanghwa Island and "presented with death," a euphemistic way of saying he was forced to take his own life. These moves triggered a short-lived revolt in the northeast by Yi Chingok, and many government officials resigned in protest. Thirty-seven of the lord of Suyang's followers were made merit subjects following these actions. Two years later in 1455, the lord of Suyang, canonized Sejo (r. 1455–1468), deposed young King Tanjong, whom he kept under guard in a separate part of the palace, and took the throne himself. Some forty-one of his supporters were awarded the prestigious title of merit subject upon this occasion.

These actions served to rally the scholar-officials of the Hall of Assembled Scholars to the cause of the young Tanjong. They carefully laid plans to carry out a restoration movement to be set in motion during the state visit of an embassy from Ming China in the summer of 1456. As this plot came to light, another restoration attempt led by one of Sejo's brothers, the lord of Kŭmsŏng, surfaced in the autumn of the same year. The severity of the purges which followed was marked not only by the elimination of the individuals directly involved but by the murder of their sons and grandsons as well. Several hundred of those involved in or linked to the restoration bids were branded as criminals, killed, or banished. Representative were the Six Martyrs (*Sayuksin*), whose number included Song Sammun. Six other high ministers who resigned from government service in protest became known as the *Saengyuksin* (Six Ministers Who Lived). Among the latter was Kim Sisŭp (1435–1493), who in retirement would write the prototype of Korea's first novel.

The lord of Kŭmsŏng was jailed in the military town of Andong in southeast Korea. Tanjong's mother, Queen Dowager Hyŏndŏk, was demoted to the status of commoner and exiled. The young monarch Tanjong was sent under military guard into exile at Yŏngwŏl, on the mountainous east coast. He was demoted to commoner status and killed. He was seventeen. The tragic death of this young ruler became the subject of a widespread literature, for example in the historical tale *Pyŏngjarok* (Record of 1456), as did the Six Martyrs and Six Ministers Who Lived as exemplars of courageous loyalty to the king.

The blood bath he instituted to secure the throne may have been an element in King Sejo's intense patronage of Buddhism. Feelings for and against the usurpation ran bitter and deep, and generations of Korean intellectuals would be profoundly influenced by these events. The cruel purges which put Sejo on the throne and kept him there opened fractures in Yi dynasty society which would never heal.

THE REIGNS OF KINGS SEJO AND SŎNGJONG

King Sejo proved to be an iron-handed ruler with a strong personal involvement in military affairs. This interest is evidenced in the many books on military matters compiled at this time. This monarch also carried out a reorganization of the military system. Perhaps the most bizarre effort along these lines was the reported issue of iron coins, *P'albang t'ongbo* (Circulating Treasure of the Eight Regions). Cast in the shape of a willow leaf, the coins were intended to serve in time of peace as coins and in time of war as arrowheads, unfortunately none has ever been found, so their actual existence is speculative.

A practicing Buddhist, Sejo established an office to print Buddhist texts and had the large monastery of Wŏn'gak-sa with its graceful and elegant thirteen-tiered granite stupa constructed inside the walls of Seoul in 1464. The state-sponsored intellectual activity of the previous decades did not diminish. Among the works compiled during Sejo's reign was Sŏ Kang's text on silkworm raising *Chamsŏ chuhae* (1458); other works appeared on cattle raising and medicine. The Yi dynasty codex, *Kyŏngguk taejŏn*, was completed in 1469, the year following his death.

Sejo was succeeded by one of his sons, a lad of eighteen, canonized Yejong (r. 1468–1469), who ruled a brief 14 months and died. During this period the government was in the hands of his mother, Queen Dowager Yun. To assist her in ruling, she instituted the system of *wŏnsang*, the title of an official who was something like a prime minister, with Sin Sukchu (1417–1475) as the first appointee. Upon the death of Yejong, Queen Yun steered another of her sons to the throne. This lad, canonized Sŏngjong (r. 1460–1494), was thirteen at the time. His lengthy reign was marked by several successful campaigns against the Jürčen tribes in the north, troubles in the royal household, and an intellectual activity surpassed in brilliance only during the reign of his remarkable ancestor King Sejong. Among the state-sponsored works of this period were the *Tongguk t'onggam* (1484), a general history of Korea; *Tongmunsŏn* (1478) and *Tongin sihwa* (1474), anthologies of verse and prose in Chinese by Korean writers; *Tongguk yŏji sŭngnam* (1486), a gazetteer of the entire nation; *Kukcho oyeŭi* (1474), which stan-dardized all ceremonies; and the *Akhak kwebŏm* (1493), a text on music, dance, and songs performed at court.

The trouble in the royal household centered around Sŏngjong's second wife, Queen Yun, who because of alleged arbitrary actions was deposed, reduced to the status of a commoner, and poisoned. This incident was to have widespread repercussions when her son Yŏnsan'gun (r. 1494–1506), later succeeded to the throne.

PURGES OF THE LITERATI

Among the many accomplishments of Sŏngjong's long and fruitful rule was the expansion of the Office of Special Counselors (*Hongmun'gwan*), which together with the Office of the Censor-General and the Office of the Inspector-General, had become a haven for an ambitious group of younger scholars. The Office of Special Counselors was closely linked with the Office of Royal Lectures (*Kyŏngyŏn*) and the National Academy (*Sŏnggyun'gwan*) and became a new organ of remonstrance, powerful through the personal contact its members had with the monarch.

The young scholars of these offices came from out-of-power clans in the countryside, particularly from the southeastern province of Kyŏngsang, and gained the name of *Sallim* (mountain and forest) group. The central figure around which this group constellated and began its rise to national prominence was Kim Chongjik (1431–1492). The *Sallim* scholars were associated with the *sŏngni* (nature and reason) school, which is to say they were strict followers of Chu Hsi orthodoxy. They traced their traditions to the Koryŏ loyalist Kil Chae (1353–1419), a disciple of the murdered Chŏng Mongju. The latter was later enshrined as the patriarch of the *sŏngni* school in Korea. The *Sallim* scholars tended to be bright, young, and idealistic, and they soon began to use the advisory and censorial offices to increase their influence. Their most powerful weapons were moral arguments based upon Neo-Confucian principles, which they used to secure appointments for their supporters, to implement changes in the existing government structure, and to impeach their enemies. Dogmatic and uncompromising, they were extremely intolerant of those who did not share their views. They increased the authority of the advisory and censorial offices and changed the political role of these organs to that of political elimination. Highly reform-minded, they based many of their recommendations on firm ground, but they also freely used character assassination and malicious and unsupported charges against even the highest officials. Their constant debate and criticism of policies, even after decisions had been reached, eroded the authority of monarch and minister alike, while their campaigns of vilification and slander resulted in the dismissal of scores of higher ministers, including merit subjects, presidents of ministries, provincial governors, and countless lower echelon officials.

When King Sŏngjong died, he was succeeded to the throne by Yŏnsan'gun (r. 1494–1506), an independent-minded monarch who was apparently determined to exercise the full authority of his position. Members of the censorial and advisory offices, however, by their constant criticism of all authority save their own effectively thwarted any such plans.

Firmly entrenched in the central government were the conservative merit subjects who were members of powerful and influential families which had risen to prominence by supporting King Sejo to the throne. In general, this group tended to look upon the *Sallim* scholars as brash upstarts. They also differed with the *Sallim* scholars over what they considered to be an overemphasis on the study of the classics and a disregard for the literary arts. These differences provided a backdrop for the four violent purges, *sahwa* (calamities of the scholars), which occurred in the years 1498, 1504, 1519, and 1545.

In 1498 Yi Kukton associated with the conservatives and then in the Bureau of Historiography (*Ch'unch'ugwan*) made an attempt to settle an old grudge against Kim Ilson, a *Sallim* member of the bureau. Kim had once submitted a memorial accusing Yi of misconduct and of factionalism while the latter was an official in Chŏlla Province. Yi now submitted his own charges to the effect that Kim was asserting a malicious slander of King Sejo which had its origins with the now-dead Kim Chongjik. This report found its way to the influential minister Yu Chagwang, who saw in it a chance to avenge an old grudge against Kim Chongjik and his followers. Yu sought the support of other ministers, and they put the matter before the monarch as a case of treason. The purge which resulted compounded ancient animosities and went further than its initiators anticipated. Five of the more prominent *Sallim* scholars were killed, and some two dozen others were either banished or dismissed from office. The coffin of Kim Chongjik was dug up, and his skeleton chopped up in posthumous punishment. Yi Kukton, who had triggered the purge, was himself dismissed from office for not reporting the matter promptly.

Since these actions were aimed at specific individuals, they did not diminish the activities of the *Sallim* members of the censorial and advisory offices, who continued as they had in the past despite numerous pronouncements by Yŏnsan'gun that he was determined to end all attacks against constituted authority. This he attempted to do by abolishing the Office of Censor-General, the Office of Special Counselors, and the Office of Royal Lectures. The result of Yŏnsan'gun's attempts to consolidate authority apparently led to an estrangement between the palace and the bureaucracy.

At this point, Im Sahŏng, a member of a clan which had furnished sons-in-law for royal princesses of the two previous monarchs, submitted a confidential report to Yŏnsan'gun concerning the death of the monarch's mother, Lady Yun. Yŏnsan'gun had been only four at the time and apparently knew none of the details behind his mother's death. Im's report implicated Lady Ŏm and Lady Chŏng, who were seized and beaten to death. Their sons the lord of Anyang and the lord of Pongan were also killed. Yŏnsan'gun appears to have been held back somewhat from further actions by his grandmother, but after her death a widespread purge began against those reportedly involved in the poisoning of Lady Yun. Once begun the purge seemed to gather its own momentum, and it was probably without precedent for the cruel ferocity with which it was carried out. Scores were killed; the dead were disinterred and their corpses hacked up. The alleged crimes of individuals were passed on to their families and clans. Finally the point was reached where the only way to restore order was to remove royal sanction for the purge. The chief court officials banded together, and with a royal order from Dowager Yun they deposed Yŏnsan'gun.

The reinstatement and return to power of the survivors of the *Sallim* group was a natural consequence of the overthrow of Yŏnsan'gun. Those who had been killed in the purges were transformed from criminals and traitors into martyrs and national heroes. Yŏnsan'gun was subsequently vilified by the historians, who accused him, among other things, of turning Wŏn'gak-sa monastery into a house of pleasure, of making a stable out of Hŭngch'ŏn-sa monastery, the headquarters of the Zen school, of violating the maiden daughters of court officials, of sending out teams of officers to select beautiful girls from towns throughout the country for his pleasure, and of seizing the land and dwellings of some 20,000 commoners on the outskirts of the capital. Yŏnsan'gun was denied the customary laudatory title of "progenitor" (*cho*) or "ancestor" (*chong*) and given the lowest title "lord" (*-gun*).

The chief ministers who deposed Yŏnsan'gun put Prince Yŏk, King Sŏngjong's second son, then eighteen, on the throne. This was Chungjong (r. 1506–1544), whose reign was marked by the opposition of the merit subjects who raised him to the throne and the *Sallim* group whose power radiated from the revived censorial and advisory offices. Chief representative of the *Sallim* group was Cho Kwangjo (1482–1519), who had through his positions in the Office of Special Counselors and the Office of the Inspector-

General won the support of Chungjong. Among the innovations which Cho and his group initiated were the *hyangyak* (village code) and the recommendation examination (*chŏn'gŏgwa*), which was held for the first and only time in 1519. Cho and his group used the recommendation examination to secure appointments for their supporters, while Cho himself secured appointment as Inspector-General in 1519 at the age of thirty-seven. Up to this point Cho and his group had attacked and removed ministers individually, but now at the height of their power they attempted a frontal attack on the merit subjects who had put Chungjong on the throne. They finally succeeded, but it soon proved to be an empty victory. Seventy-six merit subjects of the ninety-nine still living had their titles removed. Chungjong, however, refused to take any further action and pointedly insisted that they be allowed to retain their official court rank and all awards of lands, slaves, and residences which had accompanied their enrollment as merit subjects. The purge of 1519 commenced a few days later, initiated by the combined forces of such powerful figures as the Hong clan who had married into the royal family as well as other senior ministers, all with the acquiescence of Chungjong. The arrest of Cho Kwangjo brought out the students of the Sŏnggyun'gwan, who demonstrated before the palace gate for his release. Cho and some thirty members of his group were exiled, and most were later killed. Those who had tended to sympathize with Cho were dismissed from office. Ironically, the intensity and ferocity of the purge appears to have been largely the work of the censorate itself.

The last purge of the literati occurred in 1545 and was the result of a power struggle between two members of the P'ap'yŏng Yun clan, both of whom had relatives in the royal household. Yun Im (1487–1545) was the younger brother of the Changgyŏng queen, the first wife of Chungjong. She bore the crown prince, who succeeded his father to the throne. This was King Injong (r. 1545). During Injong's brief 8-month reign Yun Im, an exponent of Chu Hsi orthodoxy in the *Sallim* tradition, became a major power figure in the government.

Yun Wŏnhyŏng (?–1565) was the younger brother of the Munjong queen, the second wife of Chungjong. When King Injong died, he was succeeded by this queen's son, Prince Hwan, canonized Myŏngjong (r. 1545–1567). Yun Wŏnhyŏng and his supporters then purged Yun Im and his group from power, utilizing the authority of the censorate to impeach them on charges of lese majesty. The purges continued for several years, resulting in scores executed and hundreds dismissed from office or banished.

A bright era of intellectual activity had been washed away in rivers of blood, and divisions had been created in Korean society which would last as long as the dynasty itself.

THE JAPANESE INVASIONS

At the same time that the Yi dynasty bureaucratic elite was splintering into irreconcilable factions, Japan was undergoing a period of consolidation under Toyotomi Hideyoshi. In 1587 Hideyoshi brought the feudal lords of Kyūshū and western Japan under his control. He then planned the conquest of China. Many reasons have been suggested for this action. A new orientation abroad resulting from the far-flung commercial activities of Japanese merchants and the ranging adventures of the *Wakō* is often mentioned. It has also been said that Hideyoshi desired to turn the military strength of the Japanese feudal lords outward in order to prevent them from using their armies in power clashes inside Japan. To this might be added the paranoia of conquest. Korea was to play a key role in this plan.

In 1587 Hideyoshi sent an embassy to Korea through the offices of the Sō clan of Tsushima. The plan called for an alliance in the attack against Ming China with the vanguard leading the attack to be composed of Korean troops. The Korean officials were warned by the envoys that Korea herself might be invaded if they refused to cooperate. The Korean authorities stalled and replied that Korea would consider the matter if the *Wakō* were completely eliminated. In an attempt to find out whether the Japanese were in a position to carry out their intentions, a large embassy was sent to Kyōto, where they were received by Hideyoshi in 1590. The chief of this embassy was of the *westerner* faction at court. He returned with an alarming report of Japanese military preparations. Unfortunately, the deputy chief of the embassy was of the *easterner* faction, and his report stressed that there was no evidence to suggest that the Japanese intended to attack Korea. Factional members at court closed ranks to support the judgement of their faction's man.

With the matter entangled in the factional struggle at court a concerted national effort was impossible. Those preparations which were made seem to have been carried out largely through the efforts of Yu Sŏngnyong (1542–1607), the chief minister at court, who was of the *southerner* faction. It was Yu who insisted that a report be sent to the Ming authorities, who had already received similar reports from envoys from the Ryūkyū Islands, and this only after considerable debate. City walls were repaired, and new walls were constructed for a dozen or so towns in Kyŏngsang Province. Yu was also responsible for recommending the appointment of Yi Sunsin to be commander of the western Chŏlla naval station.

Early in 1592 Yi made his headquarters at the southeastern port city of Yŏsu and began construction of his famed "turtle ships" (*kŏbuksŏn*), the world's first ironclads. The first turtle ship was launched and outfitted with cannon only 2 days before the first Japanese troops landed at Pusan.

It would be misleading to picture Korea as being totally unprepared militarily at this time. Kyŏngsang Province, which faces Japan, had as a result of the *Wakō* raids and the military reorganization of King Sejo taken on the appearance of an armed camp in the early fifteenth century. The administrative center of the province was at Kyŏngju, the ancient Silla capital, and the military headquarters (*taedohobu*) was at the city of Andong, in the northern interior of the province near the headwaters of the Naktong River. The principal inland towns were practically all military towns (*tohobu*) and were all walled by 1591. They all had army officers appointed who drilled the local peasants twice a year in military tactics including practice with firearms. Yet as a consequence of the *Wakō* raids, the major professional military strength was concentrated in naval forces garrisoned along the coast opposite Japan. Once through the Korean coastal defense an invading army would face only poorly trained peasant soldiers.

Hideyoshi's field headquarters and the main assembly area was located in Hizen, while the advance staging base was at Tsushima, visible 40 miles across the sea from the high cliffs of Pusan. Seven divisions or some 150,000 men were mobilized for the invasion. The vanguard comprised three divisions: one of 18,000 men under the youthful Christian convert General Konishi Yukinaga, one of 22,000 men under General Katō Kiyomasa, and the third of 11,000 men under General Kuroda Nagamasa. In addition there were some 700 ships, transport vessels, naval ships, and small craft manned by 9,000 seamen, many of them said to have been former *Wakō*. Firearms—both short-range brass cannon and matchlock muskets—were used, which gave the Japanese forces a decided advantage.

Konishi's force landed at Pusan 5 days ahead of Katō and Kuroda, who were delayed. Although they fought bravely, the defenders at the port of Pusan and the administrative town of Tongnae a few miles inland were no match for the invaders and were easily overrun.

As the first news of the invasion reached the Korean court, reports of towns captured began to stream in. At this time the Japanese armies were still in the Naktong pocket. All the men the court could muster were immediately sent to block the three major mountain passes leading from Kyŏngsang Province and limit the Japanese to the Naktong area.

Konishi had taken his forces up the center of Kyŏngsang directly toward the Oryŏng Pass, passing through the towns of Miryang, Taegu, Sangju, and Mun'gyŏng. This was generally one of the three routes followed by Japanese embassies going to Seoul in more peaceful days. At Sangju, Konishi defeated a Korean force which then withdrew beyond the pass to erect a defensive line at Ch'ungju. Konishi crossed the Oryŏng Pass and descended into the lower valley of the Han. There he waited for Katō, who had taken his forces from Pusan up the coastal corridor toward Kyŏngju. Together

Konishi and Katō faced the strong Korean defensive positions at Ch'ungju which blocked their advance toward Seoul.

> For 10,000 li the waving battle-flags
> darken the sky.
> With a great roar the cries of the soldiers
> seem to lift heaven and earth.*

The Korean positions were overrun after a stiff battle, and the Japanese commanders then marched toward Seoul by different routes. Kuroda during this period had swept westward and crossed the Sobaek range at Ch'up'ungnyŏng Pass. He then proceeded through the western provinces toward Seoul.

> Higher than mountains, the bones
> pile up in the fields.
> Vast cities, great towns
> become the burrows of wolves and foxes.*

Less than 3 weeks since their departure from Tsushima, Konishi's triumphant soldiers marched through the south gate of Seoul. Katō arrived the next day. The city was in flames. The Korean court and bureaucrats had deserted the city and fled north to safety, first at Kaesŏng, where they were stoned by the people, and then on to P'yŏngyang. The defense of the capital was left largely in the hands of hastily assembled forces of commoners and outcastes. In the confusion the slaves of Seoul burned the government buildings and palaces to destroy the slave registers. Hated official offices such as the Ministry of Justice were prime targets for the torch.

By late spring the three main divisions of the Japanese vanguard had all arrived in Seoul. The remainder of the Japanese forces landed in the south and were given the task of holding the southern provinces. They also set about organizing the southern provinces into feudal holdings along the Japanese pattern for distribution to the victorious commanders.

A garrison force was stationed in Seoul and the three Japanese vanguard divisions marched north. Konishi and Katō proceeded northwest toward P'yŏngyang. Kuroda turned toward Hwanghae. After a fierce 3-day battle the stubborn Korean defense at the Imjin River was broken. Konishi then took P'yŏngyang. Katō had turned eastward on a route which would take him far to the northeast and across the Tumen River into Manchuria. The Korean court and high elite fled to the border town of Ŭiju, where they anxiously awaited assistance from Ming forces. In the autumn a woefully

*From "Song of Great Peace," Pak Nogye, 1598.

inadequate division of 5,000 Chinese soldiers crossed the Yalu and marched bravely toward P'yŏngyang, where they were swiftly routed in a night battle.

General Li Ju-sung (1549–1598), a descendant of a Korean family which had lived in Liaotung for six generations, was then appointed to duty in Korea. He had just finished subduing a Mongol rebellion and arrived in Korea in early 1593 with a sizable army. He was successful in retaking the city of P'yŏngyang, but continuing south Li suffered a defeat. Following their defeat the Chinese forces withdrew to P'yŏngyang and the Japanese to Seoul.

During this period Korean naval forces at sea and Korean irregulars, the "Righteous Armies" (Ŭibyŏng) on land, caused the Japanese severe losses.

With the onset of the Japanese invasions, Yi Sunsin had moved his headquarters northward to the modern Ch'ungmu city which takes its name from his literary appellation. During 1592 Yi Sunsin made four sweeps along the island-dotted coast toward Pusan. Several major engagements were fought offshore of Kŏje Island, during which Yi and his ironclad "turtle ships" wrecked havoc among the Japanese supply ships. On his fourth sweep in 1592 Yi attacked the main anchorage at Pusan and using fireboats sank over 100 vessels.

The effect of these activities is reflected in Konishi's continued pleas for supplies. Korean control of the southern waters also blocked entrance to the Yellow Sea and prevented the Japanese from landing men or supplies at ports on the west coast.

On land, while the Japanese had defeated both the Chinese and Korean armies, the forces of the vanguard were now drawn up in defensive positions at Seoul. The rest of the Japanese forces in the southern provinces were barely holding their own against the Korean irregulars who harassed them continually. These peasant irregulars were joined by many of the soldiers of defeated government armies and operated like guerrilla forces in open battle. One of these was Cho Hŏn, who successfully engaged Japanese forces in the Ch'ungch'ŏng area several times before his death in battle. Kwak Chaeu was another local guerrilla leader. In battles along the Naktong River he managed to drive the Japanese forces from several towns. Some of these small groups were led by monks such as Ch'ŏyŏng, whose forces fought in the Suwŏn area. Others were led by slaves. One guerrilla leader was Kwŏn Yul, whose irregulars from the Kwangju area fought several successful engagements against the Japanese in Chŏlla. The activities of these local irregulars made Japanese prospects of living off the land difficult, while Korean naval activity successfully hampered resupply efforts.

Whereas the Chinese could easily mobilize more forces, the Japanese vanguard divisions had already lost a third of their men. Therefore, when the Chinese suggested an armistice for negotiations Konishi consented. The negotiations produced several requirements of the Japanese, including the investiture of Hideyoshi as king of Japan. The Japanese agreed to withdraw to the south and await the arrival of envoys from the Ming court. In the early spring of 1593, the Japanese armies evacuated Seoul and marched south. A rearguard was left at the landing areas in the south, and the bulk of the Japanese troops withdrew to Japan. In 1594 the Chinese forces returned to Manchuria.

When the Chinese embassy, under the impression they were about to deal with a subdued minor state, finally arrived in Japan, they found the situation much different than they had been led to believe. Hideyoshi had also been misled by his negotiators apparently, for his demands were those of the victor and included the daughter of the Ming emperor as a wife, the restoration of trade relations between China and Japan, and Japanese possession of the southern provinces of Korea with the northern half of the peninsula to remain under Chinese influence. The Chinese embassy was prepared to bestow upon Hideyoshi a patent of investiture and a "seal of state" recognizing him as king of Japan. The misunderstandings, needless to say, were irreconcilable and negotiations were broken off.

In Korea the grain shortage already made serious by the war had been aggravated by the foraging activities of two foreign armies. The occupation of the rice-producing areas of the south by the Japanese had created a financial crisis within the Korean government during the first year of the war. The government had already been freely distributing titles to the *sŏŏl* and slaves who engaged in resistance to the Japanese. Now official rank was put up for sale except for the first and second ministerial ranks, which apparently never were sold. The seriousness of the crisis is underscored by the offering of the third court rank for 100 Korean bushels of rice in 1592; by early 1593 the grain shortage was such that the third rank brought only 20 bushels.

As the grain shortage worsened banditry and peasant uprisings proliferated. There was also one major revolt during this period. It was led by Yi Monghak, a *sŏŏl* descendant of the royal clan. He gathered a sizable force of peasants and monks and managed to gain control of a large area in North Chŏlla Province before his army was finally defeated at the town of Hongsŏng.

Despite the war the factional feuding continued unabated at court. The westerners remained dominant. One result of this feuding was that the naval genius Yi Sunsin, now commander Naval Forces South, was relieved of his command and jailed in early 1597. This represented a victory of the westerner faction over the easterners who had supported Yi. Yi was replaced by a westerner appointment, Wŏn Kyun (d. 1597), then commander of one of the Chŏlla naval stations, whose inept maneuvers almost eliminated the Korean fleet.

The unrealistic attitude of the court toward the war is reflected in the awards of merit subject: eighty-six of the group that accompanied the king to Ŭiju were granted this distinction and only eighteen awards were made for merit in battle.

The negotiations had limped along for over 3 years and had failed to produce results satisfactory to Hideyoshi, and in early 1597 he ordered the war resumed. General Konishi, who had returned to Japan in the summer of 1595, led his forces back to Korea. During this period he was visited by Father Gregorio de Cespedes (1551–1611). The Jesuit had spent the Christmas of 1597 with the Sō family on Tsushima and landed in Korea on December 27. The lord of Tsushima, who is said to have been converted to Christianity during a visit to Kyōto, gave the Jesuit priest a young boy taken prisoner in Korea who was said to be a son of the "secretary to the king." Father de Cespedes had the boy educated in the Jesuit seminary, and the lad, Vincent Caoun, served as a catechist, was admitted to the order of the Jesuits, and with twenty-five other Jesuits was burned at the stake in Nagasaki on June 20, 1626. Another of the prisoners brought back from the wars in Korea was sold as a slave to the Florentine Jesuit Francesco Carletti, who set him free. This Korean, baptized Antonio Corea, accompanied Carletti back to Italy in 1606.

Japanese forces in Korea amounted to perhaps 100,000 men, chiefly concentrated along the Kyŏngsang coast. With the recommencement of hostilities in the south a Chinese army of some 40,000 under General Yang Hao (d. 1629) was sent to Korea. In early 1598 a large battle near the coastal city of Ulsan ended in General Yang's defeat. The Japanese forces maintained their defensive positions, from which they launched short-range attacks that kept the more numerous Chinese and Korean forces off balance. The pickled ears of reportedly 38,000 men were sent to Kyōto as proof of the fighting prowess of the Japanese commanders in Korea, and they were buried at Kyōto in the Mimizuka (Mound of Ears).

At sea Yi Sunsin had been hastily reinstated after Wŏn Kyun's disastrous defeats, and he began to regain control of the southern seas. The last great sea battle of the war was fought in the Myŏngnyang Straits in late 1597. After his recall Yi Sunsin had been stationed in the area of the straits, which are between Chin Island and the Hwawŏn peninsula of South Chŏlla. At this time he had only twelve ships under his command. A fleet of 133 Japanese ships departed the southern Korean port of Ŏranp'o in the winter of 1597 and Yi attacked them at Myŏngnyang Straits. Because of his knowledge of the tides and the torrential current which roars through the straits, Yi

THE TURTLE SHIP OF YI SUNSIN

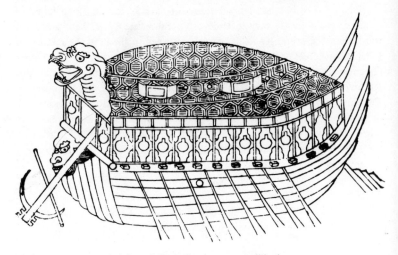

A late eighteenth-century woodblock.

managed to sink thirty-one of the ships and force the rest to turn back. He died in the battle at the age of fifty-four, but he had regained control of the southern seas for Korea.

In September 1598 Hideyoshi died. Peace talks were opened through the Sō clan, and the Japanese forces were recalled.

> *Today, after seven years searching*
> *We see the Great Peace.*
>
> . . . .
>
> *The aged and infirm scattered*
> *here and there in the mountain hollows*
> *come back looking for their old nests*
> *like young swallows on the east wind.**

For Japan the wars resulted in a large-scale cultural influx despite their adverse effect upon the economics and politics of the state. One area in which this cultural influx was particularly apparent was ceramics, as a result of the resettlement in Japan of captive Korean ceramic makers, who began the manufacture of several well-known Japanese wares. Another area was books, which were taken back in great quantity, both Korean reprints of Chinese works and the works of Korean authors. Some 2,950 books were taken and put into the Sumpu library of Tokugawa Ieyasu after the death of Hideyoshi. And it was through Kang Hang, a Korean prisoner, that Chu Hsi Confucianism gained a foothold in Japan. It is also said that through the capture of Korean technicians and fonts of type that printing with movable metallic type first entered Japan at this time, although some would credit its introduction to Europeans.

From the Korean view the Japanese had reboarded their ships and gone home, implying a Japanese failure and a Korean victory in defending their homeland.

> *When we return to the Seryu barracks*
> *to dismiss the soldiers, to rest our swords*
>
> . . . .
>
> *the drums and trumpets mingle*
>
> . . . .
>
> *and the dragon-banner*
> *waves haughtily in the west wind.**

But the wars had brought widespread destruction to Korea, particularly in the burning of many Buddhist temples and towns in the south. They were a national disaster which set in motion forces that would reshape the society.

*From "Song of Great Peace," Pak Nogye, 1598.

9
Late
Chosŏn   THE MANCHU INVASIONS

Ming China effectively controlled the rolling plains of the Liao-ssu and Liao-tung areas, but the eastern Manchurian highlands north of Korea were held by various Jürčen tribes. In the late sixteenth century the great leader Nurhaci (1559–1626) rose to unite the Jürčen people. Large-scale Jürčen attacks commenced along the northeastern borders of Korea in 1583 and continued sporadically over the following decade.

When Korean King Sŏnjo fled to Ŭiju in late 1592, Nurhaci sent envoys to meet him; he also made an offer, which was refused by the Ming authorities, to send his own forces to Korea's aid at this time. A Korean embassy was sent to Nurhaci's base at the military town of Hŭng-gyŏng-no-sŏng and returned with a detailed report of conditions in the area and a map of the city.

In 1593 when Ming garrison forces from the Liao-tung area were drawn into Korea to engage the Japanese, Nurhaci began the first of his campaigns westward against Ming outposts in Manchuria. Korea, to the extent possible, supported Ming China. But by 1616 Nurhaci was confident enough to proclaim himself "khan"; he named his state Chin (gold) to show the continuance of the earlier Chin dynasty.

In 1619 Korean forces 13,000 strong joined the Ming armies in Manchuria in a coordinated attack on Nurhaci. The advance forces of the Ming army were defeated at the battle of Sarhu on April 14. Three days later the battle of Dungge ended with the defeat of the joint Ming-Korean armies and the capture of the commander of the Korean forces, General Kang Hŭngnip (1560–1627).

The ruler of Chosŏn at this time was Kwanghaegun (r. 1608–1623), an able monarch who was supported by the northerner faction. Although pro-Ming, following the disaster of the battle of Dungge, Kwanghaegun endeavored to avoid involvement in the wars raging in Manchuria and adopted a policy of nonalignment. This policy quickly became a bone of contention in the factional struggles which had recommenced at court, and ended in 1623 with Kwanghaegun and his supporters being swept from power by the faction of westerners who put Injo (r. 1623–1649) on the throne. A strong

Chronological Overview

	China	Korea		Japan
1600	Ming	Chosŏn		Tokugawa
1644	Ch'ing			
1868				Meiji
1905				
1910		Annexation and Formal End of the Yi Dynasty		
1912	Republic			Taishō

pro-Ming policy was put into effect which included support for Ming General Mao Wen-lung (1576–1629), who had occupied Ka Island (c. P'i-tao) off the northwest coast of Korea in the spring of 1621 following the fall of the Manchurian city of Shen-yang. For the next 7 years General Mao, with Korean support, made sporadic raids on Nurhaci's flank and posed a distinct threat to his advance across Manchuria.

Just at this time the revolt of Yi Kwal erupted inside Korea. He was a military officer who with his son and brother had been active in the move which put King Injo on the throne. While Yi had been given the title of "merit subject second class," his son and brother had gone unrewarded. Yi Kwal's revolt was a reflection of widespread discontent among officials at this time. When an attempt was made to arrest his son for some alleged misdeed, Yi Kwal contacted other officials in the northwest, and in early 1624 they declared an open rebellion. The rebel army is said to have numbered about 10,000 and included a detachment of a hundred or so Japanese soldiers captured during the Hideyoshi invasions and put into the Korean army. In a well-planned revolt, the rebels were able to take the capital in less than 3 weeks. Court officials hurriedly executed several dozen officials thought to be linked with the rebel cause and then fled south with King Injo to the city of Kongju. Government troops were quickly assembled from the southern provinces, and in battles near the city of Kwangju the rebel armies were defeated decisively. Yi Kwal was captured and executed, while remnants of his army fled north to join the forces of Nurhaci.

Nurhaci had been successful in his drive across Manchuria, and in 1625 he moved his capital to the city of Shen-yang. The unstable conditions in Korea provided an excellent opportunity to remove the menace of Ming General Mao and the pro-Ming Koreans who supported him. In 1627, Manchu armies 30,000 strong crossed the Yalu River with Korean General

Kang Hŭngnip and former soldiers of Yi Kwal as guides. One army under Prince Amin (d. 1640) was sent against General Mao, while two other armies commanded by Princes Jirgalang (1599–1655) and Yoto (d. 1638) rode south toward the capital. P'yŏngyang fell, and the news of the rapid Manchu advance brought panic to the capital. The royal storehouses and offices of the Ministry of Finance and Ministry of War were put to the torch by the Seoul garrison commander. One general is reported to have loaded commandeered boats with rice and sailed off. A good deal of resistance seems to have been given by the "Righteous Armies" who were active in the northwest. There was also some unexpected assistance. When the Japanese Shogun Tokugawa Iemitsu heard of the invasions, he had the lord of Tsushima send 300 rifles, 300 long swords, and 300 *kŭn* of gunpowder niter to Korea. The Manchu armies took Seoul and sent their Korean prisoner General Kang to Kanghwa Island, where the court had taken refuge, to negotiate. There was some difficulty in the peace negotiations, since the Manchu Prince Amin had brought his forces into Seoul after attacking Ming General Mao at Ka Island, and he was now reluctant to make peace and leave the comforts of the Korean capital. The two other princes tricked him into going north to P'yŏngyang, and they concluded a peace treaty. When he discovered the ruse, Prince Amin let his troops loose to pillage for 3 days in revenge.

In an oath phrased in terms of an elder-younger brother relationship and sanctified by the sacrifice of a white horse and a black ox, Korea swore to join the Manchus against the Ming. This was in 1627.

During the ensuing decade the oath was ignored as much as possible by the Korean authorities. In 1632 a Manchu embassy arrived with the notice that henceforth Korea would be considered a tributary state and required to supply an annual tribute including 10,000 Korean ounces of gold and of silver, 10,000 rolls of fine colored cloth, an equal amount of white ramie cloth, and 3,000 cavalry mounts. Since Korea was a vital source of food and military equipment for their war against the Ming, Manchu demands were heavy and constant. The Korean authorities finally became belligerent. A notice was sent to all the provinces to prepare for war, and troops were sent to assist General Mao, then fighting along the mouth of the Yalu River. When a Manchu envoy arrived in 1636, he was given a copy of the war notice and chased back across the border.

A large army of Manchus, Mongols, and Chinese crossed the ice of the frozen Yalu River on January 4, 1637, under the personal command of Abahai (1592–1643), who had become khan in 1626 and emperor in 1636. The Manchu cavalry advance was so swift that by the time the fire beacons on the mountain tops had flashed the news to Seoul, the Manchu vanguard had already crossed the Ch'ŏngch'ŏn River at Anju, 75 miles inside the Korean border. In great haste, the queen, the princes, and all women and children of the families of the court officials were sent to the safety of a proven refuge, Kanghwa Island, with plans for the king and his ministers to join them later. That night as King Injo and the royal party prepared to leave the city, word came in that an advance unit of Manchu cavalry had already arrived and was blocking the road to Kanghwa Island. With the sanctuary of Kanghwa cut off, it was decided to join Korean army units in the mountain fastness of Namhan sansŏng, a fortified citadel of refuge some 11 miles south of the capital. While a party of officials diverted the Manchu soldiers with food and wine, the king and his ministers slipped through a small side gate in the city wall and made their way south to the citadel. In the fortress with supplies for 2 months if strictly rationed were 13,000 persons.

With little time to prepare defenses Seoul capitulated quickly and Korean relief forces hastily summoned from the provinces were defeated and scattered. Requests for aid had been sent to the Ming authorities, but a fleet sent out had been driven back by winter storms at sea. Yet all was not lost. King Injo and his forces had withstood the siege by the main Manchu armies, and their sallies into the enemy ranks showed no signs of weakening. Members of the royal household and several ministers had made it to the safety of Kanghwa Island, while Korean forces were re-forming in the provinces. This was the general state of affairs when Emperor Abahai arrived in the area of the mountain citadel on January 26, 1637.

As the siege went into its fortieth day and the Korean soldiers inside the impenetrable mountain fortress braced themselves for further attacks, an unbelievable message came in from the Manchu camp. The Manchu army had taken Kanghwa Island, and in the emperor's camp were 200 hostages, including the queen and the royal consorts, the royal princes, and the wives and children of the high court officials. There was no alternative but to surrender and accept the Manchu terms.

On February 24, King Injo rode out of the mountain citadel with a small retine silent in defeat on a submissive journey across the bleak winter fields to the camp of Emperor Abahai. A sacred nine-tiered altar had been erected for the submission ceremony, and, by the banks of the Han, amid ochre tents, King Injo bowed his head to the ground nine times before Abahai and pledged to turn over his patent of investiture and the seal of state that his ancestors had received from the Ming court, to send two princes as hostages, and to adopt the Ch'ing calendar. All relations with the Ming court were to cease, annual tribute would be submitted, and troops and supplies would be furnished on demand, including fifty vessels, for an immediate attack on Ming General Mao's base on Ka Island. In that moment Korea's destiny was sealed for $2\frac{1}{2}$ centuries as Korea became a reluctant tributary to Ch'ing China.

Korean families taken captive at this time were formed into a unit of the Manchu Yellow Banner Army. Three ministers who had urged resistance were delivered up and taken to Shen-yang, where they were executed. Two young Korean princes, Prince Sohyŏn and the lord of Pongnim, were taken as hostages as the victorious Manchu armies rode northward through the snow toward the broad plains of Manchuria.

> Fare thee well, my Samgak-san,
> Let us meet again, my River Han,
> I leave the mountains and rivers of home behind;
> In these uncertain times,
> I may return, I may not.*

The invasions devastated the Korean northwest scarcely three decades after the Japanese invasions had decimated the southern provinces. It was a bitter and humiliating defeat. When the lord of Pongnim, canonized Hyojong (r. 1649–1659), took the throne, he made elaborate plans to escape Ch'ing domination and devoted considerable national resources to military preparations. But for most Korean intellectuals it was a tragic national disgrace, and for centuries they would look nostalgically back toward relations with Ming China and the fancied golden years of the past.

FACTIONAL STRUGGLES

Many factors contributed to the factional struggles which emerged during the reign of Sŏnjo (r. 1567–1608) and which were to be characteristic of Yi dynasty society until its end. Certainly a central factor was the acquisition and retention of wealth conceived principally in terms of land. The acquisition of land, in the form of gift-lands or salary-land which rapidly became private holdings, had been dependent upon appointment to government office and political influence since the founding of the dynasty. Following the settlement of the new territories in the north and the confiscation and distribution of monastery lands, there were no longer surplus lands for the government to distribute. Stipends for government officials were paid out of tax revenues. An increase in government posts without a corresponding increase in revenue could only lower the stipends. This meant that there was a practical limit upon the number of government positions open to the yangban. While land and office were limited, the number of yangban aspirants was gradually increasing. Appointment to office, the gateway to economic power, was via the examination and selection process. Since approval of an appointment could be manipulated by political influence, political patronage became an important factor. The Ministry of Personnel and the three cen-

*From a sijo by a hostage of the Manchu, Kim Sanghŏn, 1570–1652.

soring offices were key agencies in this process, and it is not surprising to find them in the center of these struggles.

By the mid-fifteenth century the distribution of salary or position lands had ceased. This led to continued agitation by younger government appointees for land reforms. These efforts were just as vigorously opposed by the established *yangban*. The opposition of the advocates of these two positions surfaced in the purges of 1498–1545. The purges themselves created martyrs which tended to solidify existing divisions. The factions which emerged were distinguished less by philosophical differences than by their positions of dominance at court, which usually saw two principal factions struggling for supremacy while lesser factions fought for bare survival. The absence of real ideological differences made personalities and kinship relations vital, and factional affiliations came to be inherited.

In the midst of this violent maelstrom was the monarch. This in turn brought members of the royal household into the fray. Particularly active were those ministers whose clan lines had married sons or daughters into the royal family. They could be expected to advance the cause of their own clan line represented in the royal family, particularly so if there was a chance of a grandson obtaining the throne. This, in turn, meant that factional struggles often focused upon aspirants for the throne. The institutional weakness of the throne meant that only a very strong and capable monarch could hope to gain sufficient support to rule in his own right. Most Korean rulers found themselves buffeted by severe criticism at every turn.

The factional struggles and the attitudes and values they represented were reinforced by ancestor worship and the emphasis on filial piety, which contributed to family-clan cohesiveness, by strength of personal relations with strong loyalties to personalities transcending loyalty to abstract and often debatable principles, by the dominance of the role of scholar-official over other social roles, by the nature of factional politics which were an all-or-nothing-at-all struggle, and also by the *sŏwŏn* or private academies on *yangban* estates where officials in disfavor at court could retire to teach their clansmen, gossip and write poetry with their cronies, and pass along their bitterness at the opposition at court. A forebearer's fight was taken up as a duty; failure to take it up would indicate a lack of filial respect. Moral sanction for the atmosphere of self-righteous intolerance which developed was provided by Chu Hsi orthodoxy. The politics of vengeance which emerged was not lacking in religious overtones, and it was carried out with all the intensity and self-righteous conviction of a holy war.

The factional struggles reached a peak of intensity during the period 1600 to 1650. Here then, briefly outlined and without any attempt to follow the process in detail, are some of the major factions and incidents surrounding them.

In 1575, during the early years of the reign of Sŏnjo, a conflict emerged between the cliques of Sim Ŭigyŏm (1535–1587) and Kim Hyowŏn (1532–1590). Sim, a high-ranking member of the Censorate and the younger brother of the queen dowager opposed the appointment of Kim as head of the Office of Civil Appointments (Chŏllang) in the Ministry of Personnel. Although the official rank of the head of the Office of Civil Appointments was relatively low, the power of the office in appointments was such that the selection of its head was normally decided by the most influential ministers. As soon as Kim took office he promptly blocked the recommendation submitted for Sim's younger brother. As Kim lived in the eastern section of the capital his followers became known as the "easterners" (tongin). Sim's followers were known as "westerners" (sŏin), since Sim had his residence in the western section of the city.

In 1591, a clash occurred between the easterners and westerners over the investment of the crown prince. King Sŏnjo had no sons by his wives, but he did have thirteen sons by concubines. The westerners, among whom was the noted kasa verse author Chŏng Ch'ŏl (1536–1593), supported one of these sons to be the crown prince. A split occurred among the easterners over the issue and gave rise to the "southerners" (namin), who took a conciliatory position, and the "northerners" (pugin), who were vehemently opposed. The latter came to power following the Japanese invasions, and they in turn split into the "lesser northerners" (sobuk) and "greater northerners" (taebuk). The succession struggle was taken up by these two factions, each of which was divided: the lesser northerners into two factions and the greater northerners into four factions. Later the various northern groups were known generally simply as the "northerners."

The great northerners held power during the reign of Kwanghaegun (r. 1608–1623), whom they supported to the throne. At this time there occurred the incident of the seven sŏŏl. Kwanghaegun and his backers apparently feared the possibility of a coup d'etat by the supporters of the lord of Yŏngch'ang, another of Sŏnjo's sons and then a boy of eight. At this time a travelling merchant was killed in the Oryŏng Pass, and several hundred Korean ounces of silver taken from him. The actual criminal may have been a certain Sŏ Kabyang, one of several sŏŏl engaged in commerce in the town of Yŏju. The entire group was arrested, although only four of the seven accused appear to have actually been sŏŏl. Kwanghaegun's supporters were able to obtain the services of one of these men to write a memorial to the effect that the robbery was committed to obtain money for the movement to put the lord of Yŏngch'ang on the throne. Among those accused of being linked to the plot of 1618 was the talented prose writer Hŏ Kyun. The incident began a series of conflicts which finally resulted in the overthrow of Kwanghaegun by the faction of westerners led by Yun

Pang (1563–1640), whose father was the lord of Haep'yŏng and who was related to the royal family through marriage to a daughter of Sŏnjo. He later inherited his father's title, and the Haep'yŏng Yun clan to which he belonged remained actively involved in the factional struggles for some time. The westerners, who had been planning to move for some time, assembled several hundred soldiers one night and broke into the Ch'angdŏk palace and captured Kwanghaegun. In the fighting the palace was burned. The victorious westerners put Injo (r. 1623–1649) on the throne and began a bloody purge

Yi Dynasty Factions (Simplified)

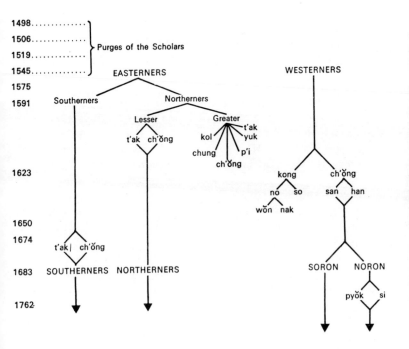

which eliminated both the greater and lesser northerner factions. The westerners then divided into two factions: the *kong* (merit) faction, who had been involved in putting Injo on the throne, and the *ch'ŏng* (clear) faction, who had not participated. A split soon occurred among the *kong* westerners over an appointment to the post of "inspector-general" and gave rise to the *no* (elder) and *so* (younger) westerner factions. The *no* faction again divided into the *nak* faction, supporters of the lord of *Nak*hŭngbu, and the *wŏn* faction, supporters of the lord of *Wŏn*p'yŏngbu in 1649.

In 1674 the southerners, who had previously challenged the westerners unsuccessfully in 1654 over the issue of the proper mourning period for Queen Dowager Cho, raised the issue of the proper mourning period to be observed for one of Hyojong's wives. In their challenge they were contending with the influential Song Siyŏl (1607–1689), head of the *ch'ŏng* westerner faction and one of the ablest Confucian scholar-officials of the period. Song had been tutor to Crown Prince Pongnim and had accompanied King Injo to *Namhan sansŏng* at the time of the second Manchu invasions. Firmly anti-Manchu, Song resigned following the humiliating peace treaty. He was recalled when Crown Prince Pongnim—King Hyojong (r. 1650–1659)—took the throne. He stood behind King Hyojong's plans to resist the Manchu Ch'ing authorities and rose to become one of the great powers at court. But the reign of his patron King Hyojong had ended 25 years before, and now the struggle was over who would succeed Hyojong's successor King Hyŏngjong (r. 1660–1674). The southerner faction was victorious, King Sukchong (r. 1675–1720) took the throne, and Song Siyŏl was stripped of power.

The southerners themselves divided into the *ch'ŏng* (clear) and the *t'ak* (muddy) factions. The *ch'ŏng* faction was led by Hŏ Mok (1595–1682), who desired the death penalty for Song Siyŏl, while the *t'ak* faction was under the leadership of Hŏ Chŏk (1610–1680). Both leaders were of the Yangch'ŏn Hŏ clan. The moderate faction prevailed, and Song was not executed.

In 1680 Song Siyŏl was recalled, and he led the *ch'ŏng* westerners back into power. Three years later this faction split into the *noron* (elder doctrine) faction, led by Song until his murder in 1689, and the *soron* (lesser doctrine) faction of Yun Chung (1629–1711).

From 1683 we can generally distinguish four factions, viz., the *noron*, *soron*, northerners, and southerners. During the majority of this later period the *noron* was generally in power, occasionally being replaced temporarily by the *soron*, who were their chief opposition.

A French missionary account of the early nineteenth century relates the following Korean tale concerning the status of the various factions at that time:

A No-ron, richly clothed, is seated at a sumptuously prepared table, and savors the best morsels at his pleasure. A Sio-ron [= soron] who is seated next to him, but a little behind him, graciously performs the function of servant, and as the price of his obsequiousness he receives part of the food. A Sio-pouk [= lesser northerner], knowing that the banquet is not for him, sits much further off with a grave, calm air. He will have a few leavings when the others have had their fill. Finally a Nam-in (= southerner), covered in tatters, stands behind the No-ron who does not see him. He is spiteful, grinds his teeth and shows his fist, like a man who is promising himself a spectacular revenge.*

PRIVATE ACADEMIES (SŎWŎN) AND SHRINES (SA)

The *sŏwŏn* (c. *shu-yüan*) were a combination of a shrine, a private study, a school, and a social gathering spot for local scholars. One of the earliest of these *sŏwŏn* was established in 1543 by Chu Sebung (1495–1554) while he was serving as Prefect of P'unggi in Kyŏngsang Province. In this case the shrine in the *sŏwŏn* was dedicated to the memory of An Hyang, revered as the scholar who had first introduced the works of Chu Hsi to Korea, and is said to have been patterned after a private academy which Chu Hsi founded. Chu Sebung was followed in this post by Yi Hwang, who was later to become Korea's most eminent scholar in the Chu Hsi tradition. Yi Hwang was able to use his considerable influence to secure royal patronage for the *sŏwŏn*, since it was in fact also a shrine to a Korean Confucian sage. As state patronage in the form of cash, grain, land, slaves, and books shifted from the regional schools (*hyanggyo*) to the *sŏwŏn*, the latter proliferated. During this same period shrines (*sa*) dedicated to local notables began to be established, some of which developed into *sŏwŏn*. Like the *sŏwŏn*, the shrines developed into small tax-free estates with grants of land, cash, and so on.

While many of the shrines at the academies were dedicated to famed Korean Confucianists such as Sŏl Ch'ong, An Hyang, Chŏng Mongju, Kil Chae, and Song Siyŏl, only three appear to have had shrines to Chinese sages and scholars, namely, one in Sŏngju to Chu Hsi, one in P'yŏngyang to Kija, and one in Hamhŭng to Confucius. The national shrine to Confucius was, of course, at the Sŏnggyun'gwan Academy in Seoul.

The establishment of shrines and private academies flourished following the Japanese and Manchu invasions, and by the late seventeenth century there were almost seven hundred *sŏwŏn* and probably as many shrines scattered throughout the country. Large concentrations were usually located around the provincial government centers, where the candidates for the government service examinations took the first part of the triennial examinations.

The ten private academies and fourteen shrines of the Taegu area disclose something of the character of that city as well as the ideals espoused by the Yi dynasty elite in their dedications. The oldest and largest private

*From HRAF translation, C. Dallet, *Histoire de l'église de Corée*.

academy in Taegu, which had begun as a shrine, was the *Yŏn'gyŏng sŏwŏn* (Polishing the Classics Academy), whose forty rooms in half a dozen buildings centered on the Hall of Benevolence and Wisdom. Most of the Taegu shrines honored the principle of loyalty and were dedicated to the memory of the heroes of the Japanese invasion or other military actions. There was also a shrine to Sin Sunggyŏm, the general who sacrificed his life to save the founder of the Koryŏ dynasty from the forces of Later Paekche in the tenth century. About half of the shrines and private academies honored ancestors of a single clan: the Sŏ clan of Talsŏng had three; the To clan, which had emigrated from Sŏngju, had two. One shrine honored the filial piety of an individual who sat beside his parent's grave for 3 years, while several honored former provincial governors and other local officials for exemplifying good government. Probably the most unusual shrine in Taegu was that dedicated to the memory of Kim Ch'ungsŏn, a Japanese soldier who had come over to the Korean side during the Hideyoshi invasions and earned merit in battle, for which he was given the surname Kim. He had originally settled at the town of Kimhae, on the lower reaches of the Naktong River, but later moved into the Taegu area, where his descendants still reside.

The *sŏwŏn* became a favorite retreat for scholars out of favor at court and a meeting place for factional associates, where animosities were passed along from father to son, from master to student. The *sŏwŏn* as the major educational institutions of the period played a role in the permeation of Chu Hsi orthodoxy through the society even as their concentration around principal regional centers both reflected and accelerated the growth of these provincial towns.

EARLY CONTACTS WITH THE WEST

During the reign of King Sŏnjo (r. 1567–1608) an envoy returned from Peking with maps of Europe. This was the beginning of a steady flow of information into Korea about Europe. In 1632 Chŏng Tuwŏn returned with an embassy from China with major works on Christianity as well as information on Western sciences in Chinese translation. Chŏng also brought back pistols, a telescope, maps, and a chronometer he had acquired in the Chinese capital. In his encyclopedic *Chibong yusŏl* (1614), Yi Sugwang (1563–1623), one of the forerunners of the *Sirhak* (Pragmatic) school, introduced an outline of Catholic doctrine prepared by Matteo Ricci (1522–1610) as well as information drawn from Chinese translations of Western works on geography and astronomy.

Prince Sohyŏn (1612–1645), taken hostage by the Manchu conquerors in 1636, met the German Jesuit Johannes Adam Schall von Bell (1591–1666) in Peking in 1644, and upon his return to Korea he brought back such items as a terrestrial globe and Christian religious images.

Not long after the brief sojourn with Hideyoshi's forces of the Jesuit priest Gregorio de Cespedes (1551–1611) in 1597, three Dutch mariners were stranded on the Korean coast in 1627. Two of these men were killed in the fighting during the invasions of 1636. The third, Jan Janse Weltevree, a tall, blue-eyed, red-bearded expert in firearms was given the Korean name of Pak Yŏn and, because of his knowledge of cannon casting, was appointed to a post in the military; he was apparently in the *chungin* class. Weltevree married a Korean girl and spent the remainder of his days in Korea, only once meeting a group of his countrymen when, in 1653 at the age of fifty-eight, he was sent to Cheju Island to interview the survivors of the shipwrecked Dutch yacht *Sparwer*. The ill-fated yacht was driven on the rocks off Cheju Island during a storm on the night of August 15, 1653. Hendrick Hamel, a secretary aboard the yacht later wrote an account of his adventures in his *Journal*. Hamel and his shipmates were detained under guard on Cheju and billeted in the house where, in 1641, the Korean ruler Kwanghaegun had spent the final years of his life in exile.

The thirty-six survivors of the crew of the *Sparwer* were sent to Seoul the following year and lodged in the Chinese section of the city. They were assigned to a military unit in the capital, which was apparently something of a foreign brigade, since it also included Chinese and Japanese soldiers. Many of the men died and in March 1656, the twenty-two men who remained were assigned to military posts in Chŏlla Province. Ten years later, eight of them escaped in a skiff from the southern naval city of Yŏsu and sailed to Japan after spending 14 years in Korea.

When Hamel and his shipmates arrived in Korea, the Chosŏn ruler was Hyojong (r. 1649–1659), the former lord of Pongmin, who had been held hostage by the Manchus for 8 years at Shen-yang. King Hyojong gathered around him ministers hostile to the Manchu and began planning to build up the Korean military to the point where a break with the Ch'ing would be possible. The plan was secretly reported to the Ch'ing, which resulted in several ministers being sent as hostages. Although Hyojong's military build-up never resulted in a Korean attack on the Ch'ing, the preparations it entailed directed sparse government resources into military preparations. The military build-up accounts for why Weltevree, a cannon caster, was treated so well and why Hamel and his shipmates were assigned to the military. Hamel mentions seeing two-masted naval vessels with banks of thirty to thirty-two oars and armed with cannon in the port cities he visited. He also wrote in his *Journal* of the general military character assumed by the country:

Every province has its General, and every place its military officer; there is scarcely a village without at least its commanding corporal. Nevertheless, the number of free persons who are exempt from being in the troops, joined to the slaves, makes about one-half of the male population.*

From those exempted from military service a levy was extracted, 1 bolt of cloth for *yangban*, 3 Korean bushels of rice for monks, and so forth. Hamel's recollections give us a rare glimpse of Korea in the mid-seventeenth century

The houses of the nobility are magnificent, and have a suite of rooms in front, in which they receive their friends; and commonly there is a square court with a fountain and garden at the entrance. The apartments of the women are at the more retired part of the house; but some women are allowed to go abroad and to see company, and are treated with great respect.

The country nevertheless is full of religious houses and temples, and they have a numerous order of monks. In some of the monasteries there are not fewer than five or six hundred monks. . . . In general the monks are not much more esteemed than are the slaves. They are not exempt from military service, and a number of them are employed in turn to guard the forts and castles.

The richer people frequent much the cloisters, to divert themselves with the public women, because generally these places are pleasantly situated and have beautiful gardens so that they ought rather to be called houses of pleasure than temples.*

In the same year that Hamel and his group entered Seoul, Korea at the request of the Ch'ing court had dispatched a company of 150 riflemen to fight the Russians who had begun to enter the Amur region. Four years later another company of Korean riflemen was sent. During a relatively short period Korea had encountered Europeans advancing both from the south and from the north.

RELATIONS WITH CH'ING CHINA

All the questions and problems existing on the Chinese side regarding Korea were handled through the Ch'ing Board of Rites in Peking until the establishment of the *Tsungli Yamen* in 1861. The tribute requirements imposed upon Korea as a condition for peace were gradually reduced until by the late seventeenth century they consisted chiefly of furs, paper, rice,

*From H. Hamel, *Journal*, translated by James Burney, London: Luke Hansard & Sons, 1813.

and textiles in manageable quantities. Korea-Ch'ing relations centered chiefly around the annual embassies, which provided an opportunity for the exchange of gifts between the two courts and for trading activities at the border, and the border question itself. All trade was strictly conducted at the border, and no trade was allowed by sea. Beyond the Yalu River a strip of land some 50 miles wide was left uninhabited, and beyond that was the Willow Palisade, also commonly known as the Barrier of Stakes, with a principal entry gate outside the Manchurian city of Feng-huang-ch'eng.

As a condition of the peace negotiations of 1637 an official market was established in 1646 on an island in the lower Yalu, where official trade was carried out. In the northeast a market was opened at the town of Hoenyŏng in 1628, and soon afterward another market was set up at the Korean frontier town of Kyŏngwŏn. Here, licensed Chinese merchants attended the semi-annual market fairs.

In the late seventeenth century wealthy Korean merchants began to accompany official embassies to China as far as the gate in the Barrier of Stakes at Feng-huang-ch'eng, where a market was held for several days. Principal Korean items of trade were ginseng, ramie cloth, gold, and silver. Ch'ing products included silks, medicines, gems, and books. This trade was strictly regulated, and severe penalties were imposed for illegal commercial activities. Ginseng was considered a Korean state monopoly; officials detected smuggling ginseng were promptly relieved of their posts and commoners of their heads. Restricted articles included arms and gunpowder niter. The Ch'ing authorities also placed a restriction on the unauthorized export of coins and the Chinese dynastic histories.

The "uninhabited" area beyond the Yalu became a haven for the illegal trading of horses and sale of products from both Korea and China, as well as a sanctuary for bandit groups.

Encounters with Russians moving eastward drew Chinese attention to Manchuria, including the ill-defined boundaries between Korea and China. Finally, in 1711 a border marker was set up on Paektu Mountain, while the uninhabited area beyond the Yalu was incorporated into China in 1875 by the Chinese statesman Li Hung-chang (1823–1901).

RELATIONS WITH TOKUGAWA JAPAN

Several years after Hideyoshi's death Tokugawa Ieyasu contacted Korea through the offices of the lord of Tsushima. The Korean authorities agreed to reopen relations for the return of several thousand Korean prisoners of war taken to Japan. In 1606 the first Korean embassy was sent to Edo, where the shogun had his residence. Three years later, in 1609, relations were normalized with the Sō clan of Tsushima. The treaty of 1609 permitted twenty ships (twenty-three from 1636) to call at Pusan annually and provided for an annual allowance of 100 Korean bushels each of rice and beans for, the lord of Tsushima.

Relations were stabilized with the Tokugawa shogunate by the second Korean embassy of 1617, which returned with 150 Koreans taken prisoner during the war. Thereafter until 1793 Korean embassies were sent to Japan to congratulate the new shoguns. In the 188 years from 1606 to 1793 eleven Korean embassies travelled the long sea route from Pusan to Tsushima to Osaka and thence overland to Edo.

The embassies were large affairs and usually numbered close to 500 persons. Since it was traditional for the host nation to pay all the costs of transportation, food, lodging, and entertainment while in their country, plus side trips such as visits to the Tokugawa Tōshō shrine at Nikko, the funds expended by the government upon each of these state visits were not insignificant.

The great expense was noted by the Japanese scholar Arai Hakuseki (1657–1725) when a large Korean embassy arrived in Edo in 1710 to congratulate the new shogun. Arai, the first scholar known to have postulated a relationship between the Korean and Japanese languages, suggested that all future official relations with Korea be conducted through Tsushima. Following the embassy of 1763, the suggestion was implemented, and for the next century Korean embassies proceeded no further than Tsushima. Japanese envoys were never permitted beyond Pusan after the Hideyoshi invasions, which increased the role of the lord of Tsushima in these relations. This may have been another reason for the Japanese restriction. Gradually the lord of Tsushima was able to monopolize the Korean trade, which he jealously protected. When Richard Cox, the head of the English factory in Japan, attempted to contact the Korean embassy of 1616 at Kyōto in order to open an English trading station in Korea, he was blocked from seeing the embassy by the lord of Tsushima. After the shogunate limited Korean envoys to calling at Tsushima, the lords of Tsushima assumed the role of political intermediary between Japan and Korea. In actuality they conducted what amounted to their own foreign policy with Korea and accepted Korean titles, which implied a tributary status to Korea.

At Pusan an official Japanese inn was maintained, and a large number of Japanese resided in the walled community in the Ch'oryang section of the city. The community was under the jurisdiction of the local government administration at Tongnae, a few miles inland, but had its own Japanese magistrate, trade supervisor, and constabulary. Market fairs of 3-days duration were permitted three times a month, a number which was soon doubled. At these markets the Japanese sold silver; alum; cinnabar; porcelain; lacquered articles inlaid with gold, such as folding screens, tables, and saddles; and surplus products from their trade with the Europeans, chiefly the Dutch after 1640, such as sandalwood, black pepper, and water buffalo horn. Through the Pusan market a variety of new plants entered Korea, including tobacco in 1621. In 1763 Kang P'illi (1713–?), the magistrate of Tongnae, obtained sweet potatoes from a Korean embassy returning from Tsushima and acquired a knowledge of their cultivation. He subsequently wrote a treatise on raising the sweet potato, and its cultivation soon spread throughout the peninsula. The potato was a latecomer, being introduced from Ch'ing China in 1824.

The Tongnae merchants traded rice, copper, cotton cloth, silks, ginseng, tiger and leopard skins, hunting birds, writing brushes, cow horn, and medicines. A tax of 10 percent was the standard legal assessment. The Koreans traded surplus items from their trade with China, which was a primary incentive for the Japanese merchants. Later, as the volume of direct trade between Nagasaki and Canton grew, the Korean trade diminished.

In addition to this trade were the official and private gifts exchanged between Koreans and the members of the annual embassies from Tsushima. Similar exchanges of gifts were also part of each annual Korean embassy to Edo until these journeys ceased. The amount of goods involved was considerable, since this was itself a type of trade.

Japanese claims to Ullŭng Island and Tŏkto, a smaller nearby island, were first advanced at this time. After several skirmishes the issue was resolved in Korea's favor in 1697 only to reemerge after the Meiji restoration of 1868. Representatives of the Chosŏn court and the Tokugawa shogunate had two final meetings on the island of Tsushima, one in 1811 and the other in 1845, but were unable to come to an agreement on the resumption of official embassies. The next Korean embassy to the Japanese capital was to be in 1876 and under entirely different circumstances.

ECONOMIC CONDITIONS

In 1510 the Department of Border Defense (*Pibyŏnsa*) was established as a temporary measure at the time of the riots of Japanese residents in the three port cities of the south. It was turned into a permanent organ of government with total control over the Korean military in 1555 following severe *Wakō* incursions in the south and Jürčen raiding in the north. During the wars this department was given complete control over all resources to meet the national emergency. Its chief officials included the presidents of the Ministries of War, Personnel, Finance, and Rites. Its broad-scale approach to the problem of national defense entailed involvement in all phases of government, particularly in finance, and a corresponding loss of power by the Six Ministries as well as a considerable expenditure of national resources on the military in the early period. This situation existed until the latter part of the nineteenth century when, during the reign of Kojong (r. 1863–1907), the regent Hŭngsŏn Taewŏn'gun (1820–1892) once again reinstituted the Joint Council (*Ŭijŏngbu*) as the highest organ of state. The central control exerted by the Department of Border Defense meant in some ways a return to elite council politics. During the years of peace which followed the wars, the Department of Border Defense devoted an increasing amount of its time to domestic problems and a correspondingly less amount of time and resources to military matters.

After the Japanese and Manchu invasions the Korean government found itself in a state of financial crisis. In addition to the loss of life and widespread destruction caused by the wars, important government records had been lost, including slave registers, census records, and land registers. By 1646 land on the tax registers had fallen to about 46 percent of the pre-Japanese invasion level, and government revenues in grain had by 1655 dropped to 13 percent of their preinvasion figure! Reform measures were adopted, but even as late as 1726, registered taxable land was only about 53 percent of the preinvasion figure.

A difficulty that continued to hamper economic reform efforts was the near impossibility of obtaining accurate population and land figures due to their manipulation for tax evasion purposes. The loss of the tax registers led to an increase in private landholdings by officials and powerful local clans, who often reported their new gains in the tax-exempt category of newly opened lands. These and other malpractices by local magistrates led to the institution of the "secret inspector" (*amhaeng ŏsa*), who travelled in disguise through the provinces and reported instances of malfeasance directly to the king.

The financial difficulties also led to the discontinuance of all land allotments in the salary-fields, which had accompanied appointment to government posts. To meet state needs, tax quotas were assigned to the provinces. In the search for new revenue sources, in 1663 more lands were confiscated from Buddhist monasteries. Then an increased burden of taxation fell upon those who remained on the tax registers or who were unable to escape re-registration. Wartime taxes intended to be temporary became permanent.

Tribute quotas given to local magistrates were enforced arbitrarily, thus increasing the power of the local magistrate and the higher elite, who managed effectively to evade the bulk of taxation. To raise additional revenues, a host of miscellaneous levies and taxes were set on salt pans, fish ponds, boats, and the like. Another burden the peasant had to bear was an overstaffed rural administration. A town of 7,000 families might have over 200 persons in the local administration.

The peasants on their own part began to band together and turn toward cooperative enterprises (*kye*) organized on a clan or village basis, often to achieve a single objective such as meeting the tribute levy, the expense of weddings and funerals, or the purchase of oxen or agricultural tools.

There was also widespread discontent among the lower echelons of the *yangban* class as well. The factional struggles, the increase in *yangban* numbers, and the sale of *yangban* status had given rise to a large group of disenfranchised *yangban* who had little if any hope of ever securing appointment to government office. It is probably these disenfranchised *yangban* that nineteenth-century French missionary accounts depict as lazy, corrupt, and given to stealing, gambling, and drinking.

Among the many reform proposals put forth to solve the government's financial crisis was the *taedong* (great equity) system. This type of system was first proposed by Yi I (1536–1584), who suggested that the tribute tax levied by household be replaced with a new tax levied on land and that the government purchase local products directly with the revenues received from the new land tax. The effect of this system was to convert payment of local tribute items into rice, cloth, or cash.

The *taedong* system was put into effect in Kyŏnggi Province in 1608, and in 1623 applied to Kangwŏn, Ch'ungch'ŏng, and Chŏlla Provinces also. Since it shifted a large share of taxes directly to the landowners and took financial control out of the hands of local magistrates, the system had some powerful opposition. Thus, it was abolished in Ch'ungch'ŏng and Chŏlla Provinces after only 3 years. Then the *taedong* system found its champion in Kim Yuk (1580–1658), who fought his entire life for its adoption nationwide. The need for revenues in the 1650's was increased by the extensive military preparations introduced by King Hyojong. Kim Yuk, an economic reformer of the first order, advocated the promotion of commerce through the establishment of permanent commercial enterprises, the utilization of a nationwide overland transport system using horse-drawn vehicles, the purchase of raw copper for issues of coinage, and reform of the tribute tax structure by adoption of the *taedong* system. The system was finally re-instituted in Chŏlla Province in 1658, the year of Kim Yuk's death, and by 1708 had been established in all save the two northern provinces. As adopted, the *taedong* system eliminated the tribute tax levied on households and fixed a standard tax payable in grain, cash, cotton, or land. The tax was payable in two installments, one in spring coinciding with the barley harvest and one in autumn following the rice harvest.

The consequences of the adoption of the *taedong* system were far reaching. It accomplished one primary mission, namely, that of increasing government revenues, and it temporarily lightened the burden of the peasants. The latter, however, were soon made liable for heavy military service taxes.

The military service tax (*kunp'o*) was a standard amount of 2 bolts of cloth annually imposed on all commoner males between the ages of sixteen and fifty-nine. The cloth was used by the government to pay the expenses of the military. The peasants bore the entire burden, which over the years proved to be an onerous one indeed. Local magistrates began to levy the tax on children as well as male adults.

In its search for new revenues the government found a new method of taxation through the "grain return" (*hwan'gok*) system. This system, instituted following a crop failure in the reign of King Sejong, was originally intended to store grain collected from farmers at harvest and then return it to them in the spring at the time the peasants called "barley summit," just before the spring crop was harvested. The grain collected from the grain return system was stored in the "Righteous Granaries" located in the provinces, the contents of which had earlier served as a grain reserve for the military. When the grain was allocated to disaster relief in Sejong's reign, another revenue source was needed to offset the loss. This led to ever-increasing charges on the peasants, who were required to put stipulated amounts of rice into the system. By the mid-sixteenth century the revenues from these charges had become significant enough to be entered as "receipts" in the state income registers. Finally, no grain was returned to the peasants at all. The amounts required of the peasant apparently varied. One record of 1656 reveals that every household in Hamgyŏng Province was required to put 100 Korean bushels of rice into the system that year. By Chŏngjo's reign the state income from this source amounted to nearly 10 million Korean bushels of grain annually, or about nine times the amount of grain collected from the land tax at its highest preinvasion point.

THE GROWTH OF COMMERCE

One result of the nationwide implementation of the *taedong* system was that it stimulated commercial economic development. The needs of the court and the government offices had previously been met by the regional tribute levies paid in specified products and by the output of the numerous government manufactories. Since the *taedong* system converted the old tribute levies into payment in grain, cloth, or cash, a new method of procuring goods for the state had to be found. The government used commercial purchasing agents (*kongin*), who operated through the provinces. The authorized commercial shops in the capital were also utilized to secure goods for government offices, and they soon developed into large-scale monopoly enterprises (*yugijŏn*) which handled certain categories of goods, e.g., some handled chiefly silks, ramie, or cottons, while others dealt in paper and marine products. To protect their monopoly, these entrepreneurs were given the right to confiscate the goods of any merchant in the city who attempted to deal in products which they were authorized to handle. Capital for the principal commercial enterprises was furnished by the state when needed, e.g., to cover the loss of inventories through fire or flood. It is believed that these state-protected enterprises were largely owned and controlled by the wealthy and powerful elite clans.

In addition to the thirty-one large-scale commercial enterprises supplying the government's needs were numerous small shops. All merchants were, of course, registered with the government control bureau (*p'yŏngsisŏ*), which regulated weights and measures, prices, and sales while collecting a stipulated amount of any products sold by the monopoly firms and a general commercial tax from all merchants.

Despite intensive efforts to control, restrict, or even prohibit the development of local markets, commerce, though overregulated, developed. The *Man'gi yoran* of 1808 mentions the existence of 1,060 provincial markets. Local markets were held every 5 days on a staggered schedule to allow for the attendance of the peddlers, who travelled on regular circuits, dealing in clothing, household items, buttons, needles, combs, tools, dried fish, and so forth. The peddlers, like the pack-horse men, who were the major commercial transport facility, organized in guild fashion. The peddlers were recognized and granted certain privileges by the state, notably the issuance of identity certificates which shielded them somewhat from being victimized by lower officials and the *ajŏn* (clerks) in the provinces. The peddlers formed a strong organization which was loyal to the state. Their members helped to win the government victory over the rebel forces of Hong Kyŏngnae in 1812 and were among those who fought the French sailors of Admiral Roze on Kanghwa Island in 1866. In the closing years of the nineteenth century the peddlers were actively used by the government in the political arena.

A number of specialized markets and trade fairs developed. The semi-annual herb markets held at Taegu, Ch'ŏngju, and Kongju drew dealers from throughout the country. The Taegu herb market (*yangnyŏngsi*) was particularly famous and developed as the principal supplier of herbs in the trade with Tokugawa Japan; the market survives today in Taegu's Medicine Lane (*Yakchŏn kolmok*).

Villages specializing in certain products, such as the Catholic village of Chech'on, which specialized in a type of pottery called *paeron*, emerged. Commercial centers began to develop. Chŏnju, the administrative center of Chŏlla Province was already a thriving and prosperous trading town in 1656 when Hamel passed through it. Communities of wealthy merchants developed in major towns such as Kaesŏng, P'yŏngyang, Taegu, Ŭiju, Miryang, and Anju. A guild of innkeepers and owners of wine shops and restaurants (*kaekchu*) emerged which became active in wholesale brokerage dealings and in moneylending. This guild formed a symbiotic commercial relationship with the peddlers, for whom they became a primary source of capital.

The land confiscations of the mid-seventeenth century had literally driven the Buddhist monasteries into commerce, and in contrast to the plentiful supply of slave labor of earlier times, the bulk of the labor for this purpose appears to have been supplied by the monks themselves. Although much of the monastery production, which included woodwork, gold- and silverwork, textiles, fans, and liquors, was intended to be utilized by the monasteries themselves, an increasing amount found its way into the commercial markets. Many monasteries developed speciality products. T'ongdo-sa, a large monastery in Kyŏngsang Province, was particularly noted for the high quality of its vermicelli and paper, which were sold in markets throughout the province.

The expansion of commercial activity meant that cotton cloth and grain were no longer adequate as mediums of exchange, and there had been periodic recommendations for new issues of coins, notably by the presidents of the Ministry of Finance. In 1625 a short-lived issue, *Chosŏn t'ongbo* (Circulating Treasure of Chosŏn), was struck and circulated in the Seoul and Kaesŏng areas. Then, in 1633 the first issue of the *Sangp'yŏng t'ongbo* (Standard Circulating Treasure) was struck. Beginning in 1678 the authority to mint coins was granted to a large number of civil and military offices both in the capital and in the provinces. Issues of the *Sangp'yŏng t'ongbo* coins in a variety of sizes flooded forth from dozens of government offices. These coins, generally known as *yŏpchŏn*, remained the standard medium of exchange in Korea until 1884. The lack of uniformity made counterfeiting relatively easy, while the size of the coins themselves tended to diminish as less metal was used for each succeeding issue.

The development of private commercial activities, particularly in local manufacturing, led to a decline in the government-operated manufactories except in a few instances, e.g., firearms and military equipment, high-quality paper, and ceramics.

Commercial agriculture increased considerably, particularly cultivation of crops with a high cash value which did not require priceless paddy land, such as tobacco and cotton. Government attention to reservoirs and irrigation projects and the adoption of double cropping on a wide scale led to increased yields. New foods, notably the sweet potato and later the potato, were introduced. Unfortunately, despite a rise in the level of agricultural production, population increases kept pace and minimized any gains made.

SOCIAL CHANGES

Concomitant with the large-scale land accumulation by the more powerful elite families was an increase in tenancy as farmers sought to escape the burdens of taxation. A corollary of this was the purchase of *yangban* status and a lapse into tenant status of many *yangban*. The façade of the rigid social structure of the Yi dynasty had been cracked beyond repair. During the period from 1690 to 1729 there was a great decrease in slavery, probably due to the disappearance of government manufactories, and a corresponding increase in the number of commoners on the government registers. Then from about 1789 to 1859 there was a decline in the number of commoners and a corresponding increase in the number of

Late Yi Dynasty Social Change – Taegu District (*pu*)

Note: These figures were compiled from government registers in *one* district. The changing conditions in Korea at this time must be kept in mind when considering the chart. Equal political and economic status is not implied, for example, between the *yangban* of 1690 and the swollen *yangban* ranks of 1858.

Source: After Shikata Hiroshi, *Chōsen keizai no kenkyū*, 3 (1938), 386.

yangban on the census records. By 1801 government slaves were legally made commoners, and the government slave registers were burned, although private slavery remained until it was abolished in 1894.

The changes in the social class structure were reflected in the loss of social control in the examination system. This breakdown first appeared just prior to the wars when the locally appointed officials, such as the *ajŏn*, began to enter the examinations. In the postwar turmoil of the seventeenth century the once rigidly controlled examination system gave way to fraudulent practices and corruption at court. Lineage and patronage proved more vital than knowledge, and at the national examinations the court-appointed examiners automatically passed their own clansmen. Corruption at the regional examinations meant an increase in the number of supposedly qualified candidates flocking into the capital for the national examinations. The large number of candidates, the importance given to lineage and patronage factors, and the limited number of government posts available for distribution meant that the majority of the candidates, many of them undoubtedly well-qualified, were left empty-handed. At times the outcome was a wild riot in the capital. The corruption of the examination system swelled the ranks of the *yangban*, since the only reward the government had left to distribute was a degree.

THE SIRHAK OR PRAGMATIC SCHOOL

Korean intellectuals in the late Yi period were stimulated by two important influences: One was the flow of Western ideas (*sŏhak*) emanating from the Jesuits in the Chinese capital, as a result of which these ideas were associated from the very beginning with Catholicism. The second was the Ch'ing school of empirical studies (c. *k'ao-cheng hsüeh*)—also known as the School of Han Learning—pioneered by the Chinese scholar Ku Yen-wu (1613–1682), whose *Jih-chih-lu* (Record of Daily Observations) was well known in Korea. These two intellectual currents contributed to the development of the Korean Sirhak or Pragmatic school of thought. The Sirhak school might be viewed as a reaction against the metaphysical bent of the philosophers of the Chu Hsi tradition. Sirhak scholars were pioneers in the utilization of the inductive method in studying problems, advocates of administrative and economic reform proposals, and interested inquirers into Western technology and science.

The Western influence coming from China declined briefly in the late eighteenth century after the Jesuits had incurred the displeasure of Ch'ing Emperor Yung-ch'eng by backing a contender for the throne. But by that time the Ch'ing school of empirical studies was flourishing. The *Sirhak* adage "to clarify the truth, seek evidence" is taken from the History of the Former Han Dynasty (*Han shu*) and serves to indicate the intellectual debt to the Ch'ing school.

The forerunners of the Sirhak school were scholars such as the geographer and classicist Han Paekkyŏm (1552–1615), the economic reformer Kim Yuk, and the encyclopedist Yi Sugwang, who had been influenced by

their experiences while members of embassies to the Ch'ing capital. *Pan'gye**
Yu Hyŏngwŏn (1622–1673) is usually regarded as the patriarch of the
Sirhak school. Yu, like the majority of the Sirhak scholars who advocated
institutional reforms, was firmly convinced of the truth of the Confucian
adage "agriculture is the basis of government." He spent the majority of
his life in the countryside and based his reform proposals on his own observations and historical research. Like Kim Yuk he was a strong advocate of
the importance of developing commerce. His major reform ideas included a
proposal to redistribute the land to all members of society in order to create
a broad base of farmers who would till government land and would in turn
contribute taxes and services to the state. In this respect Yu was advocating
the classical ideal of an agricultural state.

By the time of *Sŏngho** Yi Ik (1681–1763) the negative effects of the
taedong system were all too evident, especially in the emergence of a wealthy
commercial class which used its wealth to acquire land and to buy *yangban*
status while circulating private coinage, often debased, in the markets. The
merchants and commercial interests operated in a monetary economy,
as opposed to the barter company of the peasants. Through usurious loans
to peasants and purchase of grain at harvest time and sale of it later when
prices were high, merchants gained large profits while the peasants lost their
land. Yi Ik's reform measures would have prohibited merchants from owning
land and would have protected the peasant from loss of his land. He also
suggested that slaves be incorporated into the economic structure as agricul-
turalists who could be taxed.

The studies of the early Sirhak scholars were not limited to proposals
for reform of state institutions, but covered an extremely broad area, including works on agriculture, history, astronomy, and medicine.

Closely associated with the Sirhak school were members of the
southerner faction, who had been out of power for many years. The mere
fact of being removed from political office may have been an incentive for
such men to depart from the orthodox Chu Hsi tradition espoused by the
state.

The Wang Yang-ming (= Wang Shou-jen 1472–1528) school, founded
by the Ming philosopher, was also known in Korea at an early date. It
propounded the idea of intuitive insight gained from direct experience. Yi
T'oegye in his *Chonsumnokpyŏn* (c. *Chuan-hsi-lu-pien*) strongly refuted its
propositions, and Korean scholars of the early Yi period in general seem
to have supported T'oegye's view. The doctrines of Wang Yang-min began
to attract a following in Korea after the Japanese and Manchu invasions. The
Korean followers of this school began with Nam Ongyong in the sixteenth

---

**Pan'gye* was the literary name of Yu Hyŏngwŏn, and *Sŏngho* was the literary name of
Yi Ik.

century and were followed by *Hagok** Chŏng Chedu (1647–1736), and, finally, continued with a line of scholars such as Yi Kwangsa (1705–1777). By the time the Wang Yang-ming school had begun to gain adherents in Korea, the school of empirical studies in China and the Korean Sirhak school attracted those who might otherwise have been drawn to the Wang Yang-ming school.

The older *sŏngni* school continued to flourish with such followers of *Hwadam** Sŏ Kyŏngdŏk as *Nongmun** Im Songju (1711–1788) and the rise of another opposing monist school which emphasized the dominant role of *i* (see page 169), whose greatest representative was *Nosa** Ki Chŏngjin (1798–1876). The brilliant period of the Korean *sŏngni* philosophers had passed, and Korean intellectuals began to turn more toward the ideas advanced by the Sirhak scholars and the Ch'ing school of empirical studies.

KING YŎNGJO'S POLICY OF IMPARTIALITY

The monarch Yŏngjo (r. 1724–1776) came to the throne amidst a bloody struggle between the *soron* and *noron* factions, with the latter emerging victorious. The factional struggle led to a short-lived revolt by Yi Injwa in 1728, who was joined by a number of military officials in the provinces. These experiences stimulated King Yŏngjo to call the *noron* and *soron* faction leaders together to convince them to support a policy of "impartiality." The political armistice that followed acknowledged the primacy of the *noron* faction and the supporting role of the *soron* faction while leaving some room for political appointees from the northerner and southerner faction.

The success of Yŏngjo's policy of impartiality was chiefly due to its realistic partiality. In these measures King Yŏngjo was probably influenced by similar actions taken by his contemporary the Ch'ing Emperor Yin-chen (r. 1723–1736), who in 1725 published his *P'eng-tang-lun* (Treatise on Cliques and Factions). In 1759, King Yŏngjo took a line from the *Analects*, expanded it a bit, and then had it engraved on stone and erected in the Sŏnggyun'gwan Academy:

> To be impartial and not partisan is the nature
> of the superior man.
>
> To be partisan and not impartial is truly the
> unsanctioned opinion of the inferior man.

*Hagok, Hwadam, Nongmun, and *Nosa* are the literary names of the individuals whose names they precede.

Yŏngjo's policies had their opponents. One of them, Yi Chŏngp'o, objected on the grounds that an impartial policy left no basis for discrimination between the loyal and the disloyal, the sagacious and the base! But Yŏngjo's efforts were relatively successful, and they opened the way for the brightest period of the late Yi dynasty.

From about 1800 the factional struggles were overshadowed by power struggles involving the royal family which continued to the end of the dynasty. A late effort was made by the Taewŏn'gun, who was regent during the youth of his son King Kojong (r. 1863–1907) and acted to break the factional affiliations, but by that time other events were rapidly making the question academic. The factional struggles which debilitated the late Yi dynasty were a senseless tragedy which critically weakened the kingdom at a time when a new and unprecedented challenge was appearing on the horizon.

THE INTELLECTUAL REVIVAL

By the reign of King Yŏngjo (r. 1724–1776) the central government had recovered from the financial crisis of the seventeenth century, and a traditional society was beginning to reassert itself. Factional struggles had been partially eliminated by the retention of power by the *noron* faction for a century. The impartial policies of employing men of talent from all factions during the reigns of Yŏngjo and his successor King Chŏngjo (r. 1776–1800) brought men into government who had been associated with the Sirhak school. State patronage for compilation of works during this period led to a burst of intellectual brilliance and activity. Among the major works of Yŏngjo's reign were the hundred-volume comprehensive encyclopedia *Tongguk munhŏn pigo* (1768–1769); the legal compendiums *Sugyo chimnok* (1742) and *Sok Taejŏn* (1743); a supplement to the ceremonial code, *Sok oryeŭi* (1743); an agricultural text, the *Nongga chipsŏng* (1733); a new compilation of court music, the *Kukcho akchang* (1764); a work on general education and behavior, the *Chohun*; and works on military science, such as the *Sok pyŏngjang tosŏl* (1748). This was a period of updating and improving the administrative codes and similar texts used by officials, which had been standard for centuries. In overall terms this revitalized intellectual activity was a continuance of traditional types of scholarship. These efforts extended into the economic field also, with an attempt made to equalize the tax burden and renovate the transport system. Three coastal granaries were established in Kyŏngsang Province, extending the maritime grain transport system to that area for the first time.

In 1776, the first year of his reign, Chŏngjo established the Royal Library (*Kyujanggak*), which functioned as a research library somewhat similar to the Hall of Assembled Scholars of the reign of Sejong. At the same time, the influence of Ch'ing scholarship began to take hold in Korea. The result was an outpouring of government-sponsored works in such areas as national history (An Chŏngbok's *Tongsa kangmok*, Han Ch'iyun's *Haedong yŏksa*), local history (Yi Chunghwan's *Taengniji*), Korean language (Sin Kyŏngjun's *Hunmin chŏngun unhae*), agriculture, phonology, medicine, veterinary medicine, geography, astronomy, cartography, and epigraphy.

Also during this period of Ch'ing influence two great scholars appeared: *Tasan** Chŏng Yagyong (1762–1836), considered the greatest of all *Sirhak* scholars, and the brilliant Pak Chega (1750–1815). The latter and his followers are generally known as members of the School of Northern Studies (*Pukhak*) after the *Pukhak-ŭi* (The Meaning of Northern Studies), a work in which Pak examined aspects of the Ch'ing economic structure.

Chŏng Yagyong had been drawn to Western ideas and Catholicism and is related to have employed Western engineering techniques in the construction of the walls of the town of Suwŏn. His associations with Catholicism led to his exile in 1801 for 17 years, during which Chŏng devoted himself to studies. He drew heavily from Chinese translations of Western texts and also introduced Western glass manufacturing and smallpox vaccination techniques. He produced several reform proposals for renovation of the central and regional governmental structures and the legal system. In his *Mongmin simsŏ* (Principles of Governing the People) Chŏng presented his ideas on rural administration based on his own experiences and research. Among his other proposals was the establishment of a type of agricultural community (*yŏjŏn*). Taxes and the stipend of the farm supervisor were to be deducted from each harvest, the remainder of the harvest being divided among the peasant members based upon the amount of labor each had contributed. Like Yi Ik, and for the same general reasons, Chŏng was opposed to the development of commerce.

A completely different view was put forth by Pak Chega, the patriarch of the School of Northern Studies. He saw a relationship between the demands for products and the resources in skilled workers, tools, and so forth, necessary for their production. This led him to postulate that increased consumption would raise levels of production. Production, he believed, was the basis of national wealth without regard to whether or not it was agricultural production. These ideas led Pak to propose regionally oriented occupations; the circulation of wealth, which he felt would stabilize prices—he apparently had a notion of the multiplier effect as well—and finally foreign trade as a stimulus to domestic commerce.

Among the early scholars of the School of Northern Studies was the

---

*Tasan was Chong's literary name.

witty satirist Pak Chiwŏn (1737–1805), who ridiculed the *yangban* and praised the virtues of commercial activities in such short stories as the Story of Master Hŏ (*Hŏsaengjŏn*).

In its emphasis upon economic measures and the extent to which it drew upon Ch'ing scholarship, the School of Northern Studies represents in many respects a continuation of the same intellectual current which produced Kim Yuk and Yu Hyŏngwŏn. Most of these scholars had been profoundly influenced by trips made to Peking as members of Korean embassies. There they met both Chinese and Western scholars. Hong Taeyong (1731–1783), a noted astronomer and mathematician, is a good example. In 1765 in Peking Hong met the Jesuits Augustine de Hallerstein (1703–1774) and Antoine Gogeisl (1701–1771), who were members of the Imperial Board of Astronomy. He later wrote of this meeting in his *Yu-P'o mundap* (Conversation with Hallerstein and Gogeisl.) In drawing inspiration and knowledge from Ch'ing China, the scholars of the School of Northern Studies were following in the footsteps of generations of Korean intellectuals.

LITERARY ACTIVITY

In the seventeenth and eighteenth centuries prose and poetic writing, for several centuries the monopoly of the educated scholar-official, had finally become the common possession of the merchant, the peasant, and the housewife. And as it did so, it sapped the authority of the *yangban*.

Anonymous *kasa* poetry began to appear on romantic themes, with subject matter drawn from daily life rather than from Chinese classics and poetry. The *sijo*, now past its grand period, was turned into a slightly longer verse form appropriately called *sasŏl* or narrative *sijo*.

The popularization of literature did not mean a total escape from Chinese influence; on the contrary Chinese works continued to exert a dominant influence on Korean prose, but the Korean adaptations of Chinese works tended increasingly to be written in the Korean language. The tendency for the scholar-officials to write in Chinese did not go entirely unchallenged. *Sŏp'o* Kim Manjung (1637–1692), the author of the widely read fantasy Cloud Dream of Nine (*Kuunmong*, 1689), argued forcefully for the use of the Korean language in writing and likened scholars writing in Chinese, a foreign language, to "parrots imitating human speech."

Nevertheless one of the most widely read books in Korea following the wars was the Chinese novel *San-kuo-chih yen-i* (Romance of the Three Kingdoms), which Kim Manjung ruefully admitted was committed to memory even by women and children. Even the philosopher Yi Ik was shocked at the popularity of this historical romance, which, he relates, was "read and told in every house, and even at the civil service examination site"! This widely imitated Chinese novel influenced the form of many of the adventurous and romantic Korean military tales which appeared after the Japanese and Manchu invasions. One of the best known of these is the *Imjinnok*, a tale replete with heroic bravado, which uses the Japanese invasion period as a background. Although military stories are rather natural after a war—the outpouring of such works after the United States Civil War being a good example—there are at least three points worth mentioning regarding these Korean stories. First, most were fantasies—which distinguishes them from the American war tales—and they fulfilled a psychological need for heroes and victories, which had been all too scarce in the conflicts themselves. Second, they enabled an open expression of contempt to be directed against the *yangban*. Third, they expressed a spirit of free individualism which contained nuances of social dissatisfaction and displayed a distinct interest in popular Buddhism and Taoism.

Another adaptation from a Chinese novel was The Story of Hong Kildong (*Hong Kildong chŏn*) by Hŏ Kyun (1569–1618), often called Korea's first novel. While Hŏ Kyun admittedly modelled the work after the popular Chinese adventure tale *Shui-hu-chuan* (Water Margin), he added a distinctive Korean dimension by making the hero a member of the *sŏŏl* class. Discriminated against by society, Hong leads a Robin Hood type of bandit group which takes wealth from corrupt magistrates and distributes it to the poor. Full of fantasy, it is escapist literature of the first order and packed with astounding feats and *deus ex machina* solutions, since Hong has the ability to change form, to shorten distances, and so forth. In the end Hong becomes ruler of an island where he dispenses beneficent government for the good of all. Despite its derivation from a Chinese prototype, The Story of Hong Kildong has a distinct place in Korean literature as one of the early social protest stories, stressing the plight of the unfortunate *sŏŏl*. Its second distinction is that it was written in Korean.

The flood of popular tales that poured out in the seventeenth to nineteenth centuries was often rich with songs and lengthy dialogues, features suggesting their possible origins from story-tellers' tales. Most circulated in both Korean and Chinese editions. In content they ranged from adaptations of old *jātaka* or Buddhist fables as in The Story of the Rabbit (*T'okkijŏn*), which is also found in the thirteenth century *Samguk yusa*; imported folk-tales such as *K'ongjwi p'atchwi*, the Korean version of the Cinderella story; stories which combined both Confucian and Buddhist elements such as The Story of Simch'ŏng (*Simch'ongjŏn*), a tale of a dutiful daughter—a similar story is known in Japan under the name *Koya himi*—and the greatest of them all The Story of Ch'unghyang (*Ch'unghyangjŏn*) an anonymous romance of the eighteenth century which remains today the most popular and well-loved Korean story ever written.

These stories also circulated in oral fashion in the genre known as *p'ansori*, with all parts sung or chanted by a single male performer. In the early nineteenth century these versions were written down in individual and choral arrangements by Sin Chaehyo (1812–1884).

By the eighteenth century there had developed a considerable literature of protest and social criticism. The same themes were a principal element of the Korean *sandae* (mask) plays performed by itinerant players on market days in the countryside. Representative of these works which criticized and ridiculed the *yangban* class, objected to concubinage, protested arranged marriages, and derided the wayward Buddhist monks were the stories of Pak Chiwŏn.

PERFORMING ARTS

During the seventeenth century the central government office in charge of *sandae* mask plays for the court was closed and the performers dismissed. The reasons were probably largely the financial crisis, although court tastes seem to have shifted in favor of the graceful Boating Dance or the excitement of the Drum Dance performed by court *kisaeng* troupes as opposed to the all-male *sandae* performances. At any rate, it appears that *sandae* troupes wandered about the country giving performances on market days and at the invitation of wealthy merchants, finally settling down in some locale, and the traditions were transmitted from generation to generation. In some instances *sandae* plays apparently mingled with shamanistic *kut* performances and took on a religious character such as may be seen in the Hahoe masked performance, which is a blend of purely shamanistic ceremony and *sandae* episodes. No permanent theaters existed; rather the performances were in the open air shows, often on a hillside for the better viewing pleasure of the audience. The *sandae* performances seem to have been for the non-*yangban* element of Yi dynasty society, the *yangban* elite being drawn to such small-group activities as boating or drinking parties with *kisaeng* entertainers. Upon more formal occasions they favored performances of the sword dance or the Ch'ŏyong dance by *kisaeng* sponsored by a local magistrate or the elaborate and sophisticated dances of the court performers. The *sandae* plays of the late Yi dynasty are one further manifestation of the process of popularization which occurred in this period. It should be noted that the performers themselves were viewed as members of the outcaste class. There are two distinct styles evident in the *sandae* plays, one drawn from the Chinese poetic tradition and incorporating allusions to Chinese verse, and the second a rather bawdy folk burlesque. Structurally the plays are a series of episodes arranged into acts and given unity by a common theme, such as the apostate monk or the *yangban* who is made the butt of jokes by his servant.

These features may be seen in the following extracts from the Pongsang mask play:

The Eight Monks

FIRST MONK:

> (*Wears a long red jacket and carries a willow branch in his hand. On his back he carries a large bell and he runs onto the stage. His hair hangs in his face and he totters about, covering his face with his sleeves, he dances circling the stage keeping time with the music. Then he falls down and lies jerking his legs, arms, and body in time to the music. He tries to get up, finally makes it on the fourth try, and goes into a spirited dance.*)

SECOND MONK:

> (*Runs onto the stage, slaps the first monk in the face and the first monk exits. The second monk dances around the stage and then advances to the front of the seated musicians, looks right and left.*)
>
> "Shhhhh. . . .
>
> (*Music and dance stop. The second monk sings*)
>
> Deep in the mountains without a calendar
> the seasons pass imperceptibly.
> The flowers bloom and its spring,
> the leaves appear and its summer.
> The paulownia looses its leaves and its autumn.
> And when the snow falls its winter.
> I too, originally a wastrel
> buried deep in the mountains
> listened with joy to the call of the elegant life.
> I forgot the invocations to Buddha
> and now I've found this pleasure spot.
>
> (*Music commences and second monk dances then intones*)
>
> "Shhhhhh. . . .
>
> Serve the guests after the sacrifices are offered;
> in the affairs of man do your best
> and trust to Heaven for the rest.
> Now a word about the affairs of man . . .!
>
> (*Sings*)
>
> The heart does not grow old
> The heart does not grow old
> In the cold snow-covered mountains
> The heart does not grow old."
>
> (*The second monk dances with a lively air, then the third monk runs on stage, hits him in the face and he exits.*)

Two puppet plays popular during the late Yi dynasty were the *Mansŏk* (Ten Thousand Bushel) *Monk* play, presented in monasteries in the spring on the occasion of the birthday of Buddha, and the *Kkoktugaksi*. The former is a mimed skit with a marionette and paper animals manipulated on strings. The *Kkoktugaksi* is a much more elaborate, episodic play involving the pretentious and cowardly *yangban* protagonist Pak Chŏmji (*chŏmji* is a minor official title), his wife *Kkoktugaksi* (*-gaksi* means a recent bride), his mistress, Hong Tongji, a poor relation, and assorted other characters, including Ismi, a serpent. Hong Tongji, who lives beyond the mountain in the countryside, is continually summoned to save Pak Chŏmji from the recurring crises of the play. The ridicule of the shiftless *yangban* of the play is contrasted by the fearless and forthright manner of Hong Tongji, whose earthy language and appearance—he is stark naked and painted bright red—offers social comment in a slapstick, humorous fashion.

PAINTING

The work of the court artists such as Kim Myŏngguk continued to dominate painting during the late Yi period, primarily because of the lack of patronage beyond court circles. But in the late eighteenth and early nineteenth centuries genre painting came into its own. This trend began with the great artist *Kyŏmjae* Chŏng Son who turned his talented hand toward the Korean landscape and animal paintings and in so doing moved a pace apart from the set academic styles which dominated court painting. His pupil Sin Yunbok (1758–1820) carried this further and became known for his paintings of gentlemen of leisure at their ease with *kisaeng* entertainers. A contemporary of Sin's, Kim Tuksin (1754–1822), although he also did the more traditional landscape paintings, painted scenes of peasant life, as in his painting of a landlord watching peasants at threshing time. Kim Hongdo (b. 1760) painted scenes of urban life of the common people, of a crowd watching a wrestling match, a blacksmith at work, and the like. The changes in theme matched the temper of the time.

THE PERSECUTIONS OF THE CATHOLICS

Christianity, declared a heterodox teaching, was proscribed by the authorities in 1786, and a ban on all Christian tracts was issued. Then in 1791 an incident occurred in Chŏlla Province which occasioned a heated debate at court. A certain Yun Chich'ung and his brother-in-law, Kwŏn Sangyŏn, had observed Catholic funeral rites for Yun's mother in lieu of the traditional, orthodox Confucian rites. They had also burned the wooden Confucian tablet containing the deceased's name which was used in ancestor worship. Ancestor worship was viewed as the duty of respectful sons, while respect for one's parents was considered analogous to loyalty to the monarch.

This made the act of destroying ancestral tablets an act of disloyalty to the king. Yun and Kwŏn were arrested and executed.

At court the incident had become involved in the factional struggle. There had been a split in the dominant *noron* faction, which had been in power for a century, into the *pyŏk* and *si* factions. The *pyŏk* faction supported by the queen dowager—i.e., the Chŏngsun queen, wife of Yŏngjo—used the association with Catholicism and Western learning against members of the *si* faction and the faction of southerners. Although the incident was to pass with relative calm, the lines had been formed for a bloody struggle in the days to come. Several officials were exiled, and many Christian converts turned over to the authorities were killed; but there was no major persecution. This was due, it appears, mainly to the powerful minister Ch'ae Chegong (1720–1799), whose factional affiliations led him to support the moderate policy favored by King Chŏngjo.

In 1794 an appeal was made by Korean Christians to the diocese of Peking which resulted in the dispatch to Seoul of the Chinese priest Father Chou Wen-mo (1752–1801), a member of the first class to graduate from the Peking Theological Seminary. Father Chou, guided by Korean Christians, crossed the frozen Yalu at night in the winter of 1794 and arrived in Seoul in early 1795. The proscription of Catholicism prevented open proselytizing, and after a few months Father Chou was reported to the authorities. He managed to avoid arrest and hid in the home of a convert, where he was to live the majority of the next 6 years. During those years he made trips through the city, converted and baptized two ladies of the royal household, and met scholars such as Chŏng Yagyong, whose elder and younger brothers had become Catholics. He also travelled through Ch'ungch'ŏng and Chŏlla Provinces preaching the faith. It is estimated that within 5 years of his arrival, the Catholic community in Korea grew from 3,000 to 10,000 persons. These days were to be short-lived.

In 1801, the first persecutions began. As soon as Sunjo (r. 1800–1834) was on the throne, the *pyŏk* faction backed by the queen dowager began to move against their opposition, principally members of the *si* and southerner factions. Instructions were issued in the name of the queen strictly proscribing all heterodox teachings and ordering a rigid enforcement of the five-household mutual guarantee system, which would enable all Catholics to be discovered and arrested rapidly. In the central government, the Censorate and the Office of Inspector General were utilized to prosecute officials connected with the new and heterodox teachings.

The role of those executed would reach 300 by the year's end. They included Father Chou Wen-mo; (Peter) Yi Sunghun (1756–1801), baptized in Peking by Father Louis de Gammont in 1794; and his uncle, Yi Kahwan

(1752–1801). Southerners by factional affiliation, the Yi men were descendants of Yi Ik. Also executed were the members of a small Catholic study group formed in 1777 which included the elder brother of the Sirhak scholar Chŏng Yagyong. Chŏng Yagyong himself was banished to Kangjin, where he remained in exile 17 years; his younger brother was exiled to Hŭksan Island. The persecutions touched the royal household as well. Yi In, the lord of Ŭnŏn, his wife, and his daughter-in-law were forced to commit suicide.

In the late autumn of 1801 two messengers carrying a lengthy (13,000 characters) message written on silk and destined for the Catholic authorities in Peking were intercepted by the government. The message, dated October 21, 1801, written by Hwang Sayŏng, a follower of Chou Wen-mo, described the persecutions and appealed to the church authorities for aid. In his desperate appeal, said to have been written while he was hiding in a cave in the south, Hwang urged the Catholic authorities to call upon the Christian nations of the West for a fleet of warships and a holy army which would subdue Korea and subordinate it to the Emperor of China, who would then make the Korean authorities accept Western priests, and the faith could be spread on the peninsula. Hwang was captured a few days later and executed, while members of his family were individually exiled to widely separated islands.

The incident provided a rationale for the persecutions already carried out. A distorted account of the incident was sent to Peking to obtain Chinese authority for the actions taken.

Just as the literati purges of the early Yi period had swept away the brilliant era of the fifteenth century, the eminent achievements of the reigns of Kings Yŏngjo and Chŏngjo ended when the persecutions of the Catholics began in 1801.

When the Andong Kim clan came to power, a more moderate attitude was adopted toward the Catholics, since the head of the clan, the influential minister Kim Chosun, was a convert to the new religion. During this period several French priests set out from China for Korea, among them Father Pierre-Philibert Maubant (1803–1839) and Father Bathelemy C. Bruguière (1793–1835). Father Bruguière, who had been appointed apostolic vicar of Korea, died in Manchuria en route in the spring of 1835, and only Father Maubant managed to enter Korea. Then came Father Jacques Honoré Chastan (d. 1839) and Father Lament Joseph Marius Imbert (1797–1839) in 1837 and 1839, respectively.

Kim Chosun died in 1831, and power passed to the P'ungyang Cho clan, who attempted to eliminate the Andong Kim clan's influence by a persecution of Catholic converts. Some 130 died, including all the French priests, who were executed in the persecutions which broke out in 1839. The proscription of Catholicism remained severe for several years. Father (André) Kim Taegon (1822–1846), who returned to Korea in 1845 after training in the Portuguese seminary at Macao, was another victim of the persecutions.

Then in 1850 the persecutions abated when the Andong Kim clan regained power. More French priests entered the country, Catholic converts multiplied, and a seminary was even built at Chech'ŏn, in the northeastern part of North Ch'ungch'ŏng Province.

SOCIAL UNREST

From about 1800 the peninsula was racked with revolts large and small in every corner of the kingdom. There is a new element which distinguishes these revolts, namely, the banding together of many different social classes, reflecting the deep-rooted discontent of the period.

Adding to the many diverse factors which contributed to this widespread unrest was a series of severe epidemics, famines, and floods. During the sixteenth to nineteenth centuries epidemics affecting entire provinces appeared about every 12 years, while a nationwide epidemic struck about every 50 years. In 1728 an epidemic carried away an estimated quarter of a million people. A century later a catastrophic cholera epidemic broke out in the northwest in 1821 and burned through the countryside during the next two summers. The accumulated medical knowledge of centuries proved useless and perhaps a million or more perished. Under the growing impact of a monetary economy and the limitless extortions of avaricious local officials, the Korean peasant reacted as best he could. When possible he sought safety in those types of organizations which were allowed to exist. There is a noted rise of commercial villages, i.e., villages which specialized in the manufacture of speciality items such as brassware or pottery or engaged in mining operations. These village specializations were, of course, a response to price incentives as much as to local conditions. Mutual aid societies (*kye*) flourished. There was, however, an unfortunate lack of a means for redress of grievances, since petitions submitted would usually be refused, as higher authorities were extremely reluctant to reverse the decision or action of a local magistrate.

In a search for alternatives the peasants turned to rebellion and religion. The persecution of the Catholics in 1801, 1839, and again in the period 1866 to 1876 had only increased the unrest. Banditry became rampant, and groups such as the P'yŏngan Province Gang were bold enough to paste warnings to the government on the four main gates of the capital in 1804. Other bands, such as the West River Gang and the Old Han Commanderies Gang, flourished in the provinces as peasants swelled their ranks.

In 1811 a particularly large-scale revolt occurred under the leadership of the wealthy landowner Hong Kyŏngnae (1780–1812). This revolt, well-planned and well-organized, drew upon all social classes, including peasants, merchants, and local government officials. At one point the rebels held all the territory north of the Ch'ŏngch'ŏn River in the northwest. The rebellion was fought to the end at the walled town of Chŏngju, where Hong's 3,000 men were defeated by a government force which outnumbered them almost three to one. Survivors of Hong's group reformed under new leadership and led another abortive uprising in 1817.

The rebellion of Hong Kyŏngnae was merely a symptom of the social, economic, and political discontent which had produced it. The participation of men from every social class is particularly noteworthy, for it reveals not only the depth of the unrest but in some measure the degree to which Yi dynasty society had already changed.

The rebellion of Hong Kyŏngnae had no sooner been put down than a terrible drought struck the nation in the years 1812 to 1813, producing a famine which produced a record death toll—it was alleged that 4.5 million died. During the second year of the drought the powerful Yang clan of Cheju Island also staged a brief revolt. The nation had fallen on evil times. Thieves were reported rampant in the capital, pirates had gained control of the lower reaches of the Han River, and in 1833 rice riots erupted in Seoul, and government warehouses were stormed and looted.

Under these conditions it is not surprising to see an increase in the popularity of the shamaness and in works of prophecy such as *Chŏnggamnok*. New religions began to appear and to attract adherents. The most popular was *Tonghak* or Eastern Learning, founded by Ch'oe Cheu (1824–1864) in the Kyŏngsang area in about 1860. *Tonghak*, later called *Ch'ŏndogyo*, was a syncretic religion incorporating values and beliefs drawn from Christianity, Confucianism, Buddhism, and Taoism. One of the principal tenets of the *Tonghak* beliefs was expressed in the formula of faith *innaech'ŏn* (man is heaven).

Just as Ch'oe's teachings were gaining in popularity, the three southern provinces were consumed by rebellion. An uprising began in the early spring of 1862 in the southern town of Chinju. Several thousand peasants wearing white headbands swarmed through the city killing local officials and wealthy merchants in a mad and bloody 23-day rampage. The spirit of revolt spread quickly, and before the government soldiers and the winter snows put an end to it, the revolt had swept through eighteen cities in the south.

The following year Ch'oe Cheu was arrested. Ch'oe, it was reported, had predicted that 1864 would be a propitious year for the *Tonghak* members, and so the government executed him in that year as a warning to his followers. The movement, however, gained strength through Ch'oe's martyrdom, and in 1894 its followers launched the *Tonghak* Rebellion which almost toppled the government. The rebellion itself led the court to call on China for assistance, and the subsequent landing of Chinese and Japanese forces on the peninsula provided the *casus belli* for the Sino-Japanese War.

PALACE POLITICS: QUEENS AND THE GREAT CLANS

During the latter half of the eighteenth century the Korean monarchs were turned into figureheads. The authority and power of the state was exercised by royal relatives, usually the queen's clan, who filled important government ministerial posts with their brothers, cousins, and uncles while striving to control the succession to the throne by marrying daughters to the crown prince. These palace intrigues and court battles were being fought at a time when Yi dynasty society was undergoing a period of rapid and violent internal change and increasing pressure from abroad.

In 1749, King Yŏngjo (r. 1724–1776) was 56 years old. He had reigned for 26 years. His principal wife, the Chŏngsun queen (1745–1805), had no issue, but two sons had been born by lesser wives. One had died young. The remaining son was the Changhŏn prince (1735–1762) who, in 1749, began to represent the aging Yŏngjo on state councils. This prince was favored by the *si* faction and opposed by the *pyŏk* faction into which the dominant *noron* group had divided. The Chŏngsun queen, whose voice carried increasingly greater authority as Yŏngjo grew older, sided with the *pyŏk* faction. When the prince took a pleasure trip to the east coast in 1761, charges of licentious behavior were lodged against him. Eight officials who had accompanied him were summarily dismissed. Yŏngjo, convinced by the *pyŏk* faction ministers and the Chŏngsun queen of the truth of the charges, had the prince smothered to death in a rice chest. He later regretted the action and conferred the appelation *sado* (one who is mourned) on the prince. Yŏngjo continued to reign until his death in 1776, with the Chŏngsun queen active in the background.

During the brief reign of the monarch Chŏngjo (r. 1776–1800) power struggles began between the powerful clans. The first two clans involved were the Hong clan of P'ungsan and the Kim clan of Ch'ŏngp'ung, members of which had supported Chŏngjo to the throne. As these groups fought between themselves, the Chŏngsun queen, now the queen dowager, consolidated power herself. When Chŏngjo died, his second son, a young lad of eleven, known to posterity as Sunjo (r. 1800–1834), was steered to the throne by the queen dowager, who kept state affairs in her own hands. She appointed Kim Chosun (?–1831) to assist her in governing. Kim, a member of the Andong Kim clan of Kyŏngsang Province and a Catholic convert, was able to marry his daughter, age eleven, to King Sunjo. It was largely to this clanswoman the Sunwŏn queen (1789–1857), that the Andong Kim clan would owe its position. When Sunjo died in 1834, she became the queen dowager and reigned as regent when her grandson, the 8-year-old monarch Hŏnjong (r. 1834–1849), was put on the throne. She quickly married a clanswoman to the young king.

Then control of affairs was briefly seized by King Hŏnjong's mother, Princess Cho. She was a member of the Cho clan of P'ungyang. Through her, the chief Cho clan official at court, the powerful minister Cho Manyong (1776–1846), pushed the clan to a position of dominance. It was a brief moment of glory. Cho Manyong died in 1846. King Hŏnjong died 3 years later without heir at the age of twenty-three. Princess Cho, her influence superseded by Queen Dowager Kim, i.e., the Sunwŏn queen, quietly bided her time.

Queen Dowager Kim assembled the high ministers of the court and put the question of succession to them. After several days of debate, the queen dowager herself decided upon one of the candidates put forth. Yi Wŏnbŏm, a lad of nineteen then living on a poor farm on Kanghwa Island, was chosen. An influencing reason may have been the fact that Yi Wŏnbŏm, later Ch'ŏljong (r. 1850–1863), had lost his father some years before, which meant that he would not be present to attempt to exercise influence through his son. The result was that power was retained by Queen Dowager Kim. She married a clanswoman to King Ch'ŏljong, and power was once again firmly in the hands of the Andong Kim clan. King Ch'ŏljong, an unsophisticated farm lad placed suddenly into the rigid discipline of court ceremonial rituals and the indulgence of palace luxury, apparently drank himself to death. Queen Dowager Kim had died several years before, and King Ch'ŏljong left only one daughter.

At this point the aging Princess Cho stepped in as the most influential voice representing the royal family. It is said that she made a secret pact with Yi Haŭng (1870–1898), a distant member of the royal family, to put his son on the throne. This, at any rate, is what happened. Her primary reasons appear to have been to end the supremacy of her archenemies the Andong Kim clan. Her maneuvers were successful. Yi Myŏngbok, the second son of Yi Haŭng, known to posterity as King Kojong (r. 1863–1907), was put on the throne as the twenty-sixth and penultimate ruler of Chosŏn. He was 12 years old. His father was given the title of Hŭngsŏn Taewŏn'gun and acted as regent during his son's minority.

King Kojong was the son of Yi Haŭng by a wife of the Yŏhŭng Min clan and was himself married to a girl of the Yŏhŭng Min clan. This brought the Min clan, which had married daughters into the royal line as early as the reign of T'aejong, into a powerful position and later precipitated an intense struggle between Queen Min and the Hŭngsŏn Taewŏn'gun.

THE END OF A TRADITION

As the nineteenth century opened, Korea came under increasing pressure from abroad. Sightings of alien ships in Korean waters, previously the objects of peripheral interest to the crowd, now sent gunners running to their stations. Since the attempt of the English vessel *Lord Amherst* to open trade relations in 1832, foreign ships had become more frequent in Korean waters, and their demands for commercial privileges had become increasingly more insistent. In the northeast the Russians had built a settlement on the Tumen River and were pressing for trade relations and timber rights. The 1839 persecution of Catholics had brought a French squadron from China in 1846. Unable to obtain an answer to their inquiries the French left a note and promised to come back. When they returned in 1866 for a reply, an attack on the fortifications on Kanghwa Island ensued. In the same year a private American vessel, the *General Sherman*, sailed up the Taedong River at flood tide on a suspect mission, grounded when the tide dropped, and was burned in the fight which followed. Her anchor chains were hung in a gate in the city of Kaesŏng in triumph. An attempt was made by an international rag-tag group of European-led adventurers outfitted in China to loot the tomb of the Regent Hŭngsŏn Taewŏn'gun's father and carry off the bones for ransom. Then, in 1871 American warships in Korean waters were fired upon by the Kanghwa Island batteries, and they responded with a charging attack on the island.

The gunboat incidents, of which only a few have been mentioned, led the regent to adopt a strict antiforeign isolation policy in an attempt to preserve the kingdom. At the same time he carried out measures aimed at strengthening the state, and made an effort to eliminate factionalism. His antifaction policies raised opposition among the elite, and his levies to reconstruct Kyŏngbok Palace caused unrest among the masses. In 1874, when King Kojong reached his majority, the regent was forced to retire. This brought the Min clan into power, and a power struggle soon erupted between the crusty regent and Queen Min.

With Queen Min now the influential voice at court the Korean authorities looked to China for assistance, as they had done for centuries. Then in 1875 further gunboat incidents culminated in an engagement between Korean shore batteries and the Japanese warship *Unyō*. The outcome of the subsequent negotiations was the Treaty of Kanghwa in 1876, which, among other things, called for the opening of three ports to international trade, viz., the old Japanese trading settlement at Pusan; Chemulp'o (Inch'ŏn), the seaport for Seoul; and the port of Wŏnsan on the east coast. Upon Chinese advice the Korean authorities attempted to offset the Japanese influence in Korea by concluding treaties with a number of Western nations: the United States

(1882), England and Germany (1883), Italy and Russia (1884), and France (1886). The isolation had ended, not for the sake of embracing the new and the unknown, but as an attempt to preserve the old and the familiar.

The regent, although retired, had not been inactive politically and regained power briefly through a revolt of the Korean military in 1882. He was then removed in a rather blunt manner. A Chinese squadron sailed into Chemulp'o, and the regent was invited aboard to inspect the flagship. Once he was aboard ship, the crew hoisted anchor and sailed for China. He was later brought back to Korea, where he died in 1898 at the age of seventy-nine.

In 1894 the *Tonghak* Rebellion swept through the country and brought both Japanese and Chinese armies onto the peninsula. In 1895 Queen Min, the strong hand behind the throne, was murdered at the instigation of the Japanese minister in Korea, and power was momentarily seized by Japanese supported Korean "progressives."

These tumultuous events did not topple the Yi dynasty. On the contrary, the king, under the influence of Russian counsel, took the pretentious title of "emperor" in 1897. In one sense the tottering dynasty was held together by foreign powers, each attempting to use the monarch to place Korea firmly under its own control. It was now apparent that the Korean authorities could no longer control nor even decisively influence those events which would decide Korea's future. With the international tide of imperialism running high, it had become a question not of whether Korea would be under the dominant influence of some foreign state but rather which foreign state and under what conditions. This was settled in favor of Japan in land and naval engagements in the Sino-Japanese War of 1894–1895 and the Russo-Japanese War of 1904–1905.

In 1905, Korea was placed under Japanese protection. King Kojong naïvely attempted to place the matter before an international deliberative body at the peace conference in the Hague, for which he was speedily forced to abdicate in favor of a son more tractable to the Japanese. Kojong's second son, Yi Ch'ŏk, canonized Sunjong (r. 1907–1910), was on the throne no more than 24 days when a new treaty with Japan stripped him of all powers. The annexation of Korea by Japan in 1910, which ended both his reign and the formal existence of the old kingdom of Chosŏn and the Yi dynasty, was merely an acknowledgement of what had already happened. In 1919 Emperor Kojong died, and his funeral became the occasion for the great March First passive resistance movement. Emperor Sunjong, after being deposed in 1910, was kept under close surveillance in Ch'angdŏk palace, where he died in 1926. He was buried on a grassy knoll in a quiet valley east of the capital, near the graves of his ancestors.

The brief notation given here of these final events, which belong essentially to another era and which are recounted in greater detail elsewhere, is simply by way of completion of the record of the Yi dynasty, which lingered on for decades after traditional Korea itself had disappeared. The events of the reigns of Kojong and Sunjong simply confirmed its passing. Although few had heard them, the doors of the past had swung shut on Korea's centuries of tradition, and they would never reopen.

Appendix 1
The Korean Language

Korean is today spoken by over 40 million people, the majority of whom live in Korea proper (South, 25 million; North, 15.6 million). There are also large Korean settlements in Manchuria, in China proper, and in Japan, and lesser numbers living in the United States, the Soviet Union, and other parts of the world.

Modern Korean is a highly inflected language and does not use tones as does Chinese, although some dialects are reported to retain pitch distinctions. Several distinct dialects are recognized in Korea today, identified by the province in which they are spoken: Chŏlla, Kyŏngsang, P'yŏngan, Kangwŏn, Hwanghae–Kyŏnggi–Ch'ungch'ŏng, Hamgyŏng, and Cheju.

Modern Korean developed from Middle Korean—known through fifteenth to sixteenth century texts—which in turn developed chiefly from the language of Silla. Little is known of the ancient Korean language, although a few texts remain in which Chinese characters were used to write Korean phonetically. Middle Korean was somewhat different from modern Korean. It had a pitch accent of low, high, and low rising. Middle Korean also retained a somewhat degraded system of vowel harmony, elements of which survive in the modern language.

The hypothesis that Korean is an Altaic language—it may be closely related to Japanese as well—appears to be the most promising one at the present time.

Through the centuries Korean has incorporated a sizable vocabulary from Chinese, which belongs to the Sinitic group of languages, and lesser amounts from other languages. In the modern period English in the south and Russian in the north are prime sources of borrowing; only a few modern Japanese words remain from the period of the Japanese occupation.

Appendix 2
Foundation
Myths
Korean foundation myths could as well be called myths of culture heroes, for they are concerned chiefly with the appearance of sage-rulers. They are also cosmogonic myths, which humanize deities. They are clearly composites, sharing both theme and detail with the myths of many other lands, incorporating many ancient concepts as well as elements which are distinctly regional in nature. The myths set forth in slightly abridged form below are of anonymous ultimate authorship, products which evolved over time via multiple authorship and in which the development of oral and written versions, if not parallel following the adoption of a system of writing, were at least complementary. The result is that there are several variants of each myth.

THE TAN'GUN MYTH

The *Book of Wei* relates: Two thousand years ago Tan'gun Wanggŏm established his capital in Asadal and founded a state which he called Chosŏn. He was a contemporary of Yao [mythical Chinese emperor, third millennium B.C.]. The Ancient Records relate that in remote times, the son of Huan In by a concubine, Huan Ung, often thought of the world and desired to help man. He was called Lord of Heaven. The father was aware of his son's thoughts. Below he saw the three peaks of Mount T'aebaek by which he could generously benefit mankind. Then he gave Huan Ung the three Heavenly Seals and sent him to go and manage the world. Ung descended beneath the divine Tan tree on Mount T'aebaek leading 3,000 followers. He is the one called Huan Ung, King of Heaven. He commanded the Gods of Wind, Rain, and Clouds and ruled over the grains, life, sickness, punishments, good and evil. In all, he ruled over the 360 some affairs concerning man, and in the world he regulated change. At this time there were a bear and a tiger who lived in the same cave. They constantly prayed to the God Ung desiring to be changed into humans. Then, the God Ung gave them one stick of wonder-working mugwort and twenty stalks of garlic telling them: If you eat this and do not look at the sun's rays for 100 days, you will attain human form. The bear and the tiger took it and ate it, and avoided the sun for 21 days. The bear attained the body of woman but the tiger was unable to avoid the sun and did not attain the body of man. The bear-woman was without anyone to marry, therefore, she repeatedly went beneath the Tan tree and prayed of her desire to be pregnant. Ung then temporarily transformed himself and married her. She became pregnant and bore a son. He was called Tan'gun Wanggŏm. The capital was the walled city of P'yŏngyang. In the beginning they called it Chosŏn; they also moved the capital to Mount Paegak in Asadal. He governed the nation for 1,500 years. King Wu of Chou (dynasty of ancient China) ascended the throne and enfeoffed the Viscount of Ch'i (Kija) with Chosŏn. Tan'gun then moved to Changdang-gyŏng. Later he returned and hid himself in Asadal as a mountain god. His age was 1,908 years. (*Samguk yusa* version).

NORTHERN PUYŎ

The *Ancient Records* say: In the fourth month of 59 B.C. the Emperor of Heaven descended to the walled city of Holsŭnggol riding a five-dragon chariot. He established a capital and was proclaimed King. The nation was called Northern Puyŏ. He took the name of Hae Mosu for himself. He had a son named Puyŏ and he took Hae as his surname. Later the King moved the capital to Eastern Puyŏ due to the command of the Emperor on High (Chinese: Shang-ti). Emperor Tongmyŏng (Eastern Brightness) followed on the throne of Northern Puyŏ and the nation prospered. He established his capital at Cholbonju. This was Cholbon Puyŏ, the beginning of Koguryŏ. (*Samguk yusa* version).

EASTERN PUYŎ

Aranbul, the Chief Minister of King Hae Puyŏ of Northern Puyŏ, dreamt that the Heavenly Emperor came down and told him: "My descendants are going to establish a nation here. You should flee from them. There is a land called Kayŏbwŏn on the shore of the Eastern Sea. The soil is rich and fertile. You should establish the King's capital there." Aranbul urged the King to move the capital there. They called the nation Eastern Puyŏ. King Puyŏ was old and without a son, so one day he sacrificed to the mountains and streams to seek an heir. When the horse he was riding reached Konyŏn, he saw a stone which cried when he faced it. He marvelled at it and had a man roll the stone over. There was a small child of golden color and the form of a frog. The King was delighted and said, "Heaven has granted me a fine heir." Then he took the child and raised him. He called him Kŭmwa (Golden Frog). When he was grown he was made Crown Prince. Puyŏ died and Kŭmwa ascended the throne as king. He transmitted the throne to Crown Prince Taeso. In A.D. 22 King Muhyul of Koguryŏ subjugated Puyŏ and killed King Taeso. The nation passed away. (*Samguk sagi* 13 version).

KOGURYŎ

The surname of the First Ancestor, Tongmyŏng, the Sagacious Emperor, was Ko (High); his given name was Chumong. Prior to this King Hae Puyŏ of Northern Puyŏ fled his lands and went to Eastern Puyŏ. When Puyŏ died, Kŭmwa ascended the throne. At this time he found a girl in the Ubal River south of Mount T'aebaek. When he questioned her she said: "I am the daughter of the God of the Rivers (Habaek). My name is Yuhwa. I had gone out with my younger brothers to play. At that time there was a boy who called himself Hae Mosu, the son of the Emperor of Heaven. He enticed me to a house on the banks of the Yalu River at the foot of Mount Ungsin (Bear-Spirit) where we had relations. He went away and didn't return. My father and mother punished me for following a man without a go between. Therefore, they banished me to live here." Kŭmwa marvelled at this and secluded her in a house. The sun's reflection followed and shone upon her. She became pregnant as a consequence and laid an egg about as large as five pecks of grain. The King left it with the dogs and pigs but none of them would eat it. He left it on the road but the oxen and horses avoided it. He left it in the fields but the birds and beasts sheltered it. The King wanted to cut it open but he was unable to do so. Then he returned it to its mother who wrapped it up and placed it in a warm spot. A child broke the shell and came out. When he was seven he made himself a bow and arrows and if he shot at a target one hundred times, he hit it one hundred times. They gave him the name Chumong which in the Puyŏ vernacular means a good shot. Kŭmwa had seven sons who constantly played with Chumong but none were his equal. The King's sons and ministers plotted to harm him. Chumong's mother was aware of this and told him that the men of the nation were going to harm him and that it would be better for him to leave. Chumong with three of his friends went to the Um River and proclaimed to the river: "I am the son of the Emperor of Heaven, the grandson of the God of the Rivers. This day I flee and my pursuers will soon arrive. What shall I do?" The fish and turtles formed a bridge and they were able to cross. The bridge dissolved and his pursuers couldn't cross. He reached Cholbonju and subsequently made it his capital. The state was named Koguryŏ so he took Ko as his surname. At this time he was 20 years old. He ascended the throne in the year 37 B.C. (*Samguk yusa* version, abridged).

PAEKCHE

The Founding Ancestor of Paekche was Onjo. His father was Chumong who fled from Northern Puyŏ. When he arrived in Cholbonju Puyŏ, the King of Puyŏ was without a son; he had only three daughters. He realized that

Chumong was not an ordinary man when he saw him and he gave him his second daughter to wife. Not long after that the King of Puyŏ died and Chumong ascended the throne. He had two sons, Piryu, the eldest, and Onjo. When Chumong was in Northern Puyŏ he had a son and this boy came down and became the Crown Prince. Piryu and Onjo were angry that he was made Crown Prince and they didn't stand for it. Subsequently they went south with ten ministers, Okan and Maryo, et al., and there were many who followed them. When they arrived at Mount Han they ascended the pass and saw a habitable spot but Piryu wanted to live on the seacoast so he led some of the people to another location. The ministers and Onjo remained and established their capital south of the river. Later they gave the nation the name of Paekche. Since they were, like Koguryŏ, of Puyŏ stock, they took Puyŏ as their surname. He ascended the throne in 18 B.C. (*Samguk sagi* 23 version, abridged).

SILLA

The surname of the Founding Ancestor was Pak. His given name was Hyŏkkŏse. He ascended the throne in 57 B.C. His title was Kŏkkan. He was 13 years old at this time. The name of the state was Sŏrabŏl. Prior to this the remaining people of Chosŏn had entered the area and dwelt separately in six communities in the mountain valleys. These were the six communities of Chin han. Sir Sŏbŏl, the head of the community of Kohŏ, saw at the foot of Mount Yang in the copse beside the Wisteria Well a horse kneeling and neighing. He went to look at it but suddenly he did not see the horse any more, only a large egg. He cut it open and a handsome lad appeared. Then he took the boy and raised him. When the boy was ten or so he had marvelous accomplishments. The people of the six communities regarded his birth as a divine miracle and revered him. At this time he ascended as ruler. The people of Chin call a gourd *pak*. Since the large egg from whence he came resembled a gourd, he took Pak as a surname. Kŏkkan means King in the Chin language. (*Samguk sagi*, 1 version, abridged).

KAYA

On the bathing day in the third month of A.D. 42, a strange sound was heard on the northern part of Mount Kuji (turtle-mandate) and a crowd of several hundred gathered. The sound, like a human voice, concealed its form but projected its voice saying: "Are there people here or not?" The nine chiefs replied: "Our people are here." Then the voice asked: "Where am I?" They answered: "This is Kuji." Again the voice said, "I am to rule here, to renew your state and to be your ruler according to a Heavenly command. Dig off the mountain top and while working sing and dance to this song which will show your numbers and enthusiasm in welcome for the great King."

> *Turtle, Turtle, poke your head out.*
> *If you do not, we will roast and eat you.*

The nine chiefs did so; all were happy, and they sang and danced. Then they looked up and saw a purple rope descending from heaven with a golden box wrapped in a red cloth at the end. Inside the box were six golden eggs. The eggs were taken to the house of one of the nine chiefs. The following day the eggs were transformed into six boys and one of them became the first king of Karak, one of the six Kaya states. This was Suro. His surname was Kim (gold) because he came from a golden egg. The other boys became the rulers of the other Kaya states. (*Samguk yusa* version, abridged).

T'AMNA (CHEJU ISLAND)

T'amna was originally without human beings. Three gods, Yangulla, Koulla, and Puulla came forth from Mohŭng cave on Mount Halla. They caught animals for food and wore animal skins for clothing. One day they found a wooden box, sealed with a purple seal which had floated up on the shore of the Eastern Sea. Opening it, they found it held three girls dressed in green, colts, the seeds of the five grains, and an envoy dressed in purple robes with a red girdle. The envoy said, "I am an envoy of Japan. Our king had these three daughters. It was said that three gods had descended on the sacred mountain in the Western Sea with the intention of establishing a nation, but that they had no wives. Therefore, the king ordered me to bring these three girls as wives in order to achieve great deeds." The envoy suddenly mounted a cloud and departed. They each took a girl as a wife and maintained residences in separate locations on the island. Their descendants ruled the island. (*Koryŏsa* 57, abridged).

JAPANESE MYTHS BEARING ON KOREA

Many of the concepts seen in Korean myths occur in Japanese myths. The *Nihongi*, an eighth-century work based upon earlier traditions, for example, uses the concept of the universe as an egg. A Korean original has been postulated for the Japanese myth of Susanowo, who is banished and descends into the Japanese province of Izumo in western Japan across from Korea in the *Kojiki* (eighth century) account: in the *Nihongi* version he descends in Korea. Izumo, where Susanowo is active, is formed, in a Japanese myth in the *Izumo Fūdoki* of 733, by the god Yatsuka-mizu-omi-tsumi, who pulls away part of the land of Silla, a Korean kingdom. Okuniyushi, the offspring of Susanowo, rules Izumo until the Sun goddess sends Niningi to assume sovereignty over all of Japan. Niningi is seen as representing Yamato and holding political power while Okuniyushi is seen as representing Izumo and holding religious power. It is interesting to note that Niningi receives three sacred treasures and Takami Musubi, his grandmother, is also called *Takagi no kami* (Goddess of the High Tree). Parallels between Korean and Japanese myths other than the foundation myths cited here are numerous. In relation to these myths we might note that the oldest center of Shinto in Japan is said to be the Izumo Shrine in western Japan.

THE KIJA STORY

When the Shang-Yin dynasty of China fell in 1122 B.C. to the invading Chou (1122–245 B.C.), Kija fled to Chosŏn with 5,000 followers and made his capital at P'yŏngyang. He was later enfeoffed with the territory and drew up a code of eighteen articles for governing. His descendants ruled Chosŏn until the state was overthrown by Wiman, a refugee from the state of Yen, in 194 B.C. (*Koryŏsa* 58 version, abridged).

DISCUSSION

Comparative studies have revealed that a number of common beliefs were widespread in ancient times. It is therefore not surprising to find some of these beliefs in Korean foundation myths.

The egg is associated with the concept that heaven and earth were once somehow joined and that men and gods could intermingle. In this concept heaven and earth are often depicted as an egg, with earth the yoke surrounded by heaven. It appears in Zoroastrianism, in the *Rig Veda*, and in Chinese mythology, where it was popular during the Later Han dynasty (23–220), and in Japanese myths. The separation of heaven and earth, i.e., the separation of men and gods—which probably relates to the egg concept—made avenues of access important, both physical access, such as through mountains or trees or pillars supporting heaven, and spiritual access, through the actions of the shaman or shamaness, who were in their person or spirit able to bridge the gap between man on earth and the gods in heaven. The view has also been advanced that the egg myth may relate to a grain-spirit myth involving mother and son spirits. The separation of men and gods often involves eviction or flight.

The shamanistic *world-tree* concept, seen in the Tan'gun myth, is widespread and is found in many cultures, e.g., Iranian, Greek, Roman, and in the sacred tree of Japanese Shinto. In many north Asian myths it is linked with concepts of the bear, e.g., Mangi, the mythical first ancestor of the Evenks.

The bear, as well as the other animals mentioned in these myths, have suggested ancient, possibly totemistic, cults in Korea. The bear is found in the myths of many peoples of north Asia, e.g., Ainu, Gilyak, Evenk, and Orock, and a bear festival with the display of a bear's head is not uncommon. The bear also appears in Chinese mythology in an entry in the *Tso-chuan* dated 535 B.C. Another myth found in Chinese sources is the Koguryŏ myth. It has been speculated that it was introduced into China from the north in the early Han period. This brings up the possibility that some of the myths of the northern people may have been incorporated into Chinese mythology and then reintroduced to the northern peoples in perhaps more sophisticated versions in Chinese records.

The view has been advanced that the animals mentioned in Korean myths were clan or tribal totems. The individual clan totems were subordinated to the totem of the most powerful clan, whose totem became the tribal totem. These totems were all subordinate to the power of the shaman or shamaness who, as the religious leader, communed with them. In a similar fashion, clan myths became tribal myths, from which they could and sometimes did become "national" myths.

Linked with these concepts were animistic beliefs in sacred mountains, rocks, and trees. The three sacred mountains of Silla, Paekche, and Koryŏ are an *axis mundi* concept, reinforced in Korea by *feng-shui* (wind and water), *wu-hsing* (five elements, viz., earth, water, wood, fire, metal), and similar geomantic and nature-interpreting theories from China which blended with native Korean shamanistic-animistic beliefs.

Related is the concept of the trinity: three national spirits who inhabited these sacred mountains and who protected the state. In Silla and Paekche sacrifices were regularly performed to them. In the late Silla (668–935) period the three protecting deities are found expressed in literature as three female spirits.

During the Koryŏ period (918–1392) these concepts were expanded with the appointment of specific cities which were designated capitals and which were often chosen through prognostication or divination by Buddhist monks. Palaces were constructed in these cities, and they were considered a safe refuge for the monarch in troubled times. In this same period the Tan'gun myth became the national myth of Korea, and the Kija story was officially endorsed as Korean history. This was the result of a long evolution and political use of these myths. The acceptance of the stories of Kija and Tan'gun in the Koryŏ period is the end of an older, unofficial but widely accepted tradition and the beginning of their incorporation into a systematized and officially endorsed medieval version of Korean history.

The Kija story should be distinguished in several respects from the foundation myths by the pedigree given it by its occurrence in a number of Chinese records of ancient date, e.g., *Shu-ching*, traditionally tenth century B.C. Most historians discount the record which states that Chosŏn was given to Kija as an appanage, but many accept the record which states merely that Kija fled to Chosŏn at the time that the Shang Yin dynasty was overthrown by the Chou dynasty. Some see the Kija story as symbolizing the influx of Chinese to Korea, which undoubtedly began at an early date. Still others argue for the location of Chosŏn in southern Manchuria in this period. I believe we might also consider the possibility that the Kija story was originally a Chinese tale given Korean dress by historians of the Chinese Han dynasty to establish ancient precedence for Chinese claims to the northern portion of the peninsula, the area of Han conquests. The acceptance of the Kija story in Korea during the Koryŏ period was due to the influence of Confucianism. In 1102, Chŏng Munjin, a member of the Confucian-oriented Board of Rites, suggested that a search be made for the grave of Kija in P'yŏngyang and that a shrine be erected to him in the city. Shortly after this shrines to Tan'gun and to Tongmyŏng were also erected in P'yŏngyang in the western and eastern sectors of the city, respectively. It is interesting to note that in the *History of Koryŏ* promulgated in the fifteenth century, one of the eight regulations attributed to Kija was cited as the beginning of, and ancient authority for, the institution of slavery in Korea. The shrines to Kija, Tan'gun, and Tongmyŏng were maintained in the Yi period, and a Shrine of the Three Divinities, viz., Huan-in, Huang-ung, and Tan'gun, was built on Mount Kuwŏl. In the late nineteenth century as the Yi dynasty declined, a number of new religions arose which either centered on a particular myth, e.g., Tan'gun-gyo (Religion of Tan'gun) and Kija-gyo, or synthesized some of these concepts with ideas drawn from Buddhism, Confucianism, and Christianity, e.g., Ch'ŏndo-gyo (Religion of the Heavenly Way).

The shamanistic-animistic beliefs which are the substratum of these myths are often obscured, since similar concepts from China—which were formalized in contrast to the Korean beliefs, which were generally not so systematized—were accepted on the peninsula. And, of course, they found expression in literature and in art as well as in court ceremonies, local customs, and folk beliefs.

The Wu-k'uai-fen group of Koguryŏ tombs in Manchuria contains some excellent paintings of scenes from the mythological beliefs of the period, and includes, for example, winged male and female deities with dragon tails holding the sun and the moon (in which is drawn a three-legged bird); another scene shows two females riding dragons through the clouds, one playing a double-ended drum, the other a stringed zither; in another are a female and a male, the latter with the horned head of a mythical beast.

During the Yi dynasty carved wooden spirit-generals guarded the entrance to villages, and the mountain god still plays an important role in the lives of those who work in the mountains, for example, women who gather food products such as mushrooms and wild ginseng, and miners, who normally require a shamanistic ceremony (*kut*) performed prior to the opening of a new mine. The female shamaness (*mudang*) is still called into the homes of the dying to exorcise demons. A small shrine to the god of the mountains, depicted as an old man with a flowing white beard and a protecting tiger at his side, will also be found in Korean Buddhist temples in the mountains.

Belief in prognostication and divination, which permeated traditional Korea after a revival in late Silla times, continues today. In the late Yi dynasty there was a particularly widespread popularization of works of prophecy, the most famous of which was a work on the interpretation of omens, *Chŏnggamnok*, which enjoys some popularity in the countryside even today.

The Korean myths give us an insight, although a hazy one it is true, into some of the ancient concepts held by the peoples on the peninsula, concepts which survive in part into the present.

Appendix 3

Postscript

The assumptions upon which this work is based emanate from the view that a concern of the study of history is the analysis of societies, cultures, and human relationships through time. This work is no exception to the general notion that no matter which approach a historian chooses, he inevitably becomes a part of his product, which reflects his socio-cultural background and the intellectual climate of his time as well as the idiosyncracies of personal style. A word on my own assumptions and views of some of the major features of Korean history would, therefore, seem to be in order.

The periods adopted in a general history of this type are important, since they invariably incorporate assumptions about the process of history itself. Usually, by period is meant a chronological framework used to divide historical development into a number of periods of time during which some particular development begins and is fulfilled. The concept is used here as an analytical tool applied to a particular society rather than as an absolute statement generalizable to all societies. The periods I use for Korean history coincide with permanent changes in the existential and technological base of the society. The following table summarizes these periods with some tentative dates.

Ancient Korea	Stage (Period) of Transition	Traditional Korea	Stage of Transition	Modern Korea
	From stone to metal culture. From predominantly nonagricultural, nomadic or seminomadic, to predominantly sedentary, agricultural way of life.		From sedentary agricultural society, predominantly rural in character, to urbanized industrial society.	
First (B.C.) millennium	Fourth century		Nineteenth century	

My view of "traditional" Korea is that of a society whose energies were primarily directed to filling out the parameters of an agricultural state within the limitations imposed by the technology at its command. There were, of course, many changes taking place other than those mentioned, not the least of which were the change from a preliterate to a literate society and temporary shifts of the existential base in a commercial direction. Yet as important as these changes were, none resulted in a permanent change in the existential base of the society.

A recurring problem which faced Korean authorities and intellectuals was that of relations with other states. While Korea's relations with these states has been discussed in the text, it should be noted that following the withdrawal of T'ang forces in the early eighth century, no Chinese army ever set foot on Korean soil except by invitation. When the tragic history of invasions from Manchuria is reviewed, it might be mentioned that no other state, sedentary or nomadic, successfully dealt with those northern people who invaded Korea, and—excluding only the Mongols—none of these northern invaders occupied Korea, while the Korea authorities usually managed to achieve a relatively favorable position for their state after each invasion. Throughout Korean history Korean leaders have repeatedly demonstrated a high degree of skill in their relations with other people, while the many invasions have left a legacy of attitudes and values, amply expressed in literature, which include high social currency for the concepts of courage, perseverance, and enduring loyalty.

I have found it useful to view societies as having key structures which constellate other social institutions. In the case of traditional Korea I see the key structure as the interacting clan and caste systems around which the society constantly reconsolidated itself. Considerations of caste and clan firmly channelled educational, political, and economic opportunities and even provided the orientation for the penal system of traditional Korea. Changes in the clan and caste systems seem to have required almost a complete breakdown in social order to accomplish. A corollary of this might be seen in the apparent increase in the number of clans participating in the political and economic decision-making process which followed periods of change in the clan and caste systems. The clan and caste systems were an enduring feature of traditional Korean society, altered but never superseded.

The institutional weakness of the Korean monarchs was an important factor in Korean history. The role of Korean kings during the Yi period seems more like that of a tolerated chief administrator whose power was checked by a powerful bureaucracy who could and often did replace him but who had to be endured and occasionally indulged since he was in fact their own source of legitimacy. At the same time, the Korean ruler was a representative of lines of at least three clans, namely, the royal clan, his mother's clan, and the clan of his principal wife. Consorts for the Korean monarchs were provided by influential elite families, and since the male offspring of these unions were always possible candidates for the throne, a potential for palace intrigue and political instability was always present. And waiting in the background were those clans which had established marriage relations

with lines of the royal clan. Korean monarchs not only had to deal with a
complex bureaucratic structure, they were also personally enmeshed in a
complex network of kinship relations, the elements of which were not always
in harmony.

My interpretation of the meaning of Korea's relations with other states
in the development of Korean society and culture has been influenced by
the notion of *functionalism*. That is, I have found it useful to view societies
as having needs in the realms of the psychological, the religious, and the
esthetic, as well as the more obvious needs for internal order, defense, relationships with the environment, and the like. I have also found it useful to
view Chinese influence on Korean society and culture as a process of acculturation, with the critical variables being language, religious and ethical
systems, and, to some extent, technology. The values and attitudes incorporated in religious and ethical systems were, to the extent that they were adopted
—and they were adopted to the extent that they were believed to be congruent
with existing belief systems—influential agents in molding Korean society
and culture. I have found the concept of system imperatives useful in under-
standing some of the features of changes of this nature.

There is a persistent theme which runs through Korean history, revealed
in practically every facet of the national life, from mythology to state institutions, from attitudes and values to art forms, namely, the native and the
foreign, sometimes in harmony, sometimes in conflict. Tan'gun and Kija,
as the late George M. McCune* perceptively observed, might be seen as
symbolic of this theme. The integration of foreign inputs into Korean society
and culture in the form of religious and ethical systems, arts and letters,
technology, and administrative systems can be seen as a continuous process
throughout Korean history which posed distinct problems for Korean
intellectuals and leaders. History is filled with the bones of broken societies,
dimly remembered cultures, and forgotten states, apt testimony to the
greatest challenge that faced Korean intellectuals, namely, the task of
preserving their own socio-cultural identity, threatened less by foreign
invasion than by continuous socio-cultural influence from China.

Language was certainly a critical variable of change in Korean society
and culture, and any analysis of Korean history must consider the questions
posed by the foreign adoption of the Chinese written language. My own
assumption might be stated as follows: Once a society adopts a language
other than its own, then it will change, and it will always change in the
direction of the society and culture whose language is adopted. Due consideration must, of course, be given to a variety of factors, including whether
spoken and/or written languages are adopted, by whom, for what purpose,

*George M. McCune, *Notes on the History of Korea: Early Korea*, Research Monographs
on Korea, series 1, no. 1, Korean Research Associates, 1952.

and the degree, intensity, and duration of use. The intense use of the Chinese written language by the Korean elite over many centuries was balanced by the retention of the Korean spoken language by the entire society. Once the Korean language was widely written and began to replace written Chinese, the process of acculturation toward the Chinese model began to be reversed. Thus, the invention of the Korean alphabet, *han'gul*, was undoubtedly the most significant cultural achievement of Korean history.

If societies are seen as being in a state of continual change, with the rate and degree of change fluctuating, then some periods of Korean history stand out sharply. There are, for example, three periods of intellectual activity, which coincided with widespread commercial maritime activity in east Asia, viz., seventh to eighth centuries, eleventh to twelfth centuries, and fifteenth to sixteenth centuries. The intellectual activity of the eighteenth century occurred under somewhat different conditions and contains a new element in the form of Western ideas. Korea's exchanges with neighboring states, the states of China in particular, might be viewed from the point of membership in an ever-changing intellectual community which provided each of its members with access to the experience and learning available to all. Korean society and culture drew from and contributed to this intellectual community.

Finally, these assumptions have been set forth, not in any belief that they are right or wrong, but as analytic tools that I have found useful in generating new insights into the processes of Korean society and culture.

Appendix 4
Summary
Bibliography

This summary bibliography is the
result of two considerations: first,
a detailed bibliography listing all works utilized would be of use primarily to
specialists and out of place in a survey work of this type and, second, reading
lists are by their very nature arbitrary and soon outdated. This summary
bibliography consists of three sections:

1. *Bibliographies* to serve as guides to further materials on Korean
history.

2. *General coverage*, with some representative major works which survey
several categories, without regard to language.

3. *Chronological coverage*, with studies published since 1945 predominat-
ing, representing works written only in Western languages.

1. BIBLIOGRAPHIES

a. Western Languages
There are several available, but the two most comprehensive are:

B. Silberman, comp., *Japan and Korea: A Critical Bibliography*,
Tucson: University of Arizona Press, 1962.

G. St. G. M. Gompertz, comp., *Bibliography of Western Literature on
Korea from the Earliest Times Until 1950*, Seoul: Tonga ch'ulp'ansa, 1962.

b. Korean and Japanese Languages
B. Hazard and W. Smith, Jr., comp., *Korean Studies Guide*, Berkeley:
University of California Press, 1954.

William E. Henthorn, comp., *A Guide to Reference and Research
Materials on Korean History*, Honolulu: Research Publications and
Translations, East-West Center, 1968.

References to the major primary source materials available for the study
of Korean history may be found in the two works mentioned above.

2. GENERAL COVERAGE

a. Survey Histories

For traditional Korea survey histories were written by Westerners long before any attempts were made to study specific institutions or periods of Korean history, and they suffer accordingly. Three early works of note are W. E. Griffis, *Korea: The Hermit Nation*, New York: Scribner's, 1882; John Ross, *History of Korea*, London, 1879; and H. B. Hulbert, *The History of Korea*, Seoul: The Methodist Publishing House, 1905. The first of the Western language works of this nature to appear after 1945 was the anthropologist C. Osgood's *The Koreans and Their Culture*, New York: Ronald Press, 1951, which combined an excellent study of life on Kanghwa Island with a brief outline of Korean history. A. Eckardt's *Korea: Geschichte und Kultur*, Baden Baden, 1960, summarizes some of the major Korean cultural achievements. A concise survey of Korean history is contained in Li Ogg, *Histoire de La Corée*, Paris: Presses Universitaires de France, 1969. There are, of course, numerous general histories of Korea in Korean and Japanese.

Prior to 1945, the study of traditional Korea was dominated by Japanese scholarship, much of which bears the inevitable attitude of the conqueror toward a captive nation. Following the liberation the pendulum has swung the other way. The majority of post-1945 research has been the work of Korean scholars, with Japanese scholarship continuing to form the most notable contribution by scholars outside of Korea. General histories of the post-1945 period which were of particular value in writing this text include Yi Kibaek, *Han'guksa sillon*, Seoul: Ilchogak, rev. ed., 1967, which includes a noteworthy bibliography; Han Ugun, *Han'guk t'ongsa*, Seoul: Uryu munhwasa, 1970; and Hatada Takashi, *Chōsenshi*, Tokyo: Iwanami shoten, 1951, which emphasizes socio-economic factors. Hatada's work has recently been translated by W. E. Smith, Jr. and B. H. Hazard, *A History of Korea*, Santa Barbara: ABC-Clio Press, 1969. Also immensely valuable were a recent survey of the field by Japanese scholars, Hatada Takashi, ed., *Chōsenshi nyūmon* (Introduction to Korean History), Tokyo: Taihei shuppansha, 1966; and the seven-volume history published by the Chindan Society and written in a traditional style by a galaxy of senior Korean scholars, such as Kim Chaewŏn, Yi Pyŏngdo, Yi Sangbaek, and Yi Sŏn'gun, *Han'guksa*, Seoul: Uryu munhwasa, 1959–1965. The thirty-seven volume compendium of selected materials, *Chōsenshi*, Chōsen Sōtokufu, Keijō, 1931–1938, was also useful as a guide to primary source materials. Of great value for the standards of excellence they set as well as the information they contain were the three-volume history of Japan by Sir George Sansom (Stanford: Stanford University Press, 1961 to 1968); and Edwin O. Reischauer and John K.

Fairbank, *East Asia: The Great Tradition*, Boston: Houghton Mifflin Company, 1958.

Institutional history provides a vital base for any general history, and I have drawn heavily from a large number of these works, including Paek Namun, *Chōsen shakkai keizaishi* (Socio-Economic History of Korea), Tokyo, 1933; Cho Kijun, *Han'guk kyŏngjesa* (Economic History of Korea), Seoul: Ilsinsa, 1962; Yu Sangun, *Han'guk kodae kwanjesa yŏn'gu* (Research on the History of the Bureaucratic System in Ancient Korea), Seoul: Myŏngji University Press, 1969. Unfortunately there are no similar works in Western languages.

b. Geography

The geography of Korea was studied on a relatively wide scale during the Japanese occupation and has been the subject of a large number of technical studies. General introductions to the subject are provided in Herman Lautensach, *Korea: eine Landeskunde auf Grund eigener Reisen und der Literatur*, Leipzig, 1945, which contains sections on history, settlement patterns, and economic geography; V. T. Zaichikov, *Geography of Korea*, Albert Parry, trans., New York: Institute of Pacific Relations, 1952; and Shannon McCune, *Korea's Heritage*, Tokyo: Charles E. Tuttle, 1956. Excellent maps showing terrain features are contained in Albert Kolb, *China-Japan-Korea: Geographie eines Kulturerdteiks*, Heidelberg: Quelle and Meyer Verlag, 1963. Useful for its historical maps is Albert Hermann, *Historical and Commercial Atlas of China*, Cambridge, 1935. An excellent bibliography of recent works is contained in *Korea: A Geographical Appreciation*, Toronto: Canadian Department of Mines and Technical Surveys, 1951. A more technical bibliography is Shannon McCune, *Geomorphology of Korea: A Selected Bibliography*, P'yŏngyang, 1941. Two descriptive works which provide extremely pleasant reading are I. B. Bishop, *Korea and Her Neighbors*, London: J. Murray, 1898; and Richard Rutt, *Korean Works and Days*, Tokyo: Charles E. Tuttle, 1964.

c. Archaeology

Studies are naturally dominated by excavation reports. Beginning in 1917 Japanese scholars working in the Chōsen Sōtokufu (Government General of Chōsen) published a series of reports under the titles *Koseki chōsa hōkoku* (Report of Investigation of Ancient Sites) in sixteen titles during the period 1917 to 1937; *Koseki chōsa tokubetsu hōkoku* (Special Report on Investigation of Ancient Sites) in seven titles in the period 1919 to 1929; and *Koseki chōsa gaiho* (Summary Report of Investigation of Ancient Sites) in six titles during the years 1934 to 1940. The last were concerned primarily with the Chinese tombs of the Han period found in the area of the former walled town of Nangnang. The findings of Japanese scholars in the Kyŏngsang and P'yŏngyang areas drew the attention of the late Sir George Sansom, who recognized their importance for the study of early Japanese history. In 1929 he published a summary of these findings in "An Outline of Recent Japanese Archaeological Research in Korea and Its Bearing upon Early Japanese History," *Transactions of the Japan Branch of the Royal Asiatic Society*, Series 2, 9(1929). Korean scholars became active in 1945 and began publishing their findings in journals devoted to art and archaeology, such as *Misul charyo*; *Kogo misul*; and *Munhwa yusan*. A few reports have also appeared in *Asian Perspectives*. Special studies include Kim Wŏnyong, *Studies on Silla Pottery*, Seoul: National Museum of Korea, 1960; Arimitsu Kyōichi, *Research on Korean Polished Stone Swords*, Tokyo, 1959; and Arimitsu Kyōichi, *The Kushimemon Pottery of Korea*, Tokyo, 1962. The selected works of Soviet archaeologists have been translated into English by the Arctic Institute of North America. Of special interest is A. P. Okladnikov, *The Soviet Far East in Antiquity*, H. N. Michael, ed., Toronto: University of Toronto Press, 1965. Views of Japanese archaeologists are presented in Arimitsu Kyōichi, "Kokogaku kara mita Chōsen" (An Archaeological View of Korea), *Chōsenshi nyūmon*, Tokyo, 1966. A résumé of views advanced by Korean and Japanese scholars appears in Kim Wŏnyong "Sŏnsa munhwa nŭn ŏttŏ kannŭn'ga?" (How Is the Study of Prehistory Coming Along?), *Sindonga*, Seoul, 1966. Excavation reports from North Korea have been published in two series: *Kogohak charyo chip* (Collection of Archaeological Data); and *Yujok palgul pogo* (Report of Excavation of Sites). A summary of archaeological findings for the ancient period appears in M. N. Vorob'yev, *Drevnyaya Koreya* (Ancient Korea), Moscow, 1961.

d. Art

Ceramics in particular has attracted the attention of a number of Western scholars. In the pre-1945 period Japanese scholarship dominated the field, and there are numerous publications which, although often primarily of an archaeological nature, in their cataloguing of frescoes, stone and metal sculpture, and architectural styles are of great interest to the art historian. An early effort at a general history of Korean art was Yu Chongyŏl, *Chōsen to sono bijutsu* (Korea and Its Arts), Keijō, 1922. But for the most part the field was dominated by Japanese archaeologists of the stature of Sekino Tadashi, Fujita Ryōsaku, and Arimitsu Kyōichi. The earliest Western entry in the field was A. Eckhardt, *Geschichte der Koreanischen Kunst*, Leipzig, 1929; English translation, London: Goldston, 1929. Active in the field in the post-1945 years was Ko Yosŏp, who published five volumes devoted to studies of Korean art history and architecture in the period 1949 to 1964. A number of Western works began to appear, including W. B.

Honey, *Korean Pottery*, London: Faber and Faber, 1948; R. T. Paine, Jr., ed., *The Masterpieces of Korean Arts*, Washington, D.C., 1957 (editions in several languages); Evelyn McCune, *The Arts of Korea*, Tokyo: Charles E. Tuttle, 1961; Jaroslav Barinka, *Alte Koreanische Kunst*, Prague, 1962 (editions in several languages); G. St. G. M. Gompertz, *Korean Celadon and Other Wares of the Koryŏ Period*, New York, 1963; and G. St. G. M. Gompertz, *Korean Pottery and Porcelain of the Yi Period*, New York: Frederick Praeger, 1968, a work which firmly established Gompertz as the leading Western authority on Korean ceramics. A major work is Kim Chaewŏn and Kim Wŏnyong, *Treasures of Korean Art: 2000 Years of Ceramics, Sculpture and Jeweled Arts*, New York, 1966 (editions in several languages).

e. Linguistics

Descriptions of the Korean language in English include Samuel E. Martin, "Korean Phonemics," *Language* (1951); and Samuel E. Martin, *Morphophonemics of Korean*, Baltimore, 1954. There are, of course, numerous studies in Japanese and in Korean, the most noted recent ones being by the Korean scholars Yi Sungnyong and Yi Kimun and the Japanese scholars Konō Rokurō and Nakamura Tamotsu. The two-volume study Ogura Shimpei, *Chōsengo hōgen no kenkyū* (Research on Korean Dialects), Tokyo, 1944, is probably still the best general work of its kind, although it has been supplemented and superseded in part by a number of recent studies on individual dialects. The relationship between Japanese and Korean has been the subject of several special studies, including Yi Kimun, "A Genetic View of Japanese," *Chōsen gakuhō* (1963); Samuel E. Martin, "Lexical Evidence Relating Korean to Japanese," *Language* (1966); and Hattori Shiro, "The Affinity of Japanese," *Acta Asiatica* (1961). In the last mentioned work Hattori uses the glottochronological method to postulate a separation between Japanese and Korean 5,390 to 7,330 years ago; it should be added that this method is not generally accepted. An interesting treatment of the history of the Korean language is Yi Kimun, *Kugŏsa kaesŏl* (Outline of the History of the National Language), Seoul, 1963. A less technical introductory work in English is Frits Vos, "Historical Survey of Korean Language Studies," *Papers of the CIC FEL Institute*, Ann Arbor, 1963.

f. Literature

The history of literature has been as closely tied to philological and linguistic studies as art history has been bound to archaeology. Kim T'aejun made the earliest attempt to separate the fields with two works: *Chosŏn Hanmunhaksa* (History of Sino-Korean Literature), Seoul, 1931 and *Chosŏn sosŏlsa* (History of the Korean Novel), Seoul, 1939. The pioneering work on the Korean theater was Kim Chaech'ŏl, *Chosŏn yŏn'gŭksa* (History of the Korean Theater), Seoul, 1933, and that for Korean poetry was Cho Yunje, *Chosŏn siga sagang* (History of Korean Poetry), Seoul, 1937. The lyrics of the Korean *hyangga* attracted the attention of Japanese scholars at an early date, and in 1929 the linguist Ogura Shimpei made the first comprehensive study of these songs. This work was continued in Yang Chudong, *Koga yŏn'gu* (Studies of Ancient Songs), Seoul, 1942; Yang used his philological approach in a study of the late Koryŏ–early Yi dynasty songs known as *changga* in *Yŏyŏ chŏnju* (comments on Koryŏ Ballads), Seoul, 1947. Both of these last mentioned works remain classics in the field.

The post-liberation period has seen the appearance of a wave of literary collections, studies of individual works, including important textual studies, and general histories of literature. Representative of such works are Yi Kawŏn, ed., *Ch'unhyangjŏn*, Seoul, 1957; Kim Sayŏp, ed., *Songgang kasa*, Seoul, 1959; and Yi Sangbo, ed., *Kaego Pak Nogye yŏn'gu*, Seoul, 1962.

A number of translations and studies of Korean literature have appeared, the bulk of them in the post-liberation period, and include: Kim Manjung, *The Cloud Dream of Nine*, J. S. Gale, trans., London: O'Connor, 1922; Peter Lee, *Studies in the Saenaennorae*, Serie Orientale Roma 22 (1959), Rome; Peter Lee, *Anthology of Korean Poetry*, New York: The John Day Co., 1964; Peter Lee, *Korean Literature: Topics and Themes*, Tucson: University of Arizona Press, 1965; Richard Rutt, "Introduction to the Sijo," *Transactions of the Korea Branch of the Royal Asiatic Society* 34 (1958); Inez Kong Pai, *The Ever White Mountain*, Tokyo: Charles E. Tuttle, 1965; and Frits Vos, "Letteratura Coreana," *Le Civiltà dell'Oriente*, II (1957), Rome. The first Western history of Korean literature to appear was A. Eckardt, *Geschichte der Koreanischen Literatur*, Leiden, 1966.

g. Buddhism

General works on Korean Buddhism include Yi Nŭnghwa, *Chōsen bukkyo tōshi*, Keijō, 1918; and Frederick Starr, *Korean Buddhism*, Boston: Marshall Jones Co., 1918. Buddhism is also treated in general works on Korean thought, which include Kim Tŭkhwang, *Han'guk sasangsa* (History of Korean Thought), Seoul: Namsandang, 1958; and Hyŏn Sangyun, "Han'guk sasangsa," *Asea yŏn'gu* 1960 to 1961. More specialized studies include Peter Lee, "Fa-tsang and Ŭisang," *Journal of the American Oriental Society*, 82 (1962) 1; W. Watson, "The Earliest Buddhist Images of Korea," *Transactions of the Oriental Ceramic Society 1957–58*, (1958–1959); Takahashi Toru, *Richo bukkyo* (Buddhism in the Yi Dynasty), Ōsaka, 1929; Paul Demieville, "Les Versions Chinoises du Milidapanha," *Bulletin de l'École Francaise de'Extreme-Orient*, XXIV (1924); L. G. Paik, "Tripitaka Koreana," *Transactions of the Korea Branch of the Royal Asiatic Society*, XXXII (1951);

Frits Vos and H. Hammitzsch, *Die Religionen Japans und Koreas*, Stuttgart, 1963; and Peter Lee, trans., *Lives of Eminent Korean Monks*, Cambridge, 1969.

h. Confucianism

In Korea, one of the earliest works to appear was Chang Chiyon, *Chosŏn Yun'gyo yŏnwŏn* (Sources of Korean Confucianism), Seoul, 1922. This was followed by Eul Sou Youn, *Histoire du confucianisme en Corée*, Paris: Librairie Pierre Tequi, 1939. Post-liberation studies include a few general works, such as Hyŏn Sangyun, *Chosŏn yunhaksa* (History of Korean Confucianism), Seoul, 1949; and Han Ugun, *Yijo hugi ŭi sahoe wa sasang* (Society and Thought of the Late Yi Dynasty), Seoul, 1961. A growing number of important studies of noted Korean Confucian scholars of the Yi dynasty has also begun to appear and include Kim Kyŏngtak, *Yulgok ŭi yŏn'gu* (A Study of Yulgok), Seoul, 1960; and Hong Isŏp, *Chŏng Tasan ŭi chŏngch'i kyŏngje sasang yŏn'gu* (A Study of the Political and Economic Thought of Chŏng Tasan), Seoul, 1959. Western language works include Gregory Henderson, "Chŏng Tasan: A Study in Korea's Intellectual History," *Journal of Asian Studies* (1957) 3; and Yang Key Baek and Gregory Henderson, "An Outline of Korean Confucianism," *Journal of Asian Studies* (1958) 1 and (1959) 2. A real landmark is Dieter Eikemeier, *Elemente im Politischen Denken des Yŏn'am Pak Chiwŏn (1737–1805)*, Leiden: E. J. Brill, 1970.

i. Christianity

As the earliest missionaries to Korea were Jesuits, it might be expected that their story would be the first to appear. It did in the two-volume work Charles Dallet, *Histoire de l'église de Corée*, Paris: Librairie Victor Palme, 1874. This extremely valuable work, containing descriptions of early eighteenth-century Yi dynasty society, has been translated in part by the Human Resource Area Files of New Haven, Conn. The history of Protestants in Korea was taken up in L. George Paik, *The History of Protestant Missions in Korea 1832–1910*, P'yŏngyang, 1929. A recent interpretative view is presented in Spencer J. Palmer, *Korea and Christianity*, Seoul, 1967.

j. Shamanism and Other Religions

They have been studied to a somewhat lesser degree than the more heavily documented religions mentioned above. Most of them, it should be noted, are mentioned in general works on Korean thought or religion, e.g., Vos and Hammitzsch cited previously. Among the few Western language articles are C. Hantze, "Schamenkronen zu Han-zeit in Korea," *Ostasiatische Zeitschrift* 19 (1933); and Ch. Haguenauer, "Sorciers et sorcières de Corée,"

Bulletin de la Maison franco-japonaise (1929). Valuable materials on Korean shamanism are contained in a series of studies by scholars of the Chōsen Sōtokufu, published during the period 1923 to 1944, under the general category *Chōsa shiryo* (Research Materials). The only comprehensive English language work available on the Tonghak (Eastern Learning) or Ch'ŏndogyo religion is Benjamin B. Weems, *Reform, Rebellion and the Heavenly Way*, Tucson: University of Arizona Press, 1966.

k. Mythology

Among the few works which exist in Western languages are Kim Chaewŏn, "Han Dynasty Mythology and the Korean Legend of Ṭan'gun," *Archives of the Chinese Art Society of America* (1948–1949); Shiratori Kurakichi, "The Legend of King Tung-ming: The Founder of Fu-yu-kuo," *Memoirs of the Research Department of the Tōyō Bunko*, Tokyo, 1938; and Boleslaw Szczesniak, "The Sumu-sunu Myth," *Monumenta Nipponica*, X (1954). An excellent summary of views of ancient Korea covering Korean founding myths is contained in No Chunghŭi, "Kodae kukkaga hyŏngsŏng toegi kkaji nŭn?" *Sindonga* (1966).

3. CHRONOLOGICAL COVERAGE

a. The Chinese Han Commanderies

The Chinese Han Commanderies in Korea have been the subject of treatment primarily by archaeologists and art historians, e.g., A. Slawik, "The Chinese Prefecture in Korea during the Han, Wei, and Chin Dynasties," *Wiener Beitrage zur Kunstgeschichte Asiens*, 7 (1932). One of the more valuable articles on this period is Hans Bielenstein, "The Census of China during the Period A.D. 2–272," *Bulletin of the Museum of Far Eastern Antiquities*, 19 (1947).

b. The Three Kingdoms Period

The Three Kingdoms Period is a rather hazy one in Korean history, although notices in the Chinese records are a distinct aid. Western language studies of this period have concentrated primarily upon the stele of Koguryŏ King Kwanggaet'o and Japanese-Korean relations during this period. These studies include Maurice Courant, "Stèle chinoise du royaume de Ko Kou Rye," *Journal Asiatique*, 11 (1898); Maurice Courant, "La Corée jusqu'au IXe siècle," *T'oung Pao*, 9 (1898); E. Chavannes, "Les monuments de l'ancien royaume Coréen de Kao-keou-li," *T'oung Pao*, 9 (1908); Boleslaw Szczesniak, "The Kotaiō Monument," *Monumenta Nipponica*, 7 (1951) 1–2; and Boleslaw Szczesniak, "Japanese-Korean Wars in A.D. 391–507 and Their Chronology," *Journal of the Royal Asiatic Society* (1946). An account of the Sui invasions of Koguryŏ is contained in W. Bingham, *The Founding of the T'ang Dynasty*, Baltimore: Waverly Press, 1941. We are still far from a clear view of this period, but inscriptions on stone and metal, the Koguryŏ wall paintings, and the painstaking work of the archaeologists are providing much valuable information on this shadowy age for which the records are few and often unreliable. A good survey of the early history of Koguryŏ has been made in A. J. Gardenier, *The Early History of Korea*, Hongkong, 1969.

c. The Late Silla Period

For the Late Silla Period a good starting point is Frits Vos, "Kim Yusin, Personlichkeit und Mythos: Ein Beitrag zur Kenntnis der alkoreanischen Geschichte," *Oriens Extremus*, 1 (1954) 1 and 2 (1954) 1. An excellent account of the Silla merchant-general Chang Pogo is contained in Edwin O. Reischauer, *Ennin's Travels in T'ang China*, New York: Ronald Press, 1955. A similar study by Kim Sanggi, using the same source materials, differs only in the speculations concerning the final days of Chang. Korean communities in China and Korean maritime trade are discussed in Edwin O. Reischauer, "Notes on T'ang Dynasty Sea Routes," *Harvard Journal of Asiatic Studies*, 5 (1940–41). A study of the Silla institution of the *hwarang* is the subject of Richard Rutt, "The Flower Boys of Silla," *Transactions of the Korea Branch of the Royal Asiatic Society*, 38 (1961). A historiographical study of discrepancies between Chinese and Korean records is contained in M. C. Rogers, "Thanatochronology of Some Silla Kings," *Monumenta Serica*, 19 (1960).

d. The Early Koryŏ Period

The Early Koryŏ Period is represented by several historiographical studies by M. C. Rogers which treat Koryŏ's relations with the states of China and include: "Factionalism and Koryŏ Policy under the Northern Sung," *Journal of the American Oriental Society*, 79 (1959); "Sung-Koryŏ Relations: Some Inhibiting Factors," *Oriens*, 11 (1959); and "The Regularization of Koryŏ-Chin Relations (1116–1131), *Central Asian Journal*, 6 (1961).

e. The Late Koryŏ Period

The Late Koryŏ Period is only slightly better covered, and studies include M. C. Rogers, "Studies in Korean History," *T'oung Pao*, LCVII (1959) 1 and 2; Ko Byŏngik, "Korea's Contacts with the Western Regions in Pre-Modern Times," *Sahoe kwahak*, 2 (1958); L. Hambis, "Notes sur l'histoire de Corée a l'Epoque mongole," *T'oung Pao*, XLV (1957); and William E. Henthorn, *Korea: The Mongol Invasions*, Leiden: E. J. Brill, 1963.

f. The Early Yi Dynasty

The Early Yi Dynasty is somewhat better represented, and works include: Edward W. Wagner, "The Recommendation Examination of 1519: Its Place in Early Yi Dynasty History," *Chōsen gakuhō*, 15 (1960); Yi Kwang-rin, "Census Taking under the Yi Dynasty," *Transactions of the Korea Branch of the Royal Asiatic Society* (1959); and Choe Ching Young, "Kim Yuk (1580–1658) and the Taedongbop Reform," *Journal of Asian Studies*, 23 (1963). Two notable studies of the social structure of the Yi dynasty are contained in Herbert Passin, "Untouchability in the Far East," *Monumenta Nipponica*, IX (1955); and Herbert Passin, "The Paekchong of Korea: A Brief Social History," *Monumenta Nipponica*, XII (1956–1957). A good view of a Korean intellectual of this period outside of his own society is provided in John Meskill, *Ch'oe Pu's (1454–1504) Diary*, Tucson: University of Arizona Press, 1965. An account of the Hideyoshi invasions of Korea is contained in George Sansom, *A History of Japan 1334–1615*, Stanford: Stanford University Press, 1961. One result of the invasions is discussed in Kim Ha-tai, "The Transmission of Neo-Confucianism to Japan by Kang Hang, A Prisoner of War," *Transactions of the Korea Branch of the Royal Asiatic Society*, XXXVII (1961). Relations between Japan, Korea, and the Ryūkyū Islands are covered in Ch. Haguenauer, "Relations du royaume des Ryūkyū avec les pays des mers du Sud et la Corée," *Bulletin de la Maison franco-japonaise*, 3 (1931) 1–2. Two accounts of the development of printing in Korea are Sohn Pow-key, "Early Korean Printing," *Journal of the American Oriental Society*, 72 (1959); and Kim Wŏnyong, *Early Movable Type in Korea*, Seoul: National Museum of Korea, 1954.

g. The Late Yi Dynasty

The Late Yi Dynasty is represented by two narrative accounts of Korea. The earlier is Hendrick Hamel, *Journal*, Rotterdam, 1668, English translation in *Transactions of the Korea Branch of the Royal Asiatic Society*, 9 (1918); an account dating a century later is that of Dallet mentioned previously. A study of Yi-Ch'ing relations, which includes information on products exchanged, is contained in Haejong Chun, "Sino-Korean Tributary Relations in the Ch'ing Period," in John K. Fairbank, ed., *The Chinese World Order*, New York, 1968. A similar account of Yi-Tokugawa relations is George M. McCune, "The Exchange of Envoys between Korea and Japan during the Tokugawa Period," *Far Eastern Quarterly* (1946). The Manchu invasions are outlined from the Chinese viewpoint in W. W. Rockhill, *China's Intercourse with Korea from the XVth Century to 1895*, London: Luzac, 1905. An interesting study of a Korean mission to Japan in the late nineteenth century is found in Sohn Pow-key, "The Opening of Korea: A Conflict of Traditions," *Transactions of the Korea Branch of the Royal Asiatic Society*, XXXVI (1960).

Index

HISTORY

$3.95

WILLIAM E. HENTHORN

A HISTORY OF KOREA

*Enraptured by the evening sunset
the boys tending cattle
on the grassy banks of the clear river
trill on their flutes
while the dragon dozing beneath the water
seems to wake and rise.*

—from Songgang's *Song of Star Mountain* (c. 1590)

The first new English-language history of Korea in over half a century, this work surveys the full range of that nation's development from the pre-historical period to the end of the Yi Dynasty in 1910. Rather than merely summarize political events and social changes, the author offers his own sensitive analyses of the country's religious and ethical systems, its art and literature, its social structure and educational methods, and the changing ideas that have made it a creative, dynamic force in the Far East through the centuries.

"Far superior to any other general history of Korea written in English . . . Up-to-date, balanced, sensibly arranged, pleasantly written, easy to refer to: this is the ideal history book on Korea for reference and for dipping."—*The Korea Times*

WILLIAM E. HENTHORN is Associate Researcher in the Social Science Research Institute of the University of Hawaii.

THE FREE PRESS
A Division of Macmillan Publishing Co., Inc.
New York

Jacket design by Sam Salant

91461